ADHD Workbook for Women 5-in-1

How to Declutter, Beat Overwhelm, Sharpen Executive Function, Sync Hormones, Tame Emotions, and Strengthen Relationships

VIVIAN WHITMORE

Claim Your Free Bonus

As a thank you for reading, I've put together a powerful digital bonus pack to help you apply what you've learned — even if you only have a few minutes a day.

 Inside you'll find:

✔ Quick-access emotional reset tools
✔ A printable clarity map for focus and purpose
✔ 30 powerful journaling prompts
✔ Daily progress & reflection trackers
✔ A mini affirmation deck for calm and confidence

Access below to download your full bonus pack:

https: / / livetolearn.lpages.co / vivian-withmore-adhd-workbook-for-women-5-in-1-paperback /

Or, scan the QR code

REVIEW ON

ADHD Workbook For Women 5-In-1: How To Declutter, Beat Overwhelm, Sharpen Executive Function, Sync Hormones, Tame Emotions, and Strengthen Relationships

By: Carolina Estevez, Psy.D., Licensed Psychologist

The *ADHD Workbook for Women 5-in-1: How to Declutter, Beat Overwhelm, Sharpen Executive Function, Sync Hormones, Tame Emotions, and Strengthen Relationships* is a well-researched, compassionate, and practical guide that addresses the unique neurological, emotional, and hormonal factors affecting women with Attention-Deficit/ Hyperactivity Disorder (ADHD). As a psychologist, I found this workbook to be an empowering blend of science, therapeutic strategies, and hands-on tools for daily life. The author bridges neuroscience, psychology, and behavioral interventions with accessible language and relatable case examples that capture the lived experience of women managing ADHD amid modern demands.

The chapters on *decluttering your space* and *beating overwhelm* stand out as especially impactful. Rather than promoting rigid organizational systems that often fail for neurodivergent minds, the workbook emphasizes "micro-steps"—breaking down large tasks into tiny, achievable actions that prevent paralysis and perfectionism. Practical techniques such as "doubling" (doing two small related tasks together) and the use of visual timers help transform initiation difficulty into momentum. The chapter also introduces ADHD-friendly storage systems that reduce visual clutter and decision fatigue, reinforcing that environment strongly influences emotional regulation. The focus on *reset routines* and the acceptance that clutter will reappear normalizes the ADHD experience and supports progress over perfection.

The section on *beating overwhelm* further explores how ADHD-related time blindness undermines productivity. The workbook introduces *time blocking* and the *Pomodoro technique* as accessible methods for restoring a sense of temporal structure. It also integrates evidence-based tools to strengthen working memory, such as externalizing reminders, planning routines, and reducing digital overload to minimize cognitive fatigue. These strategies align well with cognitive-behavioral therapy principles used in clinical practice.

The chapter on *sharpening executive function* offers a comprehensive toolkit for managing deadlines, sustaining focus, and improving task follow-through. It emphasizes realistic goal- setting, environmental design, and the use of external supports—such as checklists and accountability systems—to compensate for executive weaknesses.

Perhaps the most groundbreaking section is *syncing hormones to optimize treatment*. Few ADHD resources address the hormonal fluctuations that shape cognition, energy, and emotion in women. The book guides readers to track symptoms across the menstrual cycle, identify "high- risk" hormonal phases, and collaborate with healthcare providers on stimulant dose adjustments. The author also covers perimenopause and menopause, highlighting how sleep, nutrition, and lifestyle stabilization can buffer mood and cognitive disruptions.

Finally, the chapter on *taming emotions and strengthening relationships* integrates dialectical and cognitive-behavioral techniques such as sensory grounding, opposite action, and self- validation to manage shame, rejection sensitivity, and impulsivity. Relationship-focused exercises using mirroring, "I" statements, and emotional transparency empower women to communicate more effectively and foster connection.

Overall, this workbook is a comprehensive and affirming guide that blends neuroscience, self- compassion, and real-world behavioral tools. It is a valuable therapeutic companion for clinicians and a transformative resource for women seeking to understand and work with their ADHD rather than against it.

TABLE OF CONTENTS

INTRODUCTION
WELCOME TO YOUR EMPOWERED BRAIN

The journey of an adult woman with Attention-Deficit / Hyperactivity Disorder (ADHD) is often an invisible battle, fought in silence against a world and a mind that seem perpetually misaligned. For too long, the narrative of ADHD has been dominated by an outdated, male-centric view, leading to profound misunderstanding and delayed diagnosis for countless women. This workbook is a direct response to that historical oversight, offering a comprehensive, evidence-based roadmap designed specifically to meet the unique neurobiological and psychological needs of the female ADHD brain.

Historically, ADHD research and diagnostic criteria have centered on the externalized, hyperactive symptoms more common in boys: physical restlessness, disruptive impulsivity, and constant movement. This narrow lens has failed to capture the nuanced and often internalized presentation typical of women, whose struggles frequently manifest as profound inattention, chronic disorganization, intense emotional dysregulation, and a pervasive, invisible sense of internal restlessness. This diagnostic disparity is stark: studies show the mean age of diagnosis for women can be years later than for men, leaving them to spend years, or even decades, struggling in secret before receiving the proper framework for their challenges.

The delay in diagnosis forces women into a debilitating cycle of self-blame and shame. Without a neurobiological explanation for their difficulties, they internalize their struggles, believing their chronic disorganization, poor time management, and emotional volatility are personal failings rather than symptoms of a condition. This conflict is amplified by powerful societal expectations for women to be the organized, emotionally stable, and nurturing caretakers of their homes and families. The relentless pressure to conform directly clashes with core ADHD symptoms, compelling many to engage in **masking**: the exhausting effort to develop sophisticated compensatory behaviors to appear "neurotypical" and competent to the outside world. This constant, invisible performance is an immense cognitive burden that fuels anxiety, depression, and a shattered sense of self-worth.

This workbook transforms this struggle from a personal failure into a strategic challenge. It is built on the understanding that your challenges are not a deficit of character, but a consequence of a distinct neurological operating system that demands a tailored approach. The strategies and tools presented in these five books are designed to address the six core pillars of the female ADHD experience: how to **Declutter**, **Beat Overwhelm**, **Sharpen Executive Function**, **Sync Hormones**, **Tame Emotions**, and **Strengthen Relationships**. By addressing these interwoven challenges holistically, we move beyond mere coping to achieving genuine self-mastery and integrated success.

The Neurobiological Reality: Why Your Brain Works Differently

To effectively manage ADHD, we must first understand its neurobiological roots. ADHD is fundamentally characterized by challenges in **executive functions (EFs)**, a family of mental processes essential for regulating behavior, planning, reasoning, and maintaining focus. These core deficits are not a reflection of intelligence; rather, they are rooted in variations in brain structure and, critically, **neurotransmitter activity**, particularly concerning **dopamine** and **norepinephrine**.

Dopamine, the brain's key chemical for motivation, reward, and attention, is thought to be dysregulated in the ADHD brain. This often leads to lower effective levels in the brain's synapses. This reduction makes tasks that are not inherently stimulating or immediately rewarding feel incredibly difficult to initiate and sustain. This explains why boring or repetitive tasks are met with immense resistance or paralysis, a state often confused with laziness but which is, in fact, a neurological hurdle.

This difference in brain wiring gives rise to several critical challenges that deplete mental energy and lead to the ubiquitous feeling of being perpetually "frenzied, frazzled, and overwhelmed" :

The Burden of High Cognitive Load

A key factor in the struggle is **cognitive load**, which refers to the total amount of mental effort consumed by working memory. For a neurotypical person, the brain efficiently filters out irrelevant stimuli and prioritizes information. For the ADHD brain, this filtering mechanism is often less efficient, causing it to take in and process a disproportionate amount of incoming information, both internal and external. A stray object on a desk, a pending notification, or a fleeting intrusive thought can all compete for attention with the same intensity as the main task at hand.

Research indicates that high cognitive load can have a disproportionately negative impact on performance for people with ADHD. This means that a cluttered physical or digital space isn't just an inconvenience; it is a direct contributor to reduced cognitive function, as each piece of clutter represents a subtle, but persistent, demand on a brain already struggling to filter and prioritize. This immense, continuous mental effort is the measurable **ADHD Tax** on your energy, draining your executive function reserves and leading to chronic fatigue and burnout.

The Task Activation Deficit and Time Blindness

Two of the most frustrating executive function deficits are the difficulty in starting tasks and the struggle with time perception:

1. **Task Activation Deficit (ADHD Paralysis):** You may know exactly what needs to be done, but the gap between intention and action feels immense, like an uncrossable chasm. This paralysis is a neurological hurdle rooted in the brain's reward and motivation system. The sheer scope of a large, daunting project is perceived as too complex, triggering a cognitive shutdown rather than initiation. The solution, explored in **Book 1**, is not willpower, but creating external scaffolding by breaking tasks into their smallest component parts to reduce the activation energy required.

2. **Time Blindness:** This is the inability to accurately perceive or estimate the flow of time. Time blindness makes setting realistic schedules, remembering deadlines, and transitioning between activities exceptionally challenging. Because the future often

feels less "real" than the present, the ADHD brain struggles to prioritize based on future deadlines, leading to chronic lateness and poor planning. **Book 3** focuses entirely on making abstract time concrete and visible to counteract this core deficit.

The Female Experience: Masking, Shame, and Hormonal Fluctuations

The neurobiological realities of ADHD are compounded for women by two critical factors: the pressure to conform and the dramatic influence of ovarian hormones.

The Emotional Cost of Masking and Internalization

A significant component of the female ADHD experience is the internalization of symptoms, leading to a profound sense of shame and inadequacy. While men are more likely to externalize frustration, women often turn the struggle inward, interpreting their functional difficulties, like a messy home or an impulsive outburst, as moral failings. This internalized struggle is the source of the persistent inner critic that erodes self-worth and contributes to high rates of co-occurring mental health challenges like anxiety and depression.

This internal pressure often manifests as **emotional dysregulation**, a core, significant, and often misunderstood aspect of ADHD. Emotional dysregulation is the difficulty in controlling and appropriately expressing emotions, leading to feelings that are **all-or-nothing**, where a small trigger can flip feelings from calm to an overwhelming "red" reaction without warning. This is rooted in a disconnect between the brain's emotional accelerator (the amygdala, which can be overactive) and the emotional brakes (the frontal cortex, which can be underactive), making it difficult to modulate the intensity and duration of feelings.

Rejection Sensitive Dysphoria (RSD): A Heightened Pain

A particularly debilitating manifestation of emotional dysregulation is **Rejection Sensitive Dysphoria (RSD)**, a term describing the extreme emotional pain and anxiety triggered by the perception of criticism or rejection. For women who have endured a lifetime of "chronic negative feedback" and shame, a perceived snub can unleash an immediate, overwhelming emotional pain that feels physically agonizing. This hypersensitivity often drives women to people-pleasing or perfectionism as a defense mechanism, a strategy that is ultimately exhausting and unsustainable. **Book 5** provides the tools to manage this extreme reactivity, offering strategies to create a crucial pause between emotional stimulus and intentional response.

The Critical Interplay of Hormones and Cognition

Perhaps the most overlooked factor in the female ADHD journey is the profound, dynamic influence of hormones. ADHD is not a static condition; its symptom severity changes across a woman's lifespan in concert with her hormonal cycle, a link that is often dismissed by practitioners who have not been trained on this gender-specific reality.

1. **The Neurochemical Link:** Research shows that **estrogen**, a primary female sex hormone, plays a crucial role in regulating neurotransmitters like dopamine. Because dopamine is already dysregulated in the ADHD brain, fluctuations in estrogen can significantly impact symptom severity. When estrogen levels are lower or unstable, the existing dopaminergic pathway dysregulation may intensify, leading to worsening core ADHD challenges.

2. **The Menstrual Cycle Impact:** This connection explains why many women anecdotally report that their attention, organization, and emotional volatility worsen during the low-estrogen, high-progesterone **luteal phase**—the period leading up to menstruation. During this phase, studies suggest that inattention and executive function deficits can become more pronounced. This shift can even make standard ADHD medication feel less effective.

3. **The Midlife Challenge ("ADHD Squared"):** For women entering perimenopause and menopause, the decline in both estrogen and progesterone can "unmask" a previously subtle ADHD presentation or significantly worsen diagnosed symptoms. Some experts refer to this as an "**ADHD squared**" effect—the compounding of low estrogen and low dopamine, leading to severe brain fog, increased anxiety, and unmanageable difficulties with memory and focus.

Book 4 provides the essential roadmap for tracking this hormonal roadmap, empowering you to advocate for a personalized, integrated treatment plan that addresses your unique neurobiological needs.

Blueprint for Empowerment: The 5-in-1 Book Solution

This workbook is a structured journey designed to move you from a state of chronic overwhelm and self-blame to one of strategic self-mastery. We will tackle the core challenges of living with ADHD in women by providing an evidence-based toolkit across five interconnected books, each building upon the foundational skills of the last.

Book 1: Declutter Your Space and Defeat Task Paralysis for the ADHD Woman

The first step toward beating overwhelm is establishing external order to reduce internal chaos. This book addresses organization not as a matter of moral superiority, but as a form of self-care designed to reduce cognitive load.

The primary barrier to an organized life is not laziness, but the neurological hurdle of **task paralysis** and the cognitive cost of **disorganization**. When a task is perceived as too complex, the brain shuts down. This book provides the foundational blueprint for creating "functional organization," focusing on simple, repeatable systems that work with the ADHD brain's unique wiring:

- **Conquer Paralysis:** Systematically breaking down overwhelming tasks into **micro-steps** (e.g., separating "cleaning the entire living room" into steps like "collect dishes from the living room and place them in the kitchen sink").
- **Design Your Sanctuary:** Combating the "out of sight, out of mind" phenomenon by utilizing **visible storage** (e.g., containers without lids) and designating a predictable "home" for every item to eliminate decision fatigue.
- **Sustain Momentum:** Leveraging **Body Doubling**—performing a task in the presence of another person (in-person or virtually)—to initiate and sustain focus, which acts as an external executive function.

Book 2: Beat Overwhelm for the ADHD Woman

After establishing external order, **Book 2** provides the core strategies for managing your inner landscape, your focus, attention, and mental energy, to beat the pervasive feeling of being overwhelmed and frazzled. This involves moving past the myth of multitasking and embracing intentional, single-task focus.

This book trains your brain to regulate attention and utilize its energy efficiently:

- **Visualize Time:** Directly attacking **time blindness** by making abstract time concrete and visible through structured scheduling.
- **Schedule Success:** Shifting from ineffective, vague to-do lists to **Time Blocking**, which forces you to allocate specific, finite time

durations for tasks, thereby reducing the cognitive guesswork involved in initiation and planning.

- **Customize Your Focus:** Implementing the **Pomodoro Technique** (short, focused work intervals followed by mandated breaks) to boost concentration, prevent burnout and hyperfocus, and provide the necessary novelty for the ADHD brain to remain engaged.

Book 3: Sharpen Executive Function in Women with ADHD

Building upon the foundations of organizational structure and intentional time management, **Book 3** focuses on advanced techniques to sustain focus and build the internal resilience necessary for long-term productivity. This work is fundamentally about protecting your mental energy and optimizing your cognitive resources.

The key strategies involve creating both an internal and external "attention zone":

- **Future-Proof Your Brain:** Strengthening crucial executive function skills, including inhibitory control and working memory, through structured activities and consistent routines.
- **Protect Your Energy:** Recognizing that sustained focus is a product of managing your energy, not just your time, by prioritizing sleep hygiene, nutrition (e.g., Omega-3s), and physical activity to regulate dopamine and mitigate the effects of chronic **mental fatigue**.
- **Embrace Single-Tasking:** Debunking the myth of multitasking, which is simply inefficient **task-switching** that drains the ADHD brain. You will learn to prioritize **deep work** by batching similar tasks and creating "pre-flight checklists" to smoothly transition into sustained focus.

Book 4: Sync Hormones and Optimize Treatment for the ADHD Woman

This is the gender-specific core of the workbook, providing the scientific context and practical tools to navigate the dynamic relationship between hormones and ADHD symptoms. Recognizing this link is crucial for achieving stable mental and emotional health.

This book empowers you to become a self-advocate for tailored medical care:

- **Map Your Cycle:** Learning to track your menstrual cycle and emotional / cognitive symptoms to pinpoint when the low-estrogen phases (such as the luteal phase) are likely to intensify symptoms like inattention, anxiety, and emotional volatility.
- **Advocate for Adjustment:** Gaining the knowledge to discuss **cycle dosing** of stimulant medication with your doctor, as research suggests the efficacy of treatment can fluctuate with hormonal status.
- **Manage the Transition:** Understanding the "ADHD squared" effect during **perimenopause and menopause**, where declining estrogen compounds ADHD symptoms, and exploring integrated treatment options like Hormone Replacement Therapy (HRT) combined with stimulants to support memory and focus.

Book 5: Tame Emotions and Strengthen Relationships in Women with ADHD

The emotional rollercoaster of ADHD, coupled with its profound impact on communication, requires a robust toolkit for self-regulation and interpersonal effectiveness. This book equips you with therapeutic skills to build emotional resilience and foster meaningful connection.

Drawing heavily on evidence-based approaches like Dialectical Behavior Therapy (DBT), this book teaches you how to manage intense emotional surges and communicate effectively:

- **Ground Yourself and Change the Script:** Implementing **Distress Tolerance** skills like sensory grounding (TIPP skills) to interrupt acute emotional distress and applying **Opposite Action** (doing the opposite of the emotional urge) to change the emotional trajectory.
- **Challenge the Critic:** Utilizing **Cognitive Behavioral Therapy (CBT)** tools to identify and challenge unhelpful thought patterns (cognitive distortions), such as catastrophizing or mind reading, which fuel shame and RSD.
- **Strengthen Relationships:** Mastering **Interpersonal Effectiveness** skills to reduce relational friction, including **Active Listening** (mirroring and validation) and using **"I" Statements** to express needs without blaming, thereby moving from a "parent-child" dynamic to a collaborative partnership.

Your Roadmap to Self-Mastery and Integrated Success

The journey you are about to begin is one of empowerment. It is built on the unwavering belief that your struggles are not a reflection of a personal deficit but a signal that your unique brain requires a strategic, tailored approach. This workbook provides the necessary framework to move you from a lifetime of self-blame, masking, and chaos to a life defined by intentional action and self-acceptance.

The path to integrated success is not about achieving neurotypical perfection; it is about honoring your unique needs, building a life that accommodates your brain's natural rhythms, and celebrating progress over flawlessness. The skills you cultivate here, from external organization and focused attention to hormonal awareness and emotional resilience, will work in synergy, creating a stable foundation that allows your considerable strengths and creativity to flourish.

You are no longer merely coping with ADHD; you are actively crafting a life that is aligned with your values. By embracing this holistic roadmap, you gain the knowledge, the skills, and the compassionate mindset to build the extraordinary life you are capable of living. The time for shame is over. The moment for self-mastery is now.

BOOK ONE

DECLUTTER YOUR SPACE AND BEAT
OVERWHELM FOR THE ADHD WOMAN

INTRODUCTION
THE COGNITIVE COST OF DISORGANIZATION

For the adult woman with Attention-Deficit / Hyperactivity Disorder (ADHD), organization is not merely a matter of tidiness or a reflection of personal effort; it is a profound, daily struggle that consumes mental energy and fuels a persistent, debilitating sense of overwhelm. The chronic difficulty in maintaining order, whether in physical spaces like a home or digital environments like an inbox, is a direct, measurable symptom of the disorder, stemming from inherent challenges with **executive functions (EFs)**, such as planning, sustained attention, and working memory.

This constant friction between the desire for order and the neurobiological reality of disorganization carries a devastating cognitive and emotional cost that permeates every facet of a woman's life. Valuable time is perpetually lost in frantic searches for misplaced items, crucial opportunities are missed due to forgotten deadlines or buried paperwork, and the physical and mental clutter creates a pervasive **hum of anxiety** that depletes mental reserves. This struggle is often amplified by powerful societal expectations for women to be the organized, emotionally stable caretakers of their homes, leading to a deep, debilitating sense of shame and feelings of inadequacy.

This book approaches organization not as a rigid, perfectionistic ideal, but as a form of neurobiological **self-care**. The goal is to establish **"functional organization,"** a system designed intentionally to reduce cognitive load, minimize daily friction, and work **for** the unique wiring of the ADHD brain, rather than forcing the brain to operate against its natural impulses. By creating external structure, we can compensate for internal inconsistencies and free up the mental bandwidth necessary to master the more complex challenges of focus, emotions, and relationships.

The Neurobiological Reality: Why Your Brain Struggles with Order

The internal engine of the ADHD brain operates on a different, often more demanding, set of rules than its neurotypical counterpart, making traditional organizational advice ineffective or even counterproductive. The challenges you face are not a failure of character; they are a consequence of specific differences in how your brain processes and prioritizes information.

1. Executive Function Deficits: The Organizational Brain

Core executive functions, a family of mental processes essential for regulating behavior, planning, and maintaining focus, are significantly challenged in the ADHD population. These deficits are the root cause of chronic disorganization:

- **Working Memory as a Sieve:** Working memory, often described as the brain's temporary mental scratchpad, can feel unreliable for a woman with ADHD, making it nearly impossible to hold a multi-step organizational plan in mind or to reliably recall where an item was placed moments ago. This profound challenge is the clinical basis for the ubiquitous **"out of sight, out of mind"** phenomenon. If an item is put away in an opaque container or a cluttered drawer, it ceases to exist for the ADHD brain, necessitating systems that are deliberately visual to act as consistent, reliable external cues.

- **Reduced Prefrontal Cortex Activity:** Research indicates that the parts of the brain responsible for executive functions, particularly the **prefrontal cortex** (the brain's "command center" for planning, working memory, and impulse control), tend to be less developed or less active in people with ADHD. This reduced activity makes it challenging to remember task goals, instructions, or rules, contributing to what is often described as "brain fog", a temporary sluggishness and slowdown of thinking abilities that compounds the difficulty of organizing complex environments.

2. The High Cognitive Cost of Clutter

A crucial factor in understanding why disorganization feels so debilitating is the concept of **cognitive load**, which refers to the total amount of mental effort consumed by working memory.

The neurotypical brain is designed to efficiently filter out irrelevant stimuli and prioritize information. For the ADHD brain, this filtering mechanism is often less efficient, causing it to take in and process a disproportionate amount of incoming information, both internal and external. A single stray object on a desk, an unread email notification, or an incomplete task all compete for attention with the same intensity as the main task at hand.

- **Visual Noise as Mental Drain:** This constant processing of non-essential stimuli creates a state of chronic, high cognitive load. A cluttered physical or digital space isn't just an inconvenience; it is a direct contributor to reduced cognitive function, as each piece of clutter represents a subtle, but persistent, demand on a brain already struggling to filter and prioritize. The constant effort required to fight against this neurobiological reality is a significant "ADHD Tax" on your mental energy, leading to the chronic fatigue and burnout that underpins the feeling of being perpetually "frenzied, frazzled, and overwhelmed."

3. Task Activation Deficit: The Root of Paralysis

The path to organizing is often obstructed by a profound neurological hurdle known as **task paralysis** or the "can't get started" syndrome. This paralyzing procrastination is not a moral failing or a deficit of willpower; it is a direct result of how the brain's motivation system operates.

- **Overwhelm Triggers Shutdown:** Task paralysis occurs when a project is perceived as too complex, involves too many steps, or when the task is repetitive and understimulating. The sheer scope of organizing a messy room or cleaning a cluttered inbox can trigger a feeling of overwhelm that makes task initiation nearly impossible. The brain's executive functions struggle to find a clear entry point, triggering an immediate shutdown response instead of action.

- **Dopamine and Novelty:** This deficit is tied to the dysregulation of **dopamine**, the brain's key chemical for motivation and reward. The ADHD brain craves novelty and immediate stimulation. Mundane, multi-step tasks like organizing or filing do not provide the necessary immediate reward, making them intensely difficult to initiate and sustain, which necessitates external structures to provide momentum.

The Emotional and Relational Toll of External Chaos

The organizational struggles driven by these neurobiological factors take a severe emotional and relational toll, particularly for women who face intense societal pressure to maintain a perfect home and life.

1. Shame, Self-Blame, and the Inner Critic

The emotional cost of chronic disorganization is profound and personal. Living with constant, visible messiness and the energy drain required to manage its consequences leads to low self-esteem, self-blame, and pervasive feelings of inadequacy.

- **Internalizing Failure:** Without a neurobiological explanation for their struggles, many women internalize their functional difficulties, believing their chaotic environment is evidence of a personal flaw or moral failure. This leads to a powerful **inner critic** that reinforces a narrative of shame: "I should be able to keep this house clean," or "I must be lazy if I can't even pay the bills on time." This pattern is exacerbated by the fact that women are more likely to internalize their struggles than men, contributing to high rates of co-occurring anxiety and depression.

- **The Shame of the Home:** Societal expectations for women to be the organized, nurturing caretaker often clash violently with ADHD symptoms. When a woman struggles to maintain an organized home, this failure feels like a violation of traditional feminine norms, leading to immense social anxiety and shame, often manifesting as avoidance, such as refusing to have people over due to the mess.

2. Relationship Friction and the "Mental Load"

The organizational struggles of ADHD are a frequent and profound source of friction in close relationships, often mediated by deficits in executive functions and emotional regulation.

- **The Parent-Child Dynamic:** When an organized, neurotypical partner is forced to constantly remind the ADHD partner about household tasks, a difficult and unhealthy **"parent-child" dynamic** can emerge. The ADHD partner feels scolded and shamed for their inability to initiate tasks, while the non-ADHD partner feels exhausted and unheard, leading to significant resentment and a breakdown in core partnership values.

- **Impaired Communication:** The same EF deficits that cause disorganization also affect communication. Poor working memory and impulsivity can lead to difficulty with active listening, frequent interruptions, and challenges in following through on relationship commitments, further eroding trust and intimacy.

The Strategic Shift: Building External Scaffolding

This book is dedicated to providing the cognitive scaffolding required to stabilize your external environment, reducing the debilitating effects of chaos and overwhelm. The solution is to strategically design systems that bypass the weaknesses of the ADHD brain by leveraging external structure and accountability.

The functional approach presented here relies on three core principles that will be developed in the following chapters:

1. **Externalizing the Brain:** You cannot rely on inconsistent internal memory. Instead, you must intentionally use physical and digital systems (planners, visual cues) to reliably hold information, deadlines, and the designated locations for every item, thereby offloading your working memory. This practice transforms organization from an exercise in mental effort to a reliable system of external recall.

2. **Minimizing Activation Energy:** To defeat task paralysis, every overwhelming project must be broken down into its smallest, most actionable micro-steps. This strategic reduction in complexity lowers the activation energy required to begin, transforming daunting goals into achievable, low-friction entry points that leverage the brain's need for novelty and immediate reward.

3. **Harnessing External Structure:** Overcoming the initiation deficit requires proactive, external anchors. Strategies like **Body Doubling**, performing a task in the presence of another person (in-person or virtually), provide gentle encouragement and non-judgmental accountability, acting as a temporary external executive function that anchors attention and sustains momentum. Furthermore, establishing visible, designated

"homes" for every item (e.g., containers without lids, clearly labeled areas) creates a system of predictability that reduces decision fatigue and reinforces good habits.

The work of creating functional organization is the crucial first step toward building a truly resilient and fulfilling life. By mastering these foundational systems, you move past self-blame and equip yourself with the mental bandwidth necessary to succeed in the areas of focus, emotional regulation, and deep connection explored in the rest of this workbook.

CHAPTER 1

CONQUER PARALYSIS: BREAK DOWN OVERWHELMING TASKS INTO MICRO-STEPS

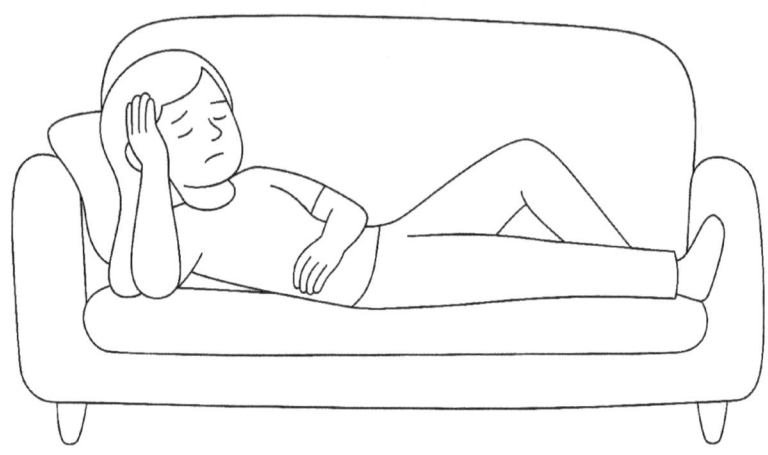

The overwhelming, chronic feeling of being "frenzied, frazzled, and overwhelmed" that many women with ADHD report is often rooted in one profound neurological hurdle: **task paralysis**. This state, often mislabeled as laziness or avoidance, is the invisible wall between intention and action, preventing you from starting or continuing projects that are crucial for creating order and stability in your life.

For the ADHD brain, organizing or initiating a demanding task is rarely about willpower. It is a neurological challenge rooted in the brain's unique wiring and its reward system. The sheer, undifferentiated scope of a large project, such as "Clean the entire house" or "Organize the finances", can trigger a cognitive shutdown, leaving you stuck in a state of avoidance and procrastination.

This chapter provides the strategic blueprint to dismantle this paralysis, transforming amorphous, daunting goals into a series of low-friction, achievable **micro-steps**. This approach fundamentally bypasses the initiation deficit, leveraging the power of momentum to move you from analysis and avoidance to consistent action.

The Neurobiology of the Paralysis Trap

To conquer task paralysis, you must first understand why your brain defaults to a frozen state when faced with a large project. This is not a character flaw, but a measurable neurobiological response tied to **Executive Function (EF) deficits** and the brain's internal reward system.

1. **Overload and Filtering Failure:** The ADHD brain struggles with filtering out irrelevant information and distractions. When faced with a cluttered room, every item, color, shape, and pending decision, *Where does this go? Do I need this? What if I toss it?*, competes for attention. The resulting sensory and visual overload exceeds the brain's capacity to process and prioritize, leading directly to a cognitive shutdown or mental paralysis.

2. **The Activation Deficit:** Task initiation, the ability to simply start a task, requires a burst of "activation energy" fueled by the neurotransmitter **dopamine**. When a project is new, complex, involves multiple steps, or is boring and repetitive, the brain struggles to produce enough dopamine to find the task stimulating or rewarding. This is why the gap between knowing *what* to do and actually *doing* it feels immense, forcing the person into procrastination and avoidance.

The solution to both overload and the activation deficit is the systematic reduction of complexity. By breaking down the daunting task, you dramatically lower the cognitive load and create clear, immediate entry points that are psychologically approachable.

Strategy: Deconstruct the Dragon into Micro-Steps

The most effective strategy to defeat paralysis is to relentlessly break down the overwhelming task into its smallest, most elemental component parts. A successful step is one that requires minimal thought, minimal movement, and generates an immediate, satisfying sense of completion.

The goal is to create steps that are so small they feel almost ridiculous to avoid. This process is structured in three phases:

Phase 1: The Brain Dump and Inventory

Before you can organize a task, you must first externalize all the thoughts, steps, and worries associated with it. This removes the mental clutter that consumes working memory and contributes to overload.

- **List Everything:** For a daunting project (e.g., "Organize the spare room"), write down every single step, thought, item, and worry related to it. Include abstract steps like "Figure out where to put the donation box" or "Call the donation center."
- **Identify Friction Points:** Review your list and circle every item that feels complex, vague, or emotionally charged. These are your "friction points" that are most likely to trigger paralysis.

Phase 2: Identify the "Next Action" (The Smallest Viable Step)

Once the friction points are identified, the objective is to simplify them into a **Next Action**, the specific, physical action that requires the least amount of energy to execute.

Overwhelming Task (Vague)	Dismantled Micro-Steps (Actionable)	Why it Works
Organize the entire living room	**Task #1: Collect dishes** from the living room and place them in the kitchen sink.	Specific and immediate. Bypasses the need to sort or find a "home."
Clean out the desk drawers	**Task #2: Empty all trash** from the desk area into a wastebasket.	Low-friction action. Provides instant visible progress.
Sort through paperwork pile	**Task #3: Find the utility bill** that needs to be paid and place it on the landing strip.	Focuses only on *one type* of item, not the entire pile.
Get started on laundry	**Task #4: Put all dirty clothes** from the bedroom floor into the hamper.	Simple physical movement. Doesn't require sorting or starting the washing machine yet.
Clear the kitchen counter	**Task #5: Wipe down one square foot** of counter space with a cleaning spray.	Time-bound and small enough to feel non-threatening.

Phase 3: Create Immediate Accountability (Toss, Donate, Keep)

When organizing items physically, the sorting process itself can induce paralysis, as the brain struggles to decide the fate of each object. A structured, predetermined set of categories eliminates decision fatigue during the active organizing phase.

1. **Designate Three Categories:** Label three distinct boxes or areas immediately: **Toss** (for true garbage), **Donate** (for items to be given away), and **Keep** (for items to be put back in a designated home).

2. **Schedule the Follow-Up:** Organizing only creates temporary clutter if the disposal steps are not completed. When a **Donate** box is full, immediately schedule the action into your calendar: "Drop off donation box at Goodwill at 2 PM Saturday". By making an appointment for that action, you maintain momentum and prevent the discarded items from becoming new, permanent clutter.

3. **The "Junk Drawer" Allowance:** To maintain a sustainable system, embrace functional organization over perfection. Designate at least one "junk drawer" in every room for temporary storage of items that do not yet have a determined home. Attempting to achieve impossible perfection often leads to immediate abandonment of the system; embracing this small allowance allows the overall system to remain sustainable.

The Dopamine Hit: Leveraging Momentum to Defeat Avoidance

The success of the micro-step strategy is rooted in the neurobiology of motivation. The ADHD brain is constantly seeking immediate feedback and reward.

By committing to, and completing, a simple micro-step, you achieve a rapid, tangible "win." This completion provides a small, satisfying burst of **dopamine** that reinforces productive behavior and makes the next step feel slightly easier to initiate. The feeling of accomplishment, even from putting a single dish in the sink, builds **momentum**, which is the most powerful antidote to task paralysis. Momentum means you rely less on inconsistent willpower and more on the positive feedback loop of immediate reward.

The mastery of this process, externalizing the cognitive load, deconstructing overwhelming tasks into their smallest actions, and utilizing the reward of momentum, is the essential first step toward reclaiming control over your environment and defeating the chronic feeling of overwhelm that defines unmanaged ADHD.

Chapter 1 Workbook: Conquer Paralysis: Break Down Overwhelming Tasks into Micro-Steps

Objective: To bypass **Task Paralysis** by reducing the **activation energy** of a single overwhelming project using the Micro-Step Strategy.

Activity 1.1: The Micro-Step Converter

1. **The Overwhelming Task:** Identify one organizing project you have been avoiding due to feeling overwhelmed (e.g., "Clean the entire closet," or "Organize the digital files").

   Task: _____

   _____

2. **Dismantle to Micro-Steps:** Break the task down into three physical actions that require **less than 2 minutes each** and **no decision-making** (minimal friction).

Action-Oriented Micro-Step	Why It Works (Low Friction)
Step 1: (Example: Find and place a trash bag next to the task zone.)	
Step 2: (Example: Clear the top three items from the surface and toss them in the bag.)	
Step 3: (Example: Set a 5-minute timer and press START.)	

Reflection 1.2: Activation Energy Audit

1. On a scale of 1 (Calm) to 10 (Paralyzed), rate your internal resistance **before** completing Step 1.

    Rating: _____

    _____

    _____

    _____

    _____

2. How did completing **Steps 1 and 2** (the physical actions) change your resistance level? (Focus on the immediate feeling of momentum).

    Change: _____

    _____

    _____

    _____

    _____

CHAPTER 2

DESIGN YOUR SANCTUARY: IMPLEMENT VISIBLE, ADHD-FRIENDLY STORAGE SYSTEMS

The immense, daily burden of overwhelm for a woman with ADHD is often amplified by the chaos of her environment. If Chapter 1 provided the blueprint for defeating the paralyzing inertia of clutter, this chapter offers the construction manual for building an external sanctuary, a physical and digital space intentionally designed to act as a **supportive ally** to the neurodiverse brain.

Traditional organizational advice often fails the ADHD population because it relies on two mental processes that are inherently compromised: robust **working memory** and seamless **executive planning**. When advice dictates that you "tuck everything away neatly," it sets you up for failure, as the moment an item is hidden, the ADHD brain registers it as permanently lost due to the "out of sight, out of mind" phenomenon.

This chapter champions **functional organization**: a strategic system built on principles of visual recall, predictable placement, and minimized decision-making. The goal is not a pristine home, but a reliably intuitive one that significantly reduces the daily friction and cognitive load that fuel internal anxiety and overwhelm. By externalizing your memory and creating visual cues, you transform your environment from a source of stress into a powerful co-regulator of your attention and emotional stability.

The Neurobiology of Visibility: Why Traditional Organization Fails

To build an effective system, we must first deeply understand the neurobiological deficits that make traditional, opaque organization, such as deep drawers, closed cabinets, or complex filing, counterproductive for the ADHD brain.

1. The Working Memory Deficit and Object Permanence

The most significant barrier to a tidy, functional home is the **working memory deficit** associated with ADHD. Working memory is the "mental scratchpad" that allows the brain to hold and manipulate information for a short period of time, such as remembering a complex instruction or where you placed your keys moments ago. For a woman with ADHD, this memory can feel inconsistent or unreliable.

This leads directly to the **"out of sight, out of mind"** experience: if an item is not in your immediate visual field, your brain essentially ceases to register its existence, location, or importance. While a neurotypical brain can easily retrieve the memory of an item's hidden location, the ADHD brain often struggles to initiate this retrieval process, particularly if the item is not needed immediately.

The implication is profound: forcing objects into opaque, hidden storage systems requires the ADHD brain to constantly expend energy fighting against its natural wiring. Every time you need an item, you must engage in a taxing cognitive search process, a task that consumes valuable mental bandwidth and contributes significantly to mental fatigue and burnout. The effective solution, therefore, is not to force the brain to remember, but to design the environment to *remember for the brain* through visual reinforcement.

2. The Cognitive Cost of Visual Noise and Clutter

While it may seem counterintuitive to advocate for more visible storage, the goal is not to create a chaotic mess but to manage **visual noise** strategically. Clutter is a direct contributor to high **cognitive load**, the amount of mental effort consumed by working memory, which is already a severe challenge for the ADHD brain.

A cluttered desk, a messy kitchen counter, or a chaotic digital desktop is not just an inconvenience; it represents a constellation of unfinished tasks, pending decisions, and unfiled items. Each of these competes for the attention of a brain that already struggles with an impaired **filtering mechanism**. The brain, unable to efficiently screen out irrelevant stimuli, processes every piece of visual input, a stray coffee cup, a pile of papers, a stack of books, as a subtle demand on its resources.

This constant, low-level mental effort is exhausting and generates a perpetual, low-grade hum of anxiety that significantly exacerbates ADHD symptoms. Studies have shown that cluttered environments can increase stress and anxiety, potentially raising stress hormones like cortisol, which can further impair executive functions like inhibitory control and emotional regulation. By strategically using clear, designated storage, we simplify the visual field. We replace the ambiguity of a messy surface with the predictable clarity of categorized storage, reducing the brain's processing burden and conserving executive function for more demanding tasks.

Section 1: The Design Strategy: Creating External Recall

The core principle of the ADHD-friendly sanctuary is to ensure that essential items remain visible and easily accessible. This strategy, known as **external recall**, compensates for compromised working memory by utilizing environmental design as an external reminder system.

1. Prioritize Visible Storage: Clear Containers and No Lids

To directly combat the "out of sight, out of mind" phenomenon, all organizational systems must favor transparency and accessibility.

- **Go Clear:** Use clear plastic or mesh containers and storage drawers wherever possible. Clear storage allows the eye to immediately register the contents, providing a constant visual cue of what is inside and eliminating the need for your working memory to recall the item's location. This is a simple yet powerful design shift that ensures items remain "in mind" even when stored.

- **Abolish the Lid:** For frequently used items or items prone to being lost (e.g., keys, mail, hats, snacks), use baskets, bins, or containers **without lids**. The friction of removing a lid, however small, can be enough to derail the moment of putting an item away, causing it to land on a nearby surface instead. Eliminating this tiny point of friction promotes the swift and easy return of the item to its designated "home," reinforcing the desired organizational habit. The basket serves as a **catch-all zone** that contains the mess without hiding the contents entirely.

- **Embrace the Tray:** Use small trays, dishes, or decorative plates on surfaces like nightstands, coffee tables, or desks. These function as miniature, contained landing zones for items that must remain visible (e.g., remote controls, reading glasses, medications). The tray visually signals that the items belong there while preventing them from spreading and creating generalized visual clutter.

2. Labeling for Specificity and Clarity

While clear storage is essential, it is often not enough. For items stored in opaque containers, or even clear containers with many similar items, clear, bold labeling is crucial. This serves two primary functions:

- **Externalizing Categorization:** The ADHD brain struggles with fluid categorization and can easily forget the specific contents or purpose of a bin once it is sealed or moved. A label, particularly one that is color-coded or uses pictures (for visual thinkers), serves as a constant, non-negotiable external reminder of the container's contents and purpose. The label prevents the mental effort of guessing or having to search through multiple drawers, thus saving precious executive function resources.

- **Promoting Consistency:** Labels reinforce the designated "home" of an item, making the act of putting things away automatic and low-friction. The label instantly communicates where an item should be returned, reducing the likelihood of it being placed on a random surface due to momentary decision fatigue. Labels should be simple and action-oriented (e.g., "Meds - AM / PM," "Office Receipts," "Car Keys / Wallet").

3. Vertical Organization vs. Piles

The ADHD brain is highly susceptible to the cognitive stress induced by piles. Piles are visually overwhelming, mentally ambiguous (is this a to-do pile or a finished pile?), and physically difficult to maintain. The solution is to move organization from a horizontal plane (piles) to a vertical one (display and file).

- **Vertical Filing:** For papers, rather than letting them accumulate in flat stacks that create visual noise, use vertical file folders, magazine holders, or wall-mounted clipboards. Displaying papers vertically keeps important documents visually accessible without creating a sense of chaotic mess. A paper on a clipboard is a visual cue for a "to-do," whereas a pile on a desk is a visual cue for "overwhelm."

- **Wall-Mounted Systems:** Utilize vertical wall space for external memory systems. Pegboards, hook racks, or command centers can keep frequently lost items (keys, headphones, backpacks) off flat surfaces and in a predictable, designated location. This leverages the principle that the ADHD brain benefits from the visual prominence of objects in its line of sight.

Section 2: Eliminating Decision Fatigue: The Power of a Designated "Home"

Once the environment is visually optimized, the next strategic step is eliminating the constant micro-decisions that plague the ADHD brain. **Decision fatigue** occurs when the sheer volume of choices, even mundane ones like *where should this pen go?*, drains mental energy, making the brain prone to poor judgment and eventual shutdown. The solution is the principle of the designated "home."

1. Give Every Item a "Home"

The foundational rule of functional organization is to commit to a specific, easily accessible "home" for every single item you own.

- **The Intentional Spot:** When organizing, you must proactively decide *where* each item belongs, and that location must be intuitive and easy to access. Putting the item away must be the simplest and lowest-friction choice available. If putting the item away is harder than leaving it out, the system will fail.

- **Anchor Points for Critical Items:** For items that are constantly lost, such as keys, wallets, phones, glasses, or medication, the **Landing Strip** is a crucial compensatory strategy. A landing strip is a small, designated zone (e.g., a dish, a tray, or a specific hook) near the entrance of your home where these items *must* be placed immediately upon entry. This intentional habit eliminates the frantic, time-consuming searches that typically accompany poor working memory and provides a vital feeling of predictability and control.

2. The Strategic Allowance: Embracing the "Junk Drawer"

The pursuit of absolute perfection is a common cause of system abandonment for the ADHD brain. Attempting to achieve impossible tidiness often leads to system failure and renewed overwhelm. To maintain sustainability, the organizational strategy must include an intentional allowance for functional imperfection.

- **The Role of the Catch-All:** The **Junk Drawer** is not a failure of organization; it is a strategically designated, contained zone of functional clutter. Designate at least one easy-to-access "junk drawer" or "miscellaneous basket" in high-traffic rooms (e.g., kitchen, office) for temporary storage of items that do not yet have a determined home, or items that are truly miscellaneous (e.g., loose batteries, rubber bands, spare change).

- **Preventing the Spillover:** The junk drawer acts as a controlled pressure release valve. It prevents small, ambiguous items from spreading onto countertops and tables, where they would otherwise create general visual clutter and increase cognitive load. It recognizes the reality that not every item can be perfectly categorized immediately, allowing the overall system to remain sustainable by channeling the chaos into a single, predictable location.

Section 3: The Sanctuary Mindset: Emotional and Cognitive Benefits

The work of designing an ADHD-friendly sanctuary yields measurable, profound benefits that go far beyond a cleaner look. These changes actively regulate the nervous system and protect valuable mental resources.

1. Reducing Anxiety and Shame

Clutter is frequently a direct source of anxiety and shame for women with ADHD. The chronic feeling that one "should" be more organized but cannot achieve it creates a relentless cycle of self-criticism and inadequacy.

- **Dismantling the Inner Critic:** Functional organization acts as a powerful antidote to the harsh inner critic. When a woman can reliably find her essential items and her space is visually calm, the evidence of her "failure" is reduced. This shift helps dismantle the toxic narrative that she is "lazy" or "incompetent," replacing it with the reality that her brain simply requires a unique, supportive system.

- **Fostering Self-Compassion:** By intentionally designing a space that accommodates her neurobiology, a woman is engaging in a powerful act of **self-compassion**: treating herself with the understanding and support she would offer a close friend facing the same challenge. This reduces the emotional isolation and self-blame that are so prevalent in the female ADHD experience.

2. Conserving Executive Function and Mental Energy

Every element of the designed sanctuary, the clear bins, the labels, the landing strips, is a tool for **conserving executive function (EF) reserves**. EF is a finite resource, and when it is depleted by fighting clutter or constantly searching for items, a woman has less capacity for high-leverage tasks like deep work, emotional regulation, and planning.

- **Frictionless Living:** The goal is to move from a state of **high friction** (where every action requires significant mental effort) to **frictionless living** (where putting things away is the easiest choice). Eliminating decision fatigue and relying on visual recall allows the woman's working memory and planning centers to operate on a simpler, more efficient level.
- **Creating Predictability:** Predictability reduces the need for the ADHD brain to constantly engage in effortful monitoring and filtering. When items are in their designated homes, the environment becomes a source of stability, not surprise. This stability frees up immense cognitive bandwidth, reducing the overall cognitive load and the persistent mental fatigue that defines chronic overwhelm.

Conclusion: Your External Brain

The organizational struggle is a profound, lifelong challenge rooted in neurobiological differences. The work of designing your sanctuary is not about achieving perfection; it is about establishing a foundational system of functional organization that consistently supports your brain's unique wiring.

The mastery of this external scaffolding, from prioritizing visible storage to strategically utilizing the junk drawer, transforms your environment from a demanding adversary into a supportive "external brain." This system of visual recall and reduced decision-making is the prerequisite for the deeper work of focus, emotional mastery, and relational stability. By reducing the visual noise and cognitive burden of your space, you free up the mental energy necessary to transition from simply surviving to proactively thriving.

Chapter 2 Workbook: Design Your Sanctuary: Implement Visible, ADHD-Friendly Storage Systems

Objective: To compensate for poor **working memory** by creating a supportive, visually accessible environment that defeats the **"out of sight, out of mind"** phenomenon.

Activity 2.1: The Visible Recall Conversion

1. **Opaque Overload Zone:** Identify one area using hidden, opaque, or lidded storage where items consistently get lost (e.g., "Bathroom cabinet," or "Toolbox").

2. **Plan the Conversion:** Detail how you will convert this area to a visual system.

Item Type	Current Storage (Hidden)	ADHD-Friendly Conversion (Visible)
(Example: Vitamins)	Tucked away in a lidded bottle in a dark cabinet.	Moved to a **clear container** without a lid on a countertop.
(Example: Mail / Paper)	Piled on the kitchen counter.	Stored **vertically** in a clear wall-mounted file folder.
(Your Item):		

Action Check 2.2: Labeling for Clarity

Commit to creating bold, simple labels for three items in your identified zone. Labels should be functional, not decorative.

Label 1: _____

Label 2: _____

Label 3: _____

CHAPTER 3

ESTABLISH PREDICTABILITY:
GIVE EVERY ITEM A DESIGNATED "HOME"

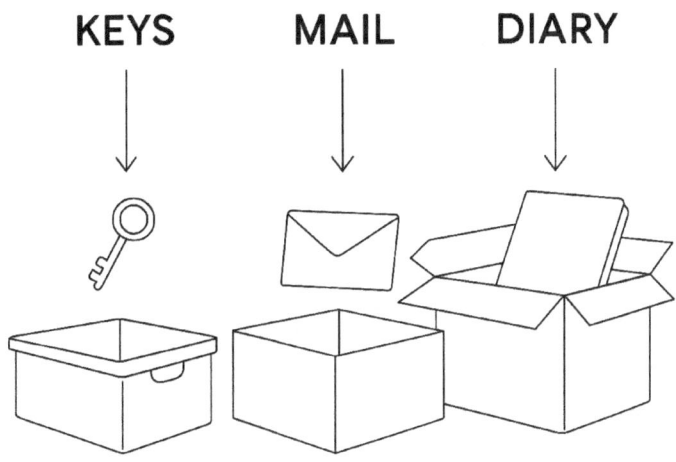

KEYS   MAIL   DIARY

Following the vital work of confronting paralysis and designing a visually accessible environment, the next critical step in achieving functional organization is establishing unshakeable **predictability**. This chapter addresses the profound daily drain caused by **decision fatigue** and the constant expenditure of mental energy required to recall or find misplaced items. The solution is elegantly simple: to commit to a specific, easily accessible, and intuitive **"home"** for every item you own.

For the woman with Attention-Deficit / Hyperactivity Disorder (ADHD), the absence of a designated home for an object, whether it's her keys, a critical piece of mail, or a pair of reading glasses, forces her brain to make a series of exhausting, minute decisions every single time she interacts with it. *Where should this go? Where did I just set it down? Which pile is the right pile?* This relentless barrage of micro-decisions is not merely an inconvenience; it actively depletes the finite resources of her executive functions, contributing significantly to chronic overwhelm, anxiety, and the pervasive feeling of being perpetually "frenzied, frazzled, and overwhelmed."

This chapter moves past simple tidiness and into a strategy of neurobiological self-management. By creating a predictable and intuitive external system, you eliminate the daily cognitive friction of choice, reduce the reliance on compromised internal working memory, and conserve your precious executive function reserves for tasks that truly require focused, complex thought.

The Neurobiological Cost of Decision Ambiguity

The struggle to keep things organized and in their place is deeply rooted in the neurobiology of the ADHD brain. Understanding *why* ambiguity drains your energy is the key to building systems that are resilient to the challenges of inattention and memory deficits.

1. Decision Fatigue: The Silent Drain on Executive Function

Decision fatigue is a state of mental exhaustion caused by having to make a high volume of choices over a sustained period. This phenomenon is particularly devastating for the ADHD brain, whose executive function (EF) skills, the "mental toolkit for success", are already prone to inconsistency and rapid depletion.

Every time you encounter an item without a clear destination, your prefrontal cortex (the brain's command center for planning and logic) has to engage in a micro-analysis: *Analyze item; Recall potential locations; Evaluate importance; Select location; Initiate movement.* This process, repeated dozens of times daily for mundane items, burns through the limited cognitive bandwidth required for higher-leverage activities like complex problem-solving, emotional regulation, or sustained focus on work.

When EF reserves are depleted by constant micro-decisions, the brain defaults to its least energy-intensive choices, which inevitably leads to:

- **Impulsivity:** Less mental energy is available to inhibit the urge to leave the item where it is or to make poor decisions later in the day (e.g., impulsive spending or emotional outbursts).

- **Avoidance / Paralysis:** The prospect of confronting a pile of ambiguous items, each demanding a decision, becomes too cognitively taxing, triggering an overwhelm response that leads to complete task paralysis.

The commitment to giving every item a designated "home" is therefore an act of preservation. It proactively eliminates ambiguity, replacing taxing analysis with automatic, low-friction placement, thus conserving executive function for when it is truly needed.

2. Compensating for Compromised Working Memory

A significant barrier to maintaining order is the well-documented **working memory deficit** associated with ADHD. Working memory, the mental "scratchpad," is essential for holding temporary information, such as the location where you just placed an item. For a woman with ADHD, this memory can feel like a sieve, making the rapid recall of a non-designated spot nearly impossible.

This is the neurobiological root of the "out of sight, out of mind" phenomenon: the item effectively ceases to exist when it is no longer in the immediate visual field, because the memory system fails to reliably store or retrieve its location.

A designated "home" acts as a reliable **external memory cue** that bypasses this internal deficit. When you train yourself to place Item X at Spot Y, the association becomes muscle memory, or an automatic process that relies on habit rather than conscious effort and recall. The external structure compensates for the internal inconsistency, creating a reliable, low-effort pathway for maintenance.

The Foundational Principle: The Rule of Intentional Placement

Functional organization for the ADHD brain must be built on the principle of minimal friction. An item's designated "home" must be the easiest, most intuitive, and least energy-intensive choice for placement. If the effort required to put an item away is greater than the effort required to leave it out, the system will fail.

1. Assigning the Home: Proximity and Logic

The act of assigning a home must be intentional and logical, taking into account the item's use and the brain's preference for immediate gratification.

- **The Proximity Principle:** An item's home should be located immediately adjacent to where it is most frequently **used**. For instance, charging cables should live directly next to the charging station, not in a box across the room. Scissors and tape should live in the most common wrapping or craft area, not in a generic utility drawer in the kitchen. This reduces the physical and mental steps required for put-away, making the organized choice the path of least resistance.

- **The "First Touch" Rule:** Commit to determining a home for every new item the moment it enters your home. If a new receipt or piece of mail lands on the counter, address it immediately by moving it to its designated home (e.g., the "To-File" bin or the "Bill Pay" folder). Allowing ambiguous items to linger creates visual clutter that contaminates the predictable system and invites paralysis.

2. The Critical "Landing Strip"

The most significant drain on time and energy for many women with ADHD comes from losing critical, frequently used items: keys, phone, wallet, or daily medication. To combat this, the **Landing Strip** is a non-negotiable strategic system designed to eliminate the decision process for these high-value, high-loss items.

- **The Designated Zone:** The Landing Strip is a small, designated, and visually prominent zone immediately near your primary entry / exit point (e.g., a specific bowl, a tray, or a dedicated hook rack).
- **The Automatic Habit:** The habit must be rigid: Every critical item *must* be placed on the Landing Strip immediately upon re-entering the home, before jackets are removed or bags are put down. This ritual transforms placement from a conscious decision into a low-effort, automatic sequence that leverages muscle memory. By eliminating the question "Where are my keys?" from your daily life, you dramatically reduce pre-departure stress, saving both time and mental energy.

The Necessity of Functional Imperfection: The Designated "Junk Drawer"

Perfection is the enemy of sustainability for the ADHD brain. Attempting to achieve a flawless organizational system that accounts for every tiny, miscellaneous item often leads to immediate abandonment and a renewed sense of failure. The strategy must include an intentional allowance for functional imperfection.

The **Junk Drawer** is not a sign of failure; it is a strategically designated, contained zone of functional clutter that acts as a controlled pressure release valve.

1. The Purpose of the Pressure Release Valve

The junk drawer serves a crucial neurobiological purpose: it provides a predetermined, low-friction "home" for items that trigger decision fatigue due to their ambiguity or size.

- **Ambiguity Reduction:** It accommodates items that do not yet have a determined "home" (e.g., a spare Allen wrench, an unidentifiable small battery, a piece of wire) or items that are truly miscellaneous (rubber bands, spare change). Without this release valve, these small items would spread onto countertops and surfaces, creating generalized visual clutter that rapidly contaminates the entire space and increases overall cognitive load.
- **Preventing Paralysis:** When encountering an item whose home is not immediately obvious, the brain might freeze, triggering task paralysis. The junk drawer eliminates this pause by offering a swift, non-judgmental destination: *If I don't know where it goes, it goes in the drawer.* This simple, clear rule prevents the spread of chaos and conserves decision-making energy for high-leverage tasks.

2. Strategic Placement and Maintenance

The junk drawer must be managed strategically to remain functional and not become an overwhelming time capsule.

- **Controlled Containment:** Designate at least one easy-to-access junk drawer or miscellaneous basket in high-traffic rooms (e.g., kitchen, office). The key is that the clutter is contained, visually separated from the organized surfaces that serve as your core memory cues.
- **Periodic Review (Low-Stakes):** Schedule a very low-stakes, non-judgmental review of the junk drawer once every six months or so. Because the contents are already contained, the task of reviewing them is less overwhelming than facing general clutter. This ensures the drawer remains a functional holding zone rather than a black hole of permanent chaos.

Sustaining Predictability: Reinforcing the "Home"

Establishing the "home" is only half the battle; the long-term success of the system depends on transforming these intentional placements into automatic, low-effort **habits**. The ADHD brain often struggles with habit formation due to the dysregulated dopamine system, which seeks immediate reward and struggles with repetitive, mundane follow-through.

1. Leverage Habit Stacking for Automaticity

Habit stacking is an evidence-based technique that links a new, desired habit (putting an item in its home) to an existing, established habit. This technique leverages the automaticity of the existing routine to anchor the new, difficult behavior, reducing the reliance on inconsistent willpower.

- **Anchor the New Habit:** Structure the placement rule around an existing, reliable cue.
  - ○ *Instead of:* "Remember to put your glasses in the case."
  - ○ *Try:* "After I put my dinner plate in the sink **(Existing Habit)**, I immediately place my reading glasses in the designated tray on the counter **(New Habit)**."
- **Anchor the Daily Transition:** Use established transition points, which are often challenging for the ADHD brain, as predictable cues.
  - ○ "After I turn off my computer for the night **(Existing Habit)**, I take my wallet and phone out of my bag and place them directly on the Landing Strip **(New Habit)**."

2. Implement the 15-Minute Daily "Reset" Ritual

Organization is not a static destination; it is a dynamic process of continuous maintenance. A key vulnerability of the ADHD brain is allowing small messes to escalate into paralyzing chaos. The solution is the **15-Minute Daily "Reset" Ritual**.

- **Prevent the Snowball Effect:** Dedicate a consistent, short period, approximately 15 minutes daily, to a focused "reset" of your core living or working areas. This is not a deep clean; it is merely an intentional effort to put things back in their designated homes, throw items out, and quickly file necessary documents.
- **Leverage Timers and Novelty:** To maintain engagement and overcome the boredom of repetition, use a timer or integrate elements of **Body Doubling** (working in the presence of a supportive partner or friend) during this 15-minute period. The short duration, enforced by a timer, makes the task feel finite and less overwhelming, leveraging the principle of the micro-step to sustain momentum.

The Emotional and Cognitive Liberation of Predictability

The commitment to establishing predictability through the "designated home" is a profound act of self-care with measurable psychological benefits that extend far beyond a tidy room.

1. Reducing Anxiety and Boosting Self-Efficacy

Chronic disorganization is a relentless source of anxiety for women with ADHD, fueling the pervasive belief that they are fundamentally incapable of self-management.

- **The Antidote to Shame:** Predictability directly counteracts the cycle of shame and self-blame that stems from lost items and chronic lateness. When a woman knows, without question, where her critical items are located, she reduces the internal stress and the subsequent external friction that often leads to outbursts or breakdowns.

- **Building Self-Efficacy:** Every successful instance of putting an item in its designated home, the keys on the hook, the mail in the basket, the remote on the tray, provides a small, satisfying "win." This consistent, positive reinforcement builds **self-efficacy**, the belief in one's own ability to succeed, which is a powerful psychological resource that bolsters overall emotional resilience.

2. Reclaiming Cognitive Bandwidth

The most important result of this work is the liberation of cognitive bandwidth. By moving the organizational burden from the brain's inconsistent internal memory to reliable external systems, a woman frees up the immense mental energy that was once consumed by searching, worrying, and deciding.

This conserved executive function can now be redirected toward high-leverage pursuits: achieving deep work, mastering emotional regulation, engaging in intentional communication, and simply enjoying moments of focused peace. The unpredictable internal chaos begins to subside, replaced by the calm, supportive rhythm of a truly predictable, intentionally designed external environment. The result is a life that is no longer dominated by low-level anxiety and micro-decisions, but by purposeful, integrated action.

Chapter 3 Workbook: Establish Predictability: Give Every Item a Designated "Home"

Objective: To eliminate daily **decision fatigue** by assigning a specific, non-negotiable **"home"** to essential items, reducing reliance on inconsistent internal memory.

Activity 3.1: The Landing Strip Commitment

1.   **High-Loss Stressors:** List the top three items you **always** search for before leaving the house.

Items: _____

_____

_____

2.   **Designate the Permanent Home:** Define the exact, exclusive location for these items near your main entrance (The Landing Strip).

Location: _____

_____

3.   **Create the Habit Stack:** Anchor the new habit of using the Landing Strip to an existing, automatic habit you do when you enter the door (e.g., taking off your coat).
     o   *Existing Habit:* "The moment I _____,"
     o   *New Habit Stack:* "I immediately place my keys / wallet on the Landing Strip."

Reflection 3.2: The Anti-Friction Allowance

1.   Name one type of ambiguous item (e.g., loose change, spare twist ties, old coupons) that often pollutes your clear spaces.

Item: _____

_____

2.   To reduce decision fatigue, you commit to routing this item directly to a **Junk Drawer** or **Miscellaneous Basket**. How does this commitment reduce the friction on your organized surfaces?

Benefit: _____

_____

CHAPTER 4

SUSTAIN MOMENTUM: USE BODY DOUBLING AND TIMERS TO START TASKS

In the journey to defeat chronic disorganization, the most difficult challenge often remains **task initiation**: the ability to simply start a demanding or tedious project. While the previous chapters laid the critical foundation by breaking down overwhelming projects into manageable micro-steps and establishing predictable homes for items, a crucial neurological barrier persists: the **task activation deficit**. For the ADHD brain, the gap between *knowing* what to do and actually *doing* it can feel immense, like an uncrossable chasm, rooted in a fundamental challenge with motivation and executive control.

This chapter provides the strategic solution to this barrier, focusing on two evidence-based techniques that create **external scaffolding** to bridge the gap between intention and action: **Body Doubling** and the disciplined use of **Timers**. These tools work by strategically bypassing the internal deficits in focus and motivation, leveraging external structure and accountability to transform a state of paralyzing inertia into one of sustained momentum. The goal is to stop fighting your internal resistance with willpower, and start designing an environment that *forces* the first step, making the organized choice the path of least resistance.

The Neurobiology of the Activation Barrier

To effectively defeat the "can't get started" syndrome, we must recognize that this resistance is not a moral failure, but a neurobiological reality. Task paralysis and the difficulty in initiation are symptoms of the ADHD brain's unique wiring, particularly concerning **dopamine dysregulation** and **cognitive overload**.

1. The Dopamine-Driven Deficit

Dopamine, the brain's primary neurotransmitter for motivation, reward, and activation, is thought to be dysregulated in the ADHD brain. This neurochemical difference makes tasks that are not immediately stimulating or inherently rewarding feel exceptionally difficult to initiate and sustain. Mundane, multi-step activities inherent in organization, such as filing paperwork or cleaning a neglected corner, do not provide the necessary immediate reward, failing to trigger the dopamine release required for activation. This deficit explains why a woman may find herself procrastinating and avoiding tasks by doing other, more stimulating activities, or simply "zoning out" instead of engaging with the task she knows must be done.

2. Cognitive Overload and Filtering Failure

The ADHD brain struggles with efficiently filtering out irrelevant information and distractions, leading to a constant state of high **cognitive load**. When faced with an organizing project, the brain is instantly overwhelmed by the sheer volume of competing stimuli—the mess, the potential steps, the emotional weight of the task—which quickly exceeds its capacity to process and prioritize. This overload triggers a cognitive shutdown, or mental paralysis, as the brain seeks to protect itself from excessive stimulation.

The two strategies presented here, Body Doubling and Timers, work by providing powerful, external cues that bypass the need for internal dopamine generation or excessive cognitive filtering, creating a non-negotiable anchor for attention and initiation.

Section 1: Body Doubling: Creating External Executive Function

Body Doubling refers to the practice of performing a task in the presence of another person to enhance motivation, focus, and efficiency. This technique, which emerged from the self-help literature of the ADHD community, is a highly effective, low-risk strategy that utilizes a social framework to compensate for internal executive function deficits.

The Mechanism: Anchoring Attention and Accountability

While controlled research on Body Doubling is limited, anecdotal evidence strongly suggests its profound utility for individuals with ADHD who struggle with consistency and initiation. The mechanism is theorized to work by creating a form of **external executive functioning** that anchors the individual to the present moment, thereby reducing distraction and enhancing motivation.

1. **Anchoring Attention:** The presence of a body double, even a silent one working on a completely separate task, acts as a consistent, non-judgmental anchor for the ADHD brain. Because the brain struggles to filter out external stimuli, the quiet, focused presence of another person becomes a central point of focus that helps the individual stay oriented to the task at hand, reducing the risk of being pulled away by internal or external distractions.

2. **Social Accountability:** The mere act of committing to work in the presence of another person, whether in-person or virtually, provides a subtle yet powerful source of accountability that bypasses the internal motivation deficit. This sense of being observed, not critically, but supportively, can supply the necessary activation energy to overcome procrastination and keep the individual engaged when the task becomes boring or difficult. The pressure is externalized and positive, making the "cost" of not starting higher than the cost of initiation.

3. **Encouragement and Momentum:** The body double can also function as a source of gentle encouragement or help with challenging steps, particularly when the ADHD individual hits a common roadblock, such as emotional overwhelm or task confusion. This external encouragement helps the person maintain momentum, which, in turn, generates the internal dopamine reward necessary to continue working.

Implementing the Body Double Strategy

To maximize the effectiveness of Body Doubling, it must be implemented strategically, ensuring the environment supports focus rather than providing a new distraction:

- **Establish the Rules:** The most successful Body Doubling requires clear ground rules. The double's role is *not* to micromanage, perform the task for you, or criticize your pace. Their primary job is simply **to be visibly present** and engaged in their *own* work. This non-judgmental presence is crucial for women with ADHD who may already struggle with immense shame and a harsh inner critic.

- **Prioritize Visibility:** Whether the session is in-person or virtual, the body double must remain visible. If working virtually, use a video call with cameras on so you can see your double working. This visual cue acts as the constant, external anchor for your attention.

- **Set a Time Limit:** The Body Doubling session should have a clear, finite duration. Because individuals with ADHD struggle with accurately estimating the time needed for a task (**time blindness**), using a timer during the session is essential to prevent overwhelm and maintain focus. Short, manageable work intervals ensure that you only have to stay focused for a limited time, making the commitment feel less intimidating.

Section 2: Harnessing Time: Timers as External Cues

The strategic use of a timer is the second crucial component of creating external scaffolding. For the ADHD brain, which struggles profoundly with the flow and estimation of time, a timer transforms abstract time into a visible, concrete, and manageable resource.

The Challenge of Time Blindness

Time blindness, the inability to accurately feel or gauge the passage of time, is a core executive function deficit that severely impacts productivity and increases feelings of overwhelm. This challenge makes it exceptionally difficult to estimate how long a task will take, or to remember deadlines without constant, conscious effort.

- **Overwhelm by Infinity:** When a task is assigned, the ADHD brain may perceive the work as an infinite, unquantifiable time sink, which triggers anxiety and paralyzes initiation.

- **The Estimation Deficit:** Individuals with ADHD consistently underestimate how long tasks will take, leading to chronic rushing, missed deadlines, and increased stress.

The Solution: Making Time Concrete

Timers directly address time blindness by creating a **visual representation of time** that bypasses the abstract, internal sense of duration. This clear structure helps bring the task into focus, eliminating the cognitive guesswork of *what to do next* and *for how long*.

The Pomodoro Technique: Structured Focus and Reward

The **Pomodoro Technique** is a highly effective timer-based system that structures work into short, focused intervals (traditionally 25 minutes) followed by mandated short breaks (5 minutes). This technique is uniquely suited for the ADHD brain due to several key neurobiological advantages:

1. **Breaks Down Overwhelming Tasks:** By requiring the user to break a large, daunting task into smaller, clearer, 25-minute chunks, the Pomodoro Technique makes the project feel manageable and achievable, directly combating the task paralysis triggered by complexity.

2. **Boosts Concentration and Reduces Fatigue:** The knowledge that the focused effort is limited to a short burst, the duration of the timer, helps keep attention sharp and prevents the deep mental fatigue often caused by continuous, unstructured effort.

3. **Prevents Hyperfocus and Burnout:** For the woman who struggles with *uncontrolled* hyperfocus, where she becomes so engrossed she neglects other responsibilities, the mandated break acts as a crucial, external circuit-breaker. The scheduled 5-minute pause provides a regular, guilt-free opportunity for the brain to seek novelty or reset, preventing burnout without derailing the entire work session.

4. **Leverages the Reward System:** Each completed interval provides a tangible sense of accomplishment, yielding a small burst of dopamine that reinforces productive behavior and builds momentum for the next interval.

Customizing the Timer for Personal Needs

While the standard 25 / 5-minute interval is a good starting point, the most powerful feature of the Pomodoro Technique for ADHD is its **customizability**. A woman must tailor the duration to match her personal attention span and energy cycle:

- If 25 minutes feels too long, start with a 15-minute interval.
- If you are deep in a flow state, extend the work block to 45 minutes, but keep the mandatory break scheduled to prevent hyperfocus from becoming avoidance or burnout.

The consistent use of structured intervals provides a reliable way to make time concrete, turning the work period into a manageable sprint rather than an overwhelming marathon.

Section 3: Leveraging Accountability and Momentum

The combination of Body Doubling and Timers does more than just start a task; it creates a structured environment for sustained momentum and proactive problem-solving, dramatically reducing the invisible energy cost of unmanaged ADHD.

Transforming Tasks into Actionable Appointments

One of the greatest struggles for the ADHD brain is translating a vague task on a to-do list (e.g., "Organize files") into a specific, executable commitment. The organizational process must treat tasks as non-negotiable, scheduled events.

- **Schedule Your Organization:** Every organizational step, whether it is a micro-step defined in Chapter 1 or a 25-minute Pomodoro interval, must be scheduled into your planner or calendar as an **actionable appointment**. For example, instead of writing "Laundry" on your list, schedule: "1:00 PM – 1:25 PM: Body Double Laundry: Sort, Load, and Start Wash Cycle." This shift provides a clear temporal cue that is crucial for a brain that struggles with internal time management.

- **Build in Buffer Time:** A key strategy to reduce stress and maintain flow is to intentionally schedule **more time than you initially estimate** for tasks, including buffers for transitions between activities. Acknowledging the estimation deficit and adding an extra 25-50% time to your scheduled appointment prevents the rush and stress that compound executive function deficits.

Defeating the "ADHD Tax" on Mental Energy

The chronic feeling of being perpetually "frenzied, frazzled, and overwhelmed" that many women with ADHD report is the emotional and mental cost of navigating daily life with compromised executive functions—often referred to as the **"ADHD Tax."** This cost includes the mental exhaustion of constantly compensating, self-correcting, and fighting internal disorganization.

By externalizing task initiation through Body Doubling and time management through Timers, you are actively mitigating this tax:

- **Reduces Cognitive Load:** These external structures reduce the mental effort required to start, stay on track, and manage transitions, thereby conserving precious cognitive bandwidth.
- **Mitigates Overwhelm:** The clear structure and defined limits combat the feelings of overwhelm that trigger paralysis, allowing the woman to operate from a place of calm control rather than panicked reaction.
- **Consistent Practice:** The use of short, scheduled intervals (like the 15 minutes recommended for daily de-cluttering) makes maintenance a consistent, low-friction routine rather than a stressful, all-or-nothing chore.

Conclusion: The Strategic Path to Action

Task initiation is the moment where the strategic work of organization meets the neurobiological reality of the ADHD brain. For the woman who has internalized her struggles as personal failings, the inability to start tasks fuels deep shame and feelings of inadequacy.

The combination of **Body Doubling** and **Timers** provides a powerful, compassionate, and evidence-based solution. You are no longer fighting internal motivation with inconsistent willpower. Instead, you are building an external system that provides the necessary social accountability to anchor your focus, and the clear structure to manage time, transforming overwhelming inertia into predictable, sustained momentum.

Mastering these tools creates a sense of confidence and control, moving you past the paralyzing gap between intention and action. This stability in task initiation is the final foundational skill in Book 1, providing the necessary platform of physical and temporal order upon which the more complex skills of focus, emotional regulation, and deep connection in the following books will be built.

Chapter 4 Workbook: Sustain Momentum: Use Body Doubling and Timers to Start Tasks

Objective: To bypass the internal motivation deficit by leveraging **external accountability** (**Body Doubling**) and **fixed time limits** (Timers) to sustain focus.

Activity 4.1: The External Scaffolding Trial

1. **The Boring Task:** Select one boring or repetitive organizing task that is difficult to start (e.g., "Filing old receipts," or "Cleaning the baseboards").

    Task: _____

    _____

    _____

    _____

2. **Set the Pomodoro Sprint:** Schedule a short, fixed work block using a timer to counteract **time blindness**.

Time Block	Activity	External Support Used
25 Minutes	Uninterrupted work on the Target Task.	**Body Double** Name:_____ _____ _____
5 Minutes	**Mandatory Break** (Stand up, stretch, get water—no social media).	Timer

Action Check 4.2: Accountability Script

1. If you get distracted or hit a wall during the 25-minute sprint, you need a non-judgmental cue. Write one sentence your Body Double can use to gently redirect you.
    *   *Body Double Script:* (Example: "You've got 15 minutes left, let's go for one more micro-step.")

CHAPTER 5

STOP THE SNOWBALL: IMPLEMENT DAILY 15-MINUTE "RESET" ROUTINES

15-MINUTE RESET

The work of achieving functional organization is not a one-time cleaning event; it is an ongoing process of strategic maintenance and habit formation. The most insidious challenge for a woman with Attention-Deficit / Hyperactivity Disorder (ADHD) is the **"Snowball Effect"**: the inevitable reality that a small, manageable mess, a few dishes in the sink, a handful of papers on the counter, an unread stack of emails, can rapidly escalate into an overwhelming, paralyzing avalanche of chaos.

This chapter addresses the final, crucial step in organization: building consistent, low-friction habits to maintain order. The solution lies in the disciplined implementation of the **Daily 15-Minute "Reset" Routine**, a non-negotiable, short burst of focused effort designed to interrupt the snowball effect before it can trigger the emotional and cognitive paralysis that leads to complete system breakdown.

For the ADHD brain, which struggles profoundly with **task initiation** and **consistency**, maintenance often feels impossible, a source of profound shame and failure. This is often because the approach is flawed: it attempts to impose rigid, perfectionistic standards that are neurobiologically unsustainable. This chapter rejects the "all-or-nothing" cycle and champions a compassionate, strategic model of **functional imperfection**, where consistency and self-forgiveness are prioritized over flawless tidiness. By consistently applying short, time-bound efforts, you transform organization from a stressful, all-consuming chore into a manageable, routine practice that systematically conserves your mental energy.

Section 1: The Neurobiological Imperative for Daily Maintenance

The struggle with consistent habit formation and maintenance for the ADHD brain is rooted in its unique neurobiology, particularly concerning its **reward system** and its vulnerability to **cognitive overload**. Understanding these mechanisms is key to building a resilient maintenance plan.

1. Dopamine, Novelty, and the Habit Deficit

Habits are typically formed and maintained through a psychological loop of **cue, routine, and reward**. For a neurotypical brain, the long-term rewards of organization, reduced stress, easier mornings, overall control, are often enough to sustain the mundane, repetitive effort of maintenance.

However, for a woman with ADHD, the **dopamine dysregulation** in her brain means that the rewards associated with routine, mundane activities are often too delayed or too small to motivate consistent follow-through. Her brain craves **novelty** and **immediate stimulation** (a fresh idea, a new project, a stimulating hobby) which provide a rapid, satisfying burst of dopamine. Mundane maintenance tasks, such as clearing the desk or filing paperwork, are repetitive, boring, and fail to generate the necessary neurochemical reward, causing the brain to struggle with activation and quickly lose interest.

This neurochemical reality explains why organizational systems fail: they demand consistent effort for a delayed, low-intensity reward. The solution is to leverage **external structure** (like a timer and a fixed routine) to force initiation, and then utilize **internal momentum** (the feeling of accomplishment from a quick win) to act as an immediate reward that reinforces the habit, bypassing the long-term dopamine deficit.

2. The Cognitive Cost of Clutter and the Snowball Effect

The core organizational principle established in previous chapters is that **clutter equals cognitive load**. The ADHD brain struggles with efficiently filtering out irrelevant stimuli. Every object without a home, every unfiled paper, and every dirty dish on the counter demands a fraction of mental attention, increasing the overall **cognitive load** on already limited **executive function (EF) reserves**.

The "Snowball Effect" occurs when small, initial points of clutter, which, individually, require minimal effort to address, begin to accumulate. This visual and mental mess quickly overwhelms the brain's filtering capacity, leading to a critical threshold where the cognitive load becomes unbearable.

At this threshold, the brain defaults to **task paralysis** and **avoidance**. The project of cleaning is perceived as too complex and daunting, triggering a neurological shutdown rather than initiation. Therefore, the strategic purpose of the Daily 15-Minute Reset is to **interrupt the accrual of cognitive debt** every single day, ensuring the clutter never crosses the threshold into paralyzing overwhelm.

3. Defeating the "All-or-Nothing" Perfectionism Trap

A significant emotional barrier to maintenance for women with ADHD is **perfectionism**, which is often a compensatory strategy developed to mask symptoms and avoid the deep pain of criticism or shame. If a woman believes a chore must be executed flawlessly or that the entire home must be perfectly organized, the task quickly becomes too large and intimidating to start.

- **The Shame Cycle:** The failure to meet this unrealistic, perfectionistic standard fuels shame and the inner critic: *"I missed one day of cleaning, so the whole system is ruined, and I'm a failure anyway."* This shame then leads to the abandonment of the entire system, reinforcing the cycle of chaos, self-blame, and renewed overwhelm.

- **The Daily Reset as a Compromise:** The Daily 15-Minute Reset is designed to be intentionally imperfect. Its goal is **functionality**, not perfection. It focuses only on high-leverage areas (like the sink or the bedside table) and deliberately leaves larger, less critical messes for another time. This small, consistent win builds resilience and teaches the brain that partial effort is valuable effort, breaking the debilitating "all-or-nothing" mindset.

The Daily Reset must be implemented as a non-negotiable **ritual** that is built on strict limits of time and scope. This structure compensates for the ADHD brain's difficulty with time estimation and initiation.

1. The Critical Role of the Timer

The timer is the single most important tool in this routine, transforming abstract time into a concrete, visible, and manageable resource.

- **Combating Overwhelm:** By limiting the task to 15 minutes, the timer prevents the project from feeling infinite or overwhelming, lowering the activation energy required to start. The brain knows the effort is finite and temporary.

- **Preventing Hyperfocus and Burnout:** For the woman who struggles with *uncontrolled hyperfocus* (getting lost in one area for hours), the timer acts as a crucial, external circuit-breaker. When the alarm sounds, the task **stops**, even if it's unfinished. This prevents the maintenance routine from consuming the entire evening and causing burnout.

- **Creating Urgency:** The presence of the timer creates a necessary sense of urgency, often referred to as "external deadlines," which provides the burst of activation energy that the ADHD brain struggles to generate internally.

2. Defining the "High-Leverage" Reset Zones

The 15 minutes must be directed toward the highest-impact areas, the **Landing Zones** that quickly accumulate clutter and cause the most stress.

- **The Kitchen Sink / Counter:** The kitchen counter and sink are often the fastest "chaos breeding grounds" in the home. The reset must prioritize clearing all dishes, wiping the counter, and putting away misplaced mail or groceries. A clean counter significantly reduces visual noise and cognitive load at the start and end of the day.

- **The Digital Desktop / Inbox:** The digital space must be included. Dedicate a few minutes to closing unnecessary browser tabs, moving files off the desktop into a single "To Sort" folder, and applying the **"Two-Minute Rule"** to the email inbox (delete, do immediately, or defer). This reduces the invisible mental clutter that fragments attention.

- **The Bedside Table / Landing Strip:** These are crucial high-loss zones. The reset ensures that keys, wallets, phones, and any essential medications are placed immediately on their designated "Landing Strip" home, preventing the frantic, time-consuming search that increases morning stress.

3. Scheduling the Reset as a Non-Negotiable Appointment

The routine must not be treated as an optional task on a vague list; it must be scheduled as a fixed, non-negotiable **actionable appointment** in your planner or calendar.

- **Fixed Time Slots:** Schedule the reset during a natural transition point, such as "immediately after dinner" or "the last 15 minutes before work ends." This utilizes **Habit Stacking** by anchoring the new routine to an established, automatic habit (eating dinner, finishing the workday) that already has momentum.
- **Visual Reminder:** Write the reset in your planner or on a whiteboard as "15-Min System Reset - Kitchen / Desk." This provides a clear, actionable visual cue that requires minimal decision-making.

Section 3: Strategies for Building and Sustaining the Maintenance Habit

Sustaining a habit requires leveraging the ADHD brain's need for reward and external cues. The following strategies ensure the Daily Reset becomes an automated, low-effort part of your life.

1. Leveraging the Momentum of Micro-Wins

The success of the Daily Reset lies in its ability to create frequent, rapid **micro-wins** that provide immediate, tangible feedback and a necessary dopamine hit.

- **Immediate Reward Loop:** When you complete a micro-step—clearing the sink, putting three items back in their designated home—the visible progress and the mental satisfaction act as an immediate reward that reinforces the productive behavior. This reliance on **momentum** makes the continuation of the task easier than the initial start.
- **The Visual Cue of the Timer:** The sound of the timer going off after 15 minutes is itself a reward, signaling that the difficult task is over and the focused effort was successfully completed. This concrete ending reinforces the brain's ability to engage with finite tasks.

2. Utilizing External Scaffolding: Body Doubling

When initiation is difficult, the organizational system must utilize external anchors. The practice of **Body Doubling**, typically used for large projects, can also be highly effective for anchoring the Daily Reset.

- **Accountability in Routine:** Working in the presence of another person (a supportive partner, friend, or virtual accountability buddy) provides a subtle, non-judgmental form of accountability that bypasses the internal motivation deficit. The body double's presence acts as a consistent anchor for the ADHD brain, making it easier to start the 15-minute routine and preventing distraction.

- **Simple Implementation:** The body double need only be present and engaged in their * own* quiet task (reading, paying bills, working). Their role is not to help clean, but simply to provide a stable, non-distracting presence that helps the individual stay oriented to the 15-minute task at hand.

3. Embracing the "Junk Drawer" for Functional Imperfection

To ensure the maintenance habit remains sustainable, the system must tolerate functional imperfection.

- **The Pressure Release Valve:** The **Junk Drawer** (or designated "Miscellaneous Basket") is the essential companion to the Daily Reset. It provides a controlled, low-friction "home" for ambiguous items that do not yet have a determined destination. When the clock is ticking during the 15-minute reset, instead of pausing to decide where a stray item goes (triggering decision fatigue and slowing momentum), the rule is simple: *Put it in the junk drawer.*

- **Controlled Containment:** This strategy channels the natural chaos and ambiguity of daily life into a contained, visually separate zone, preventing the spread of clutter onto organized surfaces where it would increase cognitive load and trigger overwhelm. It is a deliberate choice to accept imperfection in one small area to maintain functionality in the entire system.

Section 4: Long-Term Resilience and Self-Compassion

Sustained organization is inherently tied to emotional resilience. A consistent maintenance routine reduces the shame associated with chaos and builds long-term self-efficacy.

1. The Weekly Review: Maintaining the Integrity of the System

While the Daily Reset tackles surface clutter, the deeper organizational integrity must be maintained through a periodic, low-stakes review.

- **Processing the Holding Zones:** Schedule a low-pressure **Weekly Review** session (e.g., 30 minutes on Sunday afternoon). This session focuses specifically on processing the **holding zones** created by the Daily Reset—the "To Sort" file, the Digital Downloads folder, and the Junk Drawer.

- **Low-Stakes Decluttering:** Because the items are already contained, the task of reviewing them is less overwhelming than facing generalized chaos. This periodic review prevents the holding zones from becoming permanent black holes and ensures the overall organizational structure remains functional and sustainable.

2. Reframing Failure with Self-Compassion

The greatest threat to long-term maintenance is not the mess itself, but the shame that arises when the routine is inevitably missed. A woman must consciously replace the automatic self-criticism with strategic self-compassion.

- **Mistakes as Data:** When the 15-minute reset is missed— whether due to fatigue, hyperfocus, or distraction—the moment must be reframed from a personal failure into a source of **valuable data**. Instead of: *"I'm lazy and ruined the system,"* ask: *"What was the friction point today? Was I too tired? Did I miss the alarm? Should I move the reset time slot?"*

- **Self-Kindness and Recovery:** This compassionate inquiry preserves the emotional energy that self-blame would have consumed. It allows the woman to return to the system without the crushing weight of guilt, making recovery easier and quicker. The goal is to start the next 15-minute reset immediately, without waiting for the "perfect" moment to restart the routine.

3. The Emotional Payoff: Sustained Calm and Control

The reward for building this resilient maintenance system is far greater than a tidy home. The most profound benefit is the sustained reduction in **chronic anxiety** and the daily feeling of being perpetually overwhelmed.

- **Reduced Anxiety:** A predictable, functional environment reduces the brain's need to constantly monitor for potential disaster (the lost keys, the forgotten bill, the overwhelming mess). This reduction in internal monitoring frees up immense mental bandwidth.
- **Sustained Self-Efficacy:** Every successful 15-minute reset provides consistent, positive reinforcement, building **self-efficacy**—the belief in one's own ability to succeed. This sustained feeling of competence is the antidote to the shame and inadequacy that characterize unmanaged ADHD, transforming a life of frantic reaction into one of intentional control.

Conclusion: Your Foundational Systems

This book has provided a comprehensive blueprint for constructing a resilient, ADHD-friendly organizational system. The core of this work has been about externalizing the burdens of your brain, creating physical and temporal structures that compensate for internal challenges with planning, working memory, and task initiation.

By committing to the **Daily 15-Minute Reset Routine**, you systematically interrupt the emotional and cognitive paralysis caused by the Snowball Effect. This final foundational skill ensures that the stability and order you have built are not just temporary states but sustainable features of your life.

This hard-won stability is the prerequisite for the more complex work that follows. A brain that is no longer consumed by the low-level noise of disorganization and the frantic search for lost items is a brain that has gained the mental bandwidth necessary for **sharpened focus** (Book 2), **emotional mastery** (Book 4), and **deepening relationships** (Book 5). You have moved beyond mere coping to building a reliable, supportive structure for a truly empowered life.

Chapter 5 Workbook: Stop the Snowball: Implement Daily 15-Minute "Reset" Routines

Objective: To systematically interrupt the **Snowball Effect** by making low-friction maintenance a consistent, manageable **ritual**, not a stressful chore.

Activity 5.1: The Daily Reset Blueprint

1. **Identify High-Impact Zones:** List the three areas that accumulate clutter fastest and cause the most anxiety.

   Zone 1: _____

   Zone 2: _____

   Zone 3: _____

2. **Define the Reset Routine:** Create a fixed, three-step checklist that takes **no more than 5 minutes per action** and targets only high-leverage maintenance.

Reset Action	Task (Specific, e.g., "Load all dishes from the sink")
Action 1:	
Action 2:	
Action 3:	

3. **Anchor the Routine:** Commit to performing this 15-minute routine at a fixed, anchored time each day.

   Anchored Time: "Immediately after _____

   _____

   _____

   _____

   _____

   _____

   _____

   (e.g., I shut down my computer for the day), I start my 15-Minute Timer."

Reflection 5.2: The Recovery Plan

1. **The All-or-Nothing Trap:** When you inevitably miss the 15-Minute Reset, the feeling of "I've ruined the system" can strike. Write a **Compassionate Recovery Plan** that rejects this shame and gets you back on track immediately.

   o *Recovery Statement:* (Example: "It's okay. Setbacks are data. I will not try to catch up, but I will do a **5-minute micro-reset right now** to stop the snowball.")

CHAPTER 6
REFLECT AND INTEGRATE:
YOUR DECLUTTERING JOURNEY SO FAR

You have completed the foundational phase of your journey. The five preceding chapters were dedicated to constructing a stable, supportive external environment, a prerequisite for managing the more complex internal challenges of the ADHD brain. This chapter marks a moment of intentional pause, a crucial opportunity to **reflect and integrate** the organizational systems you have built, recognizing the profound transformation that has occurred in your emotional and cognitive landscape.

This work was not about achieving neurotypical perfection, but about embracing **functional imperfection**: creating external structures that work *for* your brain's unique wiring, rather than forcing your brain to operate against its natural impulses. By systematically implementing the tools of breaking down tasks, creating designated "homes," leveraging visual storage, utilizing external accountability, and performing daily resets, you have moved beyond the paralyzing cycle of chaos and shame. You have learned that your struggle was never a character flaw, but a neurobiological reality that required a strategic, tailored solution.

The integration of these skills, from defeating the initiation deficit to neutralizing the snowball effect, yields measurable, powerful results in three interconnected domains: the cognitive, the emotional, and the relational. This reflection is designed to solidify those gains, ensuring that the habits you have built are not temporary fixes, but sustainable, resilient features of your self-management toolkit.

Section 1: The Transformation of the Cognitive Landscape

The most immediate and profound impact of functional organization is the reduction of **cognitive load** and the recovery of previously consumed mental energy. Unmanaged ADHD creates a state of chronic, high cognitive demand, where the brain is perpetually exhausted from fighting against the chaos of its environment and its own internal inconsistencies. The systems built in this book directly counteract this drain.

1. Mitigating the ADHD Tax and Overwhelm

The pervasive feeling of being "frenzied, frazzled, and overwhelmed" is the emotional manifestation of continuous cognitive exhaustion. This chronic feeling of being perpetually behind is often referred to as the **"ADHD Tax"**, the measurable cumulative cost, financial, emotional, and mental, of navigating a world designed for neurotypical brains.

This tax is rooted in the constant effort required to mentally process and filter irrelevant stimuli. Every piece of visual clutter, every ambiguous pile, and every item without a designated "home" acts as an "open loop" in the brain, demanding a fraction of your working memory and attention.

By applying the principles of Book 1, you have fundamentally altered this equation:

- **Reduced Visual Noise:** Utilizing clear storage, bold labels, and ruthlessly clearing high-traffic surfaces minimizes the visual inputs that trigger overload, freeing up the brain's impaired filtering mechanism to focus on priority information.

- **Eliminated Decision Fatigue:** Giving every item a designated, predictable "home" and creating low-friction "Landing Strips" eliminates the dozens of micro-decisions (e.g., *Where does this pen go? Where did I put my keys?*) that were previously required every day. This conservation of executive function (EF) reserves significantly reduces overall cognitive load.

- **Defeated Paralysis:** The technique of breaking down overwhelming tasks into **micro-steps** and utilizing the structure of the **Daily 15-Minute Reset** systematically addresses the **task activation deficit**. This ensures that the brain is not triggered into paralysis by the perception of an infinite, daunting task, but is instead motivated by the low-friction initiation and the immediate dopamine reward of a small, achievable "win."

The result is a reclaimed sense of intellectual clarity. The mental energy that was once consumed by frantic searching, anxiety over deadlines, and fighting clutter is now available for higher-leverage activities like sustained focus, emotional regulation, and deep work. You have created an "external brain" that reliably holds the organizational load for you, allowing your internal mental energy to be conserved.

2. The Shift from Willpower to System

A major insight of this organizational journey is the understanding that consistent follow-through is not a matter of **willpower**, but of **system design**. For years, the struggle felt like a moral failing, a lack of motivation or discipline. Now, you recognize it as a neurobiological challenge that required strategic compensation.

The systems you built, the shared planner as an actionable document, the Body Doubling appointment as external accountability, and the timer as a concrete representation of time, act as external scaffolding, reliably performing the planning and initiation functions that are inconsistent in the ADHD brain. This move from inconsistent internal effort to reliable external structure is the key to long-term sustainability and reduced stress.

Section 2: The Emotional Liberation: Healing the Shame Cycle

The work of decluttering is inherently emotional work. For women with ADHD, chronic disorganization is one of the most significant sources of shame, self-blame, and inadequacy, largely due to intense societal pressure to be the organized caretaker. The systems built in Book 1 serve as a powerful antidote to this emotional burden.

1. Countering Shame and the Inner Critic

The emotional cost of chronic disorganization is profound, leading many women to endure years of feeling that they are "not an adequate human being" because their external chaos conflicts with neurotypical and gendered expectations. Without a framework for their struggles, they internalize their difficulties as personal flaws, fueling an aggressive inner critic that compounds anxiety and depression.

Functional organization directly counteracts this shame by creating irrefutable **evidence of competence** and by establishing a compassionate allowance for imperfection:

- **Evidence of Self-Efficacy:** Every time you successfully find your keys on the **Landing Strip** or successfully complete the **15-Minute Reset**, you generate a small, tangible win. This consistent, positive reinforcement builds **self-efficacy**, the belief in your own ability to manage tasks, which is the direct antidote to the feelings of helplessness and inadequacy that define shame.

- **Compassionate Design:** Embracing **functional imperfection**, such as the intentionally organized chaos of the designated **"Junk Drawer"**, actively rejects the toxic, "all-or-nothing" perfectionism that leads to system failure and renewed shame. By acknowledging that chaos is a neurobiological reality and channeling it into a contained zone, you practice self-kindness, reducing the emotional friction caused by self-judgment.

2. Reducing Relational Friction

Organizational challenges are a major source of friction in close relationships, often leading to an unhealthy **"parent-child" dynamic** where the non-ADHD partner becomes the taskmaster or reminder. This dynamic erodes intimacy and increases feelings of shame and resentment on both sides.

The establishment of clear, external systems serves as a mechanism for **de-personalizing** the struggle and promoting collaboration:

- **Externalizing Responsibilities:** By using shared calendars, chore charts, and systems that clearly externalize the organization of tasks, the burden of "remembering" is shifted from the neurotypical partner's mind to a neutral system. This reduces the need for constant verbal reminders, which mitigates the resentment and criticism that fuels the parent-child dynamic.

- **Fostering Partnership:** This move allows the relationship to shift from arguing over perceived failures (e.g., "Why didn't you put the keys away?") to problem-solving the system (e.g., "The key bowl must be moved closer to the door to reduce friction"). The focus shifts from blame to a collaborative effort toward a shared goal, which is essential for repairing disconnections and strengthening the core partnership.

Section 3: Sustaining the System: The Three Laws of Maintenance

The ultimate measure of organizational success is not how clean your home is today, but how easily you can recover when chaos inevitably creeps back in. The organizational systems you have mastered adhere to three core laws of long-term maintenance for the ADHD brain.

Law 1: The Law of External Scaffolding

The systems must always rely on external structures and human connection rather than inconsistent internal motivation. You cannot simply *wish* for motivation; you must **design** it into your environment.

- **Timers and Finite Effort:** The use of timers (e.g., Pomodoro, 15-Minute Reset) transforms amorphous, infinite tasks into finite, manageable sprints, which is a powerful antidote to both the estimation deficit and the activation deficit.

- **The Power of Presence (Body Doubling):** When inertia hits, Body Doubling leverages the power of social anchoring, providing external accountability that bypasses the internal motivation deficit and helps sustain focus.

Law 2: The Law of Low-Friction Design

The system must be designed to make the organized choice the path of least resistance. Friction points, small barriers like removing a lid, deciding where an item goes, or searching for a tool, are the primary cause of system breakdown for the ADHD brain.

- **Designated Homes:** Every item must have a predictable, accessible home, eliminating daily decision fatigue.

- **Visible Access:** Utilizing clear bins and open containers compensates for compromised working memory, ensuring that items remain "in mind" even when stored.

- **The Containment Valve:** The intentional use of the **Junk Drawer** channels ambiguous items into a controlled zone, preventing them from spreading onto high-leverage surfaces and maintaining the functional integrity of the overall space.

Law 3: The Law of Iteration (Review and Adaptation)

The system must be viewed as an ongoing, living process, not a rigid, fixed state. Failure is inevitable; recovery is strategic.

- **Consistent Reset:** The Daily 15-Minute Reset ensures that clutter is addressed before it reaches the paralyzing threshold of the "Snowball Effect," turning maintenance into a manageable ritual, not a major project.

- **Compassionate Review:** When the system fails (e.g., you miss a week of resets), the response is not self-criticism, but curious inquiry: *What was the friction point? Was the "home" too far away?* This stance treats setbacks as valuable **data collection** rather than moral judgment, allowing you to make strategic adjustments that lead to greater resilience over time.

Section 4: The Bridge to Internal Mastery

The foundational work of Book 1 is now complete, and it serves as the essential launchpad for the rest of your journey toward self-mastery. You have successfully externalized the chaos, creating a stable platform from which to address the complex internal challenges that follow.

1. From External Structure to Internal Focus

The cognitive bandwidth you conserved by systematizing your environment must now be actively redirected toward **sharpened focus** and **executive function training** (Book 2).

- **Reduced Distraction:** A clutter-free, predictable workspace directly minimizes sensory overload and visual distraction, which is crucial for a brain that struggles with filtering. The quiet of an organized desk is the necessary prerequisite for achieving deep, sustained concentration.

- **Redirected EF:** The EF resources freed up from searching for lost items and battling decision fatigue can now be used to engage in the cognitively demanding work of **time blocking**, **single-tasking**, and strengthening working memory—the core focus of the next book. You are moving from managing your *things* to managing your *attention*.

2. The Foundation for Emotional and Relational Stability

Organizational stability is the prerequisite for emotional and relational health. When a woman's daily life is a constant battle against chaos, her stress levels are chronically elevated, which severely impairs her capacity for self-regulation and emotional tolerance.

- **Stress Reduction:** The reduction in daily friction (e.g., no longer frantically searching for keys or worrying about the mess) lowers the overall physiological arousal in the nervous system, creating a more stable emotional baseline.

- **Bandwidth for Connection:** When you are less consumed by shame, anxiety, and task overwhelm, you have greater mental and emotional bandwidth available to engage in the sensitive, intentional work of **emotional regulation** (Book 4) and **active listening** within your relationships (Book 5).

The journey continues by shifting the focus inward. You are now equipped with the physical and temporal control needed to begin the challenging, but rewarding, work of mastering your attention, regulating your emotions, and building the resilience required for lasting success.

Chapter 6 Workbook: Reflect and Integrate: Your Decluttering Journey So Far

Objective: To solidify the cognitive and emotional gains, transforming the external systems into internal self-acceptance and strategic action.

Activity 6.1: The System vs. Shame Scorecard

Instructions: Rate the severity of your anxiety and shame related to two core organizational challenges, comparing your perspective **before** this book (relying on willpower) to **now** (relying on systems). (Scale: 1 = Low Shame / Anxiety, 5 = High Shame / Anxiety)

Challenge	Shame / Anxiety **Before** Systems	Shame / Anxiety **Now**	Reflection: The Tool That Helped
Finding Lost Keys / Wallet			(Example: Landing Strip)
Starting a Major Household Chore			(Example: Micro-Steps)

Reflection 6.2: Reclaiming Your Narrative

1. Identify one specific self-critical thought you had before this book (e.g., "I'm lazy because I can't keep a clean house").

   Old Thought: _____
   _____
   _____
   _____

2. Rephrase this thought using the compassionate language and neurobiological understanding you gained (e.g., "My brain is wired for novelty and needs external cues to initiate boring tasks. I am strategic, not lazy.").

New, Empowered Narrative:_____

_____

_____

_____

3. **Bridge to Focus (Book 2):** In one sentence, state what you will do with the mental energy you conserved by eliminating clutter and searching.

Action Plan: _____

_____

_____

_____

CHAPTER 7

PRACTICE AND APPLY:
YOUR DECLUTTERING ACTION TOOLKIT

You have completed the foundational work of understanding *why* disorganization plagues the ADHD brain. You now recognize that your struggles are not moral failures, but neurobiological realities rooted in challenges with **executive function (EF)**, **task activation**, and **working memory**. The previous chapters provided the neuroscientific framework and the theoretical principles for building functional organization: breaking down overwhelming tasks, creating visually supportive systems, establishing predictability, leveraging external accountability, and sustaining momentum with daily maintenance routines.

This chapter is the **Action Toolkit**, the essential bridge that moves you from theory and reflection to embodied, practical skill development. The goal is to take the abstract concepts of Chapters 1 through 5 and transform them into concrete, low-friction systems that are integrated into your daily rhythm. By systematically applying these tools, you are actively creating the external scaffolding required to consistently defeat overwhelm and sustain mental clarity.

The power of this practice lies not in achieving rigid perfection, but in achieving **consistent, intentional imperfection**. Every small action you take using these tools reinforces a positive feedback loop, provides a necessary **dopamine hit** (the reward your brain craves), and builds the self-efficacy that is the antidote to shame and paralysis.

Toolkit 1: The Task Activation Blueprint

Objective: Defeat Task Paralysis and Minimize Activation Energy

The largest barrier to organization is often the **task activation deficit**, the inability to simply start a complex or boring task. The sheer scope of an undifferentiated project triggers **cognitive overload** and an immediate **shutdown response** (paralysis). This toolkit utilizes the **Micro-Step Strategy** to systematically reduce the cognitive load, creating an entry point so small and low-friction that initiation becomes the path of least resistance.

Scientific Anchor: Dopamine and the Small Win

Task initiation requires a burst of "activation energy" that is often lacking in the ADHD brain due to dopamine dysregulation. Breaking a large project into minuscule, actionable steps creates more opportunities for **rapid feedback** and **immediate reward**. Each completed micro-step generates a small, satisfying "win," which provides the necessary dopamine reinforcement to fuel the subsequent step, creating **momentum** that bypasses reliance on inconsistent willpower.

Action Toolkit: The Brain Dump to Micro-Step Converter

This exercise requires you to externalize your mental clutter, identify a paralyzing project, and systematically dismantle it into low-friction actions.

Step 1: Externalize the Chaos (The Brain Dump)

- **Target:** Identify one major organizing project that you have been avoiding for weeks or months (e.g., The Garage, The Files, The Digital Inbox).

- **Action:** Take 10 minutes to write down *every single thought, step, worry, and task* associated with that project. Do not worry about order or logic; just empty the mental clutter onto the page. Include vague items (e.g., "Figure out what to do with the old tax papers," "Find the key to the cabinet," "Wipe the shelves").

Step 2: Isolate the Paralysis Point (The Friction Audit)

- **Action:** Review your list from Step 1. Circle the three tasks or worries that feel the most vague, most complicated, or most emotionally charged. These are your paralysis points.
- **Example Friction Point:** "Clean out the old filing cabinet."

Step 3: Convert to Micro-Steps (The Next Action Principle)

- **Action:** For your single most paralyzing friction point, break it down until the first two steps are undeniably simple, so small they require **no decision-making** and **no more than 2 minutes** of effort. The goal is to create steps that are entirely physical and immediate.

Paralyzing Friction Point	Low-Friction Micro-Steps (The Next Action)	Why It Bypasses Paralysis
Clean out the old filing cabinet	**Step 1:** Get one trash bag and place it next to the cabinet.	Requires zero mental decision-making; only physical movement.
	Step 2: Open the top drawer and pull out the first three folders.	A tiny, finite commitment (only three folders).
	Step 3: Immediately drop the three folders into the pre-placed trash bag. (Assume they are garbage for now).	Creates immediate, visible reduction in clutter.
Organize the laundry pile	**Step 1:** Grab the hamper and place it next to the pile.	Low initiation energy.
	Step 2: Pick up all socks and put them *in* the hamper. Do nothing else.	Focuses on one specific, easy-to-identify item.
	Step 3: Place the hamper outside the laundry room door.	Transfers the next required action to an external location.

Commitment: By converting the overwhelming goal into these low-friction micro-steps, you are supplying the necessary **activation energy** required for the ADHD brain to engage. Commit to completing only **Step 1** and **Step 2** right now, then immediately proceed to **Toolkit 3** to anchor the action with a timer.

Toolkit 2: The Environmental Memory Protocol

Objective: Establish Predictability and Externalize Working Memory

The "out of sight, out of mind" phenomenon is a direct consequence of a compromised **working memory** and the ADHD brain's struggle to retrieve memories of hidden objects. This toolkit designs the environment to reliably *remember for you*, reducing the daily friction caused by searching and decision ambiguity.

Scientific Anchor: Reducing Decision Fatigue

Giving every item a designated, predictable "home" eliminates constant **decision fatigue**, the daily mental exhaustion from deciding where an item belongs. This conserves the highly limited executive function resources that were previously wasted on searching and debating placement, reserving them for high-leverage tasks like planning and emotional regulation.

Action Toolkit A: The Landing Strip Audit

The Landing Strip is a crucial system for high-loss, high-stress items.

Step 1: Identify High-Loss Stressors

- **Action:** List the top three items you **always** spend time searching for before leaving the house. (Common examples: Keys, Wallet, Phone, Daily Medication, Work ID).

Step 2: Designate the Permanent Home (The Landing Strip)

- **Action:** Physically establish one small, contained, dedicated zone for these items near your main exit point (e.g., a specific decorative bowl, a small wall-mounted hook rack, or a dedicated spot on a shelf near the door).
- **Rule:** This zone must be **clear of all other clutter** to ensure the crucial items remain visually prominent and easily accessible.

Step 3: Implement the Habit Stacking Cue

- **Action:** Anchor the habit of using the Landing Strip to an existing, non-negotiable habit.

- **Example Habit Stack:** "The moment I unlock the door and drop my keys **(Existing Habit)**, I immediately place my wallet and keys in the blue bowl on the console table **(New Habit)**." This low-friction link makes the desired organizational action automatic.

Action Toolkit B: The Visual Recall Conversion

This exercise challenges the traditional, unhelpful approach of hidden storage by converting one space into a supportive, visual system.

Step 1: Identify an Opaque Overload Zone

- **Target:** Select one small, cluttered area that currently uses opaque storage and causes friction (e.g., the medicine cabinet, the utility closet shelf, a junk drawer, or a kitchen cabinet where spices are stored).

Step 2: Convert to Visible Containment

- **Action:** Replace opaque storage with **clear containers, open baskets, or trays** for the items (e.g., clear spice containers, a clear first-aid box).
- **Rule:** For frequently used items, ensure the containers are **without lids** to reduce the friction of opening / closing, making put-away easier and quicker.

Step 3: Label and Define

- **Action:** Use large, bold labels on the containers to define the contents. The labels must be simple and specific. (Example: Instead of "Stuff," use "Batteries - AA / AAA" or "Receipts - To File.")
- **Neuro-Benefit:** This intentional labeling externalizes the categorization process, eliminating the cognitive guesswork of retrieving the item and reinforcing the designated "home".

Toolkit 3: The Momentum Accelerator

Objective: Leverage External Accountability to Sustain Focus

Even with tasks broken down (Toolkit 1) and a clear environment (Toolkit 2), sustaining effort on boring, repetitive, or complex tasks remains challenging due to the internal motivation deficit. This toolkit provides the crucial external structures necessary to maintain attention and momentum.

Scientific Anchor: External Executive Functioning

The presence of a non-judgmental partner, or **Body Double**, acts as a source of **external executive functioning** that anchors the attention of the ADHD brain to the present moment, thereby reducing distraction and enhancing motivation. Similarly, timers compensate for **time blindness** by making abstract time concrete and visible, preventing the work from feeling infinite or overwhelming.

Action Toolkit A: The Body Double Protocol

This exercise sets the framework for a successful, non-judgmental Body Doubling session, whether in-person or virtual.

Step 1: Define the Task and Duration

- **Action:** Choose a single, defined task from **Toolkit 1** (e.g., "Sort paperwork from the red basket") and commit to a fixed duration.
- **Goal:** The goal is to work alongside a supportive partner or friend who is focused on their own work.

Step 2: Establish the Non-Negotiable Contract

- **Action:** Share this contract with your Body Double and commit to it:

My Role (The Worker)	Your Role (The Body Double)
I commit to working on the task for **30 minutes** without checking my phone.	You commit to being visibly present and working on *your own* task.
My check-in question is: "What is the very next tiny step?"	You agree to provide **zero criticism**, only gentle, factual support.
If I get up to wander, you gently say, "Timer is still running."	You agree **not to do the task for me** or judge my pace.

Step 3: Anchor with Visibility

- **Action:** If working virtually, ensure cameras are on. If in-person, sit in the same room. The visible presence of the Body Double acts as the continuous, external anchor for your attention.

Action Toolkit B: The Pomodoro Planning Grid

Use this grid to plan an organizing task, converting the abstract effort into timed, manageable sprints.

Step 1: Select and Estimate

- **Action:** Take a medium-sized organizing task (e.g., organizing a drawer) and estimate its duration in Pomodoro intervals (25 minutes of work).

Step 2: Schedule with Buffers

- **Action:** Create a time-blocked schedule for this task. **Crucially,** add 5-minute breaks after each Pomodoro and **add 25% extra time** to your total estimate to compensate for **time blindness**.

Time Block	Activity	Neuro-Benefit
3:00 – 3:25 PM	Pomodoro 1: Sort items in the right-side drawer (Work / Focus)	Finitude reduces overwhelm and task initiation deficit.
3:25 – 3:30 PM	**Break:** Stand, stretch, get water (Reward / Reset)	Prevents mental fatigue and hyperfocus.
3:30 – 3:55 PM	Pomodoro 2: Label containers and discard garbage (Work / Focus)	Creates momentum through a visible, tangible "win."
3:55 – 4:00 PM	**Break:** Listen to one song, quick mind-reset	Accommodates brain's need for novelty.
4:00 – 4:15 PM	Final 15-Min Push: Put items back in labeled containers (Completion)	Ensures the task is finished while energy is still high.

Commitment: By scheduling tasks this way, you are treating your organizing efforts as non-negotiable **appointments**, which the ADHD brain handles much better than abstract to-do list items.

Objective: Ensure Long-Term Maintenance and Prevent the Snowball Effect

The biggest threat to organization is the rapid accumulation of small items, the **Snowball Effect**, which quickly triggers overwhelming chaos. This toolkit creates a low-stakes, highly effective maintenance ritual.

Scientific Anchor: The 15-Minute Rule

The **Daily 15-Minute Reset** works by utilizing the principle of **low-friction maintenance**. Since organization fails when it demands excessive mental energy or time, limiting the routine to 15 minutes ensures the effort is finite and low-stakes. This consistent interruption prevents small clutter points from reaching the overwhelming threshold that triggers paralysis and contributes to chronic cognitive load.

Action Toolkit: Customizing Your Daily Reset Checklist

Step 1: Identify Your Three High-Impact Zones

- **Action:** List the three areas in your home that accumulate clutter the fastest and cause the most anxiety (e.g., The Kitchen Counter, The Digital Inbox, The Living Room Coffee Table).

Step 2: Create the Customized 15-Minute Checklist

- **Action:** Design a three-step checklist that takes no more than 15 minutes to complete, focusing only on the highest-leverage actions. This is your non-negotiable daily commitment.

Reset Zone	Action (Maximum 5 Minutes Each)	Completion Cue
Kitchen / Sink	Load all dishes from the sink and counter into the dishwasher.	Counter is cleared.
Landing Strip	Ensure keys, wallet, and phone are placed *on* the designated strip.	All high-loss items are secured.
Digital Space	Close all unnecessary browser tabs (leaving only 3 open) and file 5 emails (Delete, Do, Defer) into the "To Sort" folder.	Desktop / Inbox is visually calm.

Step 3: Integrate and Allow for Imperfection

- **Action:** Commit to performing this 15-minute sequence at the **same time** each day (e.g., right before starting the coffee maker, or immediately after turning off the TV).
- **Rule of the Junk Drawer:** If an item's "home" is not immediately obvious, place it in the designated **Junk Drawer / Basket** rather than stopping to make a decision. This maintains the momentum of the reset ritual and prevents decision fatigue from derailing the 15 minutes.

Conclusion: Your Commitment to Sustainable Action

The chaos of unmanaged ADHD is not a burden you must carry alone; it is a complex system that requires complex, compassionate, and strategic solutions. By working through this Action Toolkit, you have created a powerful suite of external structures that compensate for internal inconsistencies in focus, memory, and motivation.

Your commitment moving forward is to **consistency over perfection**. There will be days when the timer is ignored, and days when the Landing Strip is missed. The key is not to succumb to shame, but to engage the principle of **self-compassion** and return to your customized checklist immediately, treating the setback as valuable **data** for refining your system. The ultimate reward for this work is the liberation of your mental energy, creating the cognitive bandwidth necessary to engage fully with the deeper work of sharpening focus and emotional mastery that awaits you in the next books. Commit to using one tool from this kit every day for the next week.

CONCLUSION:

SUMMARY: YOUR FOUNDATIONAL SYSTEMS

You have completed the foundational work of Book 1, moving through the essential stages of confronting chaos, establishing predictability, and anchoring sustainable habits. This work was dedicated to addressing the most significant external barrier to a fulfilling life with Attention-Deficit/ Hyperactivity Disorder (ADHD): **chronic disorganization** and the resulting **overwhelm** that characterizes the female experience of the condition.

The core principle of this entire process has been to recognize that your struggle was never a character flaw or a reflection of incompetence. Instead, it was a neurobiological reality stemming from predictable deficits in **executive function (EF)**—namely, working memory, task initiation, and filtering capacity. By completing this foundational phase, you have successfully moved away from the debilitating cycle of self-blame and avoidance, and you have constructed a resilient, external scaffolding that is designed to perform the organizational tasks your inconsistent internal memory cannot reliably manage.

This chapter synthesizes the five key organizational pillars into a cohesive, integrated system, demonstrating the profound **neurobiological payoff** of this hard work. This stability in your external life is the necessary prerequisite—the "clean desk"—that frees up the mental bandwidth required to master the more complex internal challenges of focus, emotions, and relational stability that await you in the subsequent books.

Section 1: The Integrated System: Five Pillars of External Scaffolding

The systems you have built over the course of this book work in synergy, with each chapter addressing a specific neurobiological deficit to systematically reduce the overall **cognitive load** and **task activation energy** that once led to paralysis.

1. Pillar of Initiation: Defeating Paralysis (Chapter 1)

The most immediate hurdle to organization is the **task activation deficit**—the inability to initiate tasks, which is often mistaken for laziness but is rooted in dopamine dysregulation and cognitive shutdown.

- **The Problem:** The overwhelming scale of a messy room or daunting project triggers an immediate **paralysis response** as the brain's filtering mechanisms struggle to find a single, manageable starting point.
- **The Solution:** The methodical breakdown of overwhelming tasks into **micro-steps** and the identification of the **"Next Action"** (an action so simple it requires minimal effort and no decision-making) provides the necessary **activation energy**.
- **Neurobiological Payoff:** This process creates rapid, tangible "wins," each providing a small but necessary burst of **dopamine** that reinforces productive behavior and builds **momentum**, thus bypassing the reliance on inconsistent internal motivation.

2. Pillar of Memory: Designing for Visibility (Chapter 2)

Once you begin a project, maintaining order requires that items remain "in mind" and accessible, a process challenged by the working memory deficit.

- **The Problem:** The **"out of sight, out of mind"** phenomenon, a direct consequence of compromised working memory, leads to chronic loss, constant searching, and the feeling that items cease to exist the moment they are put away in hidden storage.

- **The Solution:** The implementation of **visible storage**—prioritizing clear containers, open baskets without lids, and transparent labeling—transforms the environment into a functional **external memory system**.
- **Neurobiological Payoff:** This strategy ensures that items remain visually prominent, reducing the mental effort required for retrieval and actively compensating for the internal memory deficit. By eliminating the ambiguity of hidden spaces, you reduce the **cognitive cost of visual noise** in your immediate environment.

3. Pillar of Clarity: Establishing Predictability (Chapter 3)

The daily interaction with objects without a designated place consumes significant mental bandwidth. Predictability is the key to automating placement.

- **The Problem:** The absence of a defined destination for every item forces the brain to engage in constant, taxing micro-decisions (e.g., *Where does this pen go?*), leading to systemic **decision fatigue** that drains executive function reserves.
- **The Solution:** The commitment to a specific, low-friction **designated** "home" for every item, coupled with the establishment of the **"Landing Strip"** for high-loss items (keys, wallet, phone), eliminates ambiguity. The **"Junk Drawer"** strategically manages inevitable chaos by providing a contained release valve for items without a determined home, preventing their spread onto high-leverage surfaces.
- **Neurobiological Payoff:** This creates reliable **automaticity**. Placement becomes a simple habit rather than a conscious decision, conserving precious executive function for higher-leverage tasks like planning and sustained focus.

4. Pillar of Accountability: Sustaining Momentum (Chapter 4)

Internal motivation is notoriously inconsistent. Maintaining momentum requires strategic, external support to anchor attention.

- **The Problem:** The difficulty in maintaining sustained attention, coupled with **time blindness** (the inability to accurately gauge the passage of time), makes follow-through challenging and often results in abandonment of tasks before completion.
- **The Solution:** Leveraging **Body Doubling**—working in the presence of a supportive partner or peer—provides the **external accountability** needed to anchor attention and bypass the

internal activation deficit. Simultaneously, using **Timers** (such as the Pomodoro Technique) transforms abstract time into **concrete, finite blocks**, preventing the work from feeling overwhelming.

- **Neurobiological Payoff:** The Body Double acts as an **external executive function**, and the timer ensures that effort is finite and rewarded quickly (dopamine hit from completion), which fuels sustained engagement and prevents the deep mental fatigue caused by unstructured work.

5. Pillar of Resilience: Stopping the Snowball (Chapter 5)

Even the best systems fail if small messes are allowed to escalate into paralyzing chaos. Long-term success relies on low-friction maintenance.

- **The Problem:** The **"Snowball Effect"**, where minor clutter rapidly accumulates, quickly crosses a threshold that triggers **paralysis** and a full system shutdown, often exacerbated by the **"all-or-nothing"** perfectionism trap.
- **The Solution:** The implementation of the **Daily 15-Minute "Reset" Routine**, focused only on the highest-leverage areas (e.g., kitchen counter, Landing Strip), ensures that the accumulation of clutter is interrupted before it becomes cognitively paralyzing.
- **Neurobiological Payoff:** This ritual prioritizes **consistency over perfection**, training the brain that **partial effort is valuable effort**. By performing frequent, short bursts of maintenance, you prevent the chronic accrual of **cognitive debt**, sustaining a lower, more manageable level of background anxiety.

Section 2: The Neurobiological Payoff: Reclaiming Your Mental Bandwidth

The integration of these five pillars yields a profound transformation that goes far beyond a tidy home. The organizational systems built in Book 1 are the foundational mechanism for achieving internal stability, reducing the **shame** that has accompanied unmanaged ADHD, and conserving the vital resources necessary for focused work.

1. The Critical Reduction of Cognitive Load

The most significant payoff of functional organization is the dramatic reduction in the brain's chronic **cognitive load**. Unmanaged, this load is the sum of mental effort consumed by:

- Searching for lost items (working memory drain).
- Filtering competing visual stimuli (filtering deficit).
- Making unnecessary micro-decisions (decision fatigue).
- Worrying about deadlines and forgetting tasks (time blindness anxiety).

By externalizing these burdens, you free up immense cognitive bandwidth. This liberation of mental energy is directly tied to an increased capacity for other executive functions. When the brain is no longer consumed by low-level chaos, its resources can be redirected toward the sustained, complex effort required for **deep work** and **emotional regulation**.

2. The Antidote to Shame and the Inner Critic

For a woman with ADHD, chronic disorganization is one of the most significant sources of shame, fueled by the societal pressure to maintain an organized home and family. The systems in Book 1 provide tangible, undeniable **evidence of competence** that actively counters the narrative of the inner critic.

- **Building Self-Efficacy:** Every successful use of the Landing Strip or completion of the Daily Reset provides a small, positive neurochemical reinforcement, building **self-efficacy**—the belief in one's ability to succeed—which is the direct psychological antidote to the shame and feelings of inadequacy that characterize unmanaged ADHD.
- **Practicing Self-Compassion:** The intentional design of a system that accommodates neurobiological challenges (e.g., clear containers, low-friction entry points) is a profound act of **self-compassion**. By rejecting the toxic ideal of perfectionism and embracing functional imperfection, you are treating yourself with the kindness and understanding you would offer a struggling friend, reducing the emotional friction caused by self-judgment.

3. Stabilizing the Nervous System and Relationships

Organizational friction is a direct cause of chronic stress and relational tension. Stability in the environment leads to predictability in relationships.

- **Reduced Anxiety:** A predictable environment reduces the brain's need to be constantly on high alert, monitoring for potential disasters (the lost keys, the forgotten chore). This stability calms the nervous system, reducing the **physiological arousal** that exacerbates emotional dysregulation and anxiety.

- **De-personalizing Conflict:** By externalizing shared household tasks onto a neutral system (e.g., a chore chart or a shared calendar), the couple can move from arguing over perceived failures ("You never put that away!") to collaboratively solving a system problem ("The home for this item is not clear enough, let's fix it"). This shifts the dynamic from an unhealthy "taskmaster / scolded child" relationship to a partnership, fostering greater empathy and trust.

Section 3: The Bridge to Internal Mastery (Book 2)

The work of Book 1 is a crucial first step, but it is not the destination. Its primary purpose is to clear the runway so that you have the mental resources, the structural platform, and the physical space necessary for the demanding work of **internal mastery**. The stability you have created provides the essential bridge to the focus strategies in Book 2.

- **The Foundation for Focus:** A brain that is constantly distracted by visual noise and the low-level anxiety of disorganization is a brain incapable of deep, sustained concentration. The clear desk, the organized digital space, and the reduced background anxiety achieved in Book 1 are the necessary prerequisites for achieving the state of **deep work** addressed in the next phase.

- **The Conserved Executive Function:** The EF resources you conserved by eliminating decision fatigue and task paralysis must now be actively redirected. Book 2, **Beat Overwhelm and Sharpen Executive Function for the ADHD Woman**, will teach you how to use this reclaimed mental bandwidth to engage in the cognitively demanding work of **Time Blocking**, strengthening your **working memory**, and mastering **single-tasking** to achieve intentional attention.

- **The System for Emotional Growth:** The emotional stability gained from a less chaotic external environment provides the bandwidth necessary for the intensive internal work of **emotional regulation** (Book 4) and **relational effectiveness** (Book 5). You have built the vessel; now you will learn how to steer it.

Commit to maintaining the foundational systems you have built. Consistency is the goal; self-compassion is the method. This mastery of your external world has transformed your relationship with overwhelm, paving the way for the profound transformation of your focus and emotional landscape.

BOOK TWO

BEAT OVERWHELM FOR THE ADHD WOMAN

INTRODUCTION:

THE PARADOX OF FOCUS
AND THE MASTERING OF TIME

The foundational work of organization (Book 1) created a sanctuary in your external world by clearing visual clutter, defeating task paralysis, and establishing predictable systems. This stability reduced the debilitating pressure of external chaos. Now, the journey shifts profoundly inward. This book is dedicated to mastering the internal landscape of the ADHD brain: regulating attention, conquering the elusive nature of time, and strengthening the core processes of **Executive Function (EF)** that are essential for long-term productivity and self-efficacy.

For many women with Attention-Deficit / Hyperactivity Disorder (ADHD), the concept of "focus" is a profound paradox, a double-edged sword that can feel both like a superpower and a cruel burden. On one hand, a woman's attention can be so fragmented that she experiences a "thousand-yard stare," daydreaming, or "zoning out" during conversations or meetings, which leads to forgotten details and a pervasive sense of being perpetually in a fog. This fragmented attention makes it difficult to remember instructions, organize a schedule, or stay on task, all vital components of daily functioning. On the other hand, when a task is intensely stimulating, novel, or engaging, the ADHD brain can lock into a state of intense, almost obsessive **hyperfocus**. While this state can lead to incredible bursts of productivity and creative output, it is often uncontrolled: a woman may lose track of time, forget to eat, and fail to attend to critical responsibilities, creating significant friction in her life.

The fundamental challenge is not a lack of ability to pay attention, but rather a profound **difficulty in regulating it**. The issue lies in the brain's struggle to control its "on / off" switch, preventing it from consistently directing its mental spotlight where it needs to be and sustaining it for mundane, but necessary, tasks. This inherent **dysregulation of attention** is a primary driver of the chronic overwhelm that defines the female ADHD experience, leading to a profound sense of mental fatigue, inadequacy, and being perpetually "frenzied, frazzled, and overwhelmed."

This book provides the strategic, evidence-based roadmap to move beyond this paradox. It is built upon the understanding that achieving control over your attention is the key to defeating overwhelm and unlocking your full potential.

The Neurobiological Reality: Executive Function and the Time Barrier

To master focus and time, we must first confront their neurological roots. The difficulties with planning, productivity, and sustained attention are not signs of poor intelligence or character; they are direct consequences of how the ADHD brain is wired, specifically in the areas governing executive functions and motivation.

1. Executive Function (EF) Deficits: The Command Center

Executive functions (EFs) are the high-level mental processes that allow us to regulate behavior, think before acting, meet new challenges with flexibility, and stay focused and concentrate. These functions, which include planning, goal setting, working memory, inhibitory control, and time management, are so essential to well-being that they have been described as the **"mental toolkit for success,"** often proving more predictive of academic and career success than either socioeconomic status or IQ.

For the significant percentage of adults with ADHD who experience EF deficits, the brain's **prefrontal cortex**, the "command center" for these skills, is often less developed or less active than in neurotypical individuals. This deficit leads to measurable difficulties in nearly every aspect of organization and productivity, from struggling to hold multi-step instructions in mind (poor working memory) to the inability to start a task (task activation deficit). This constant struggle creates a feeling of profound functional inadequacy, contributing directly to the shame and anxiety so common in women with ADHD.

2. The Dopamine-Driven Dysregulation

The ADHD brain's relationship with attention is distinct and deeply rooted in its **dopamine system**. Dopamine, the key neurotransmitter for motivation, reward, and activation, is thought to be dysregulated in the ADHD brain, often resulting in lower effective levels in the synapses.

This deficit creates a powerful, persistent craving for **novelty and immediate stimulation**. When a task is under-stimulating (boring, repetitive, or requiring sustained, effortful attention), the brain struggles to produce enough dopamine to find it interesting, leading to distraction, mind-wandering, and task avoidance. The opposite is true for hyperfocus. The strategies in this book are designed to strategically introduce external structure, like fixed time limits, novelty simulation, and immediate feedback, to supply the necessary cues and reward required to sustain attention on necessary tasks, thereby bypassing the internal dopamine deficit.

3. Time Blindness: The Invisible Barrier to Planning

Perhaps the most disruptive deficit for productivity and life management is **time blindness**, the inability to accurately perceive or estimate the flow of time. Time does not feel like a consistent, measurable resource; instead, the ADHD brain lives predominantly in the "now," making the future feel abstract and less urgent.

This difficulty in feeling the passage of time creates several critical challenges:

- **Estimation Deficit:** Individuals with ADHD consistently underestimate how long tasks will take, leading to chronic rushing, missed deadlines, and the inevitable stress that results from constant lateness.
- **Prioritization Failure:** Because the future is abstract, the urgency of a deadline that is a week away feels equal to the urgency of a deadline that is three months away. The brain struggles to prioritize based on true time sensitivity.

- **Overwhelm by Infinity:** When faced with a task, the time needed to complete it feels amorphous and infinite, which instantly triggers an overload response and **paralysis**.

The comprehensive solution explored in this book is to stop relying on inconsistent internal time perception and instead use **concrete, visual tools** and **intentional scheduling** to make time palpable, measurable, and manageable. This involves mastering techniques like **Time Blocking** to enforce duration and utilizing **Timers** to make abstract time visible.

The Emotional and Cognitive Toll of a Fragmented Mind

The daily struggle with attention dysregulation and EF deficits takes a significant toll on a woman's emotional and cognitive well-being, leading directly to the pervasive sense of overwhelm that this book seeks to defeat.

1. High Cognitive Load and Mental Fatigue

The ADHD brain often struggles with an impaired **filtering mechanism**, meaning it registers all incoming stimuli, a flickering light, a phone notification, a fleeting thought, with almost equal importance. This results in a constant, effortful struggle to filter distractions, creating a state of chronically high **cognitive load**: the mental effort consumed by working memory. Research indicates that this high cognitive load disproportionately impacts performance for people with ADHD.

This continuous mental fight leads to profound **mental fatigue**, a temporary sluggishness and slowdown of thinking abilities that results in poor focus, forgetfulness, and exhaustion. This chronic effort to manage an overstimulated mind is the **"ADHD Tax"** on energy reserves, leading to burnout and a diminished capacity for sustained effort. The strategic management of attention and task structure is designed to dramatically lower this baseline cognitive load, reserving mental energy for the actual work of focus.

2. Shame, Masking, and the Loss of Self-Worth

The persistent difficulties with focus, time management, and follow-through often lead a woman with ADHD to internalize her struggles and blame herself, interpreting her symptoms as moral or character failings. This internalized struggle is amplified by the intense societal pressure on women to be organized, calm, and effortlessly competent.

This conflict drives **masking**, the exhausting practice of developing sophisticated compensatory behaviors (e.g., meticulously over-preparing, building in extreme time buffers) to hide the internal chaos and appear "neurotypical" to the outside world. For instance, a woman might pretend to take notes in a meeting to mask the fact that she has a "thousand-yard stare" or is "zoning out." This continuous performance is an invisible burden that leads to a lifetime of internalized shame, anxiety, and a shattered sense of self-worth. By providing a clear, neurobiologically-grounded roadmap for focus and EF mastery, this book empowers a woman to replace the narrative of shame with a foundation of strategic self-efficacy.

The Strategic Roadmap for Sustained Focus

The path to defeating overwhelm involves strategically creating external and internal structures that compensate for EF deficits. This book guides you through a process of learning to work *with* your brain's unique wiring, not against it, through evidence-based practices drawn from Cognitive Behavioral Therapy (CBT) and specialized ADHD coaching.

1. Making Time Concrete and Visible: The primary barrier of **time blindness** must be solved with external tools. You will learn to use visual, concrete scheduling systems, such as **Time Blocking**, to enforce duration and assign a fixed time slot to every activity, task, and transition. This contrasts sharply with vague to-do lists, which the brain can easily skip because they lack context and duration. Time Blocking forces planning and prioritization, directly mitigating the time estimation deficit by scheduling intentional time buffers.

2. Creating Focused Sprints: Initiation and sustained attention must be anchored by structure. You will master the **Pomodoro Technique**, breaking work into short, focused sprints followed by mandatory breaks, customizing the duration to match your personal attention span. This structured interval provides the necessary **finitude** to reduce the overwhelm that triggers paralysis, while the scheduled breaks prevent burnout and interrupt the cycle of uncontrolled hyperfocus, serving as a critical external circuit-breaker for attention. The visible timer makes time palpable and reinforces productive effort.

3. Strengthening Internal Resilience: Sustained EF mastery requires building the internal mental muscles responsible for planning and recall. This involves utilizing structured, consistent planning routines and cognitive exercises designed to improve **working memory** and **inhibitory control** (thinking before acting). By establishing fixed, actionable daily and weekly planning rituals, you externalize task goals and instructions, supporting the prefrontal cortex. Furthermore, intentional practices, such as **single-tasking**, are employed to minimize the draining **context switching cost** that is so taxing on the ADHD brain.

4. Protecting Your Cognitive Sanctuary: True focus is maintained by ruthlessly eliminating external and internal noise that depletes your finite mental energy. You will learn to recognize and proactively minimize the sources of **digital noise** and unnecessary **stimuli** that fragment your attention and increase cognitive load. This includes strategies like **Notification Annihilation** across all devices and reducing the number of open browser tabs, which are all "open loops" consuming precious working memory. Sustaining focus is a product of protecting your energy through prioritizing fundamental well-being factors, such as optimizing sleep hygiene and incorporating intentional physical activity, to regulate dopamine and mitigate the effects of chronic **mental fatigue**.

The culmination of this strategic work is a profound sense of self-efficacy and control. You are replacing the frantic, reactive cycle of overwhelm with a calm, strategic rhythm of intentional action. The stability achieved in Book 1 (external structure) provides the critical platform, and the EF mastery achieved here (internal structure) provides the necessary skill set to move toward integrated success and prepare you for the complex work of emotional regulation and relational depth that lies ahead.

CHAPTER 1

VISUALIZE TIME: BANISH TIME BLINDNESS WITH CONCRETE SCHEDULING TOOLS

The foundational stability created by organizing your external environment (Book 1) now clears the path for the deepest internal challenge of Attention-Deficit / Hyperactivity Disorder (ADHD): the mastery of attention and time. For the woman with ADHD, the most insidious barrier to productivity and the primary driver of chronic stress is a core executive function deficit known as **Time Blindness**.

Time blindness is the neurological inability to accurately perceive, estimate, or feel the passage of time. Time does not feel like a consistent, measurable resource; instead, the ADHD brain operates predominantly in the "now," making the future feel abstract, distant, and therefore, less urgent. The consequence of this temporal vacuum is devastating: chronic lateness, perpetual underestimation of task durations, missed deadlines, poor long-term planning, and a debilitating feeling that deadlines emerge suddenly, as if out of nowhere. This struggle is not a character flaw or a failure to prioritize; it is a measurable neurocognitive reality that requires strategic, external compensation.

This chapter provides the critical first step in mastering Executive Function (EF): a shift in time management from abstract internal perception to **concrete, visible, and tangible tools**. By learning to externalize time and make it visually palatable, you systematically counteract the symptoms of time blindness, turning time from a source of anxiety and chaos into a predictable ally that you can manage and trust. The goal is to move from a reactive state, constantly rushing and playing catch-up, to a proactive, calm rhythm of intentional scheduling and focus.

Section 1: The Neurobiological Reality of Time Blindness

To effectively banish time blindness, we must first understand its neurobiological origins. The difficulty with time perception is a direct symptom of EF deficits rooted in the brain's "command center" for planning and self-regulation.

1. The Prefrontal Cortex and Time Perception

Executive functions, the suite of high-level mental processes that govern self-control, planning, and goal-directed behavior, are primarily controlled by the **prefrontal cortex**. Research indicates that in individuals with ADHD, this region is often less developed or less active, leading to compromised functioning in time-related skills.

- **Impaired Working Memory:** Time management requires **working memory**, the ability to hold and manipulate transient information, such as remembering how long a similar task took last time, or keeping multiple steps of a schedule in mind. A deficit here means the ADHD brain cannot reliably retrieve past temporal data, leading to a consistent struggle with accurate duration estimation.

- **Deficit in Inhibitory Control:** Time management also relies on **inhibitory control**—the ability to resist immediate gratification and prioritize long-term, abstract rewards (like future career success or financial security) over immediate, short-term rewards (like scrolling social media). Because the future feels abstract to the time-blind brain, the motivation to delay gratification for a distant reward is significantly weakened, contributing to chronic procrastination and poor future planning.

2. The Dopamine-Driven Urgency Gap

The struggle with time blindness is profoundly influenced by the ADHD brain's **dopamine dysregulation**. Dopamine, the neurotransmitter for motivation and reward, is released in anticipation of a reward, driving goal-directed action.

For the ADHD brain, the dysregulated dopamine system means that the sense of **urgency** required to initiate a task is not generated internally unless the reward is immediate or the consequence of avoidance is imminent (i.e., a looming deadline). Because the future is abstract:

- **Low Perceived Reward:** Tasks scheduled a week from now carry little to no emotional or chemical reward, making them impossible to initiate.

- **The Procrastination Loop:** Action is delayed until the deadline transforms the task into an immediate, high-stakes crisis, which finally triggers the intense dopamine / adrenaline response required for activation—a state often mistaken for working best under pressure, but which is neurobiologically driven crisis management.

The result is that the time-blind woman exists in a perpetual state of stress and shame, constantly rushing to meet self-imposed or external deadlines. The solution must provide external, visible cues that consistently generate the necessary sense of urgency and reward *before* the crisis hits.

Section 2: The Strategy Shift: Making Time Concrete and Visible

The core therapeutic strategy for time blindness is to stop relying on inconsistent internal perception and to replace it with a dependable **external visualization system**. Time must be made tangible—something the eye can see, the hand can touch, and the brain can anchor to.

1. Timers as External Cues

Timers are the most direct way to transform abstract time into a concrete, visible, and manageable resource. The ticking, counting-down clock bypasses the internal struggle with time estimation and provides a non-negotiable anchor for attention.

- **Finitude vs. Infinity:** The greatest source of overwhelm in time blindness is the feeling that a task requires an amorphous, infinite amount of time, which instantly triggers **paralysis**. A timer imposes **finitude**, a clear, visible end point (e.g., "This task requires only 25 minutes"), which significantly lowers the activation energy required to start. The commitment becomes manageable and approachable.

- **External Pacing:** For the brain that struggles with staying on task, the timer acts as a constant external reminder and pacer, reducing mind-wandering and sustaining concentration. It is a necessary external executive function that monitors the passage of time for you.

- **Visual Analog Clocks:** For deeper work on time blindness, visual analog clocks (like the Time Timer), which physically show the passage of time disappearing, can be profoundly helpful. These tools translate the duration into a visible, diminishing space, which is far easier for the time-blind brain to grasp than abstract numbers on a digital display.

2. Time Blocking: The Ultimate Visualization Tool

While traditional to-do lists serve a necessary purpose by simply externalizing tasks, they are fundamentally inadequate for the time-blind brain because they lack two crucial elements: **context and duration**.

Strategy	ADHD Challenge Addressed	Why It Often Fails the ADHD Brain
Traditional To-Do List	Working Memory Deficit (forgetting tasks)	Lacks time context, fails to enforce duration, and tasks feel equally urgent, leading to overwhelm and skipping.
Time Blocking	Time Blindness, Prioritization, Estimation	Forces the user to allocate a finite, visible block of time for *every* activity, making time concrete and scheduling transitions.

Time Blocking is the essential visualization strategy that directly addresses time blindness. It is a scheduling method that requires you to block out specific periods for activities, providing a clear, visible structure for the entire day.

- **Forces Estimation:** Time Blocking mandates that you pre-allocate a duration for every task (e.g., "Email Triage: 9:00 AM–9:45 AM"). This intentional allocation forces the engagement of the planning aspect of EF, mitigating the estimation deficit that plagues the ADHD brain.

- **Minimizes Guesswork:** When time is visually blocked, you eliminate the cognitive guesswork of "What should I do next?" The schedule becomes a clear, non-negotiable roadmap, which reduces feelings of overwhelm and supports better transitions between activities—a common sticking point for the neurodivergent brain.
- **Prioritizes by Finitude:** Instead of prioritizing by abstract importance, Time Blocking prioritizes by the finite reality of time. A task that is blocked from 10:00 AM to 11:00 AM has a clear boundary, which reduces the anxiety of the task feeling infinite.

Section 3: Structuring Your Time Blocks for ADHD Success

Implementing Time Blocking effectively requires customizing the system to accommodate the inherent neurobiological deficits of the ADHD brain, turning a rigid schedule into a flexible, supportive framework.

1. Compensating for the Estimation Deficit

People with ADHD consistently underestimate how long tasks will take—a phenomenon that fuels rushing, stress, and eventual system abandonment. The scheduling must proactively build in buffers to neutralize this deficit.

- **Schedule with Buffers:** The cardinal rule of ADHD time blocking is to **schedule more time than you think you need**. Intentionally add a time buffer of 25-50% to your initial estimate for every major task. If a report should take two hours, schedule 2.5 to 3 hours. This simple adjustment provides crucial breathing room, reducing the stress that comes from self-imposed, unrealistic temporal constraints.
- **Block Transitions:** Do not schedule tasks back-to-back. The process of shifting focus from one task to the next, known as **context switching**, is highly draining for the ADHD brain, which incurs a measurable cognitive cost each time it switches attention. Schedule specific, intentional transition periods (e.g., "5-Minute Break / Reset") between major blocks. This supports a smoother mental shift and maintains momentum.
- **Color-Coding:** Use a simple, consistent color-coding system to visually categorize blocks (e.g., blue for Work / Deep Focus, green for Health / Self-Care, yellow for Administrative / Errands). This visual cue allows the brain to quickly process and

prioritize the schedule at a glance, minimizing the cognitive effort required to interpret the schedule.

2. Externalizing the Schedule (Visual and Digital Anchors)

The schedule must live in a location that is impossible to ignore, thereby acting as a constant **external working memory cue** that bypasses internal forgetfulness.

- **Visual Prominence:** Place your time-blocked schedule in a location of high visual traffic, a large wall calendar, a whiteboard in your office, or a prominent digital calendar view on your desktop. If the schedule is hidden away in a notebook or a deep folder, the time-blind brain will forget it exists.

- **Digital Reminders:** Leverage technology to provide automated, external cues. Use digital calendars (like Google Calendar) that provide multiple, automated reminders for transitions and task completion. Set alerts for a week before, a day before, and an hour before major deadlines to anchor the abstract future into the urgent present.

3. Structuring Work with Finitude (The Pomodoro Precursor)

While the full implementation of the Pomodoro Technique is covered in Chapter 3, the principle of **finite effort** must be integrated into your time blocks now. When scheduling a task, the time block must feel like a commitment to a manageable sprint, not an overwhelming marathon.

- **The Sprint Structure:** When you block out an hour for a project, mentally commit to that hour as a **focused sprint**. Break the hour down into smaller intervals (e.g., two 25-minute periods with a 10-minute break in between). This strategy reduces the urge to procrastinate because the commitment to start is short and finite, making the project psychologically approachable.

- **Clear Boundaries:** The most powerful rule of Time Blocking is to **respect the block**. When the scheduled time is up, the task stops, whether it is finished or not. This protects your boundaries and ensures that one hyperfocused task does not bleed into and derail the subsequent appointments, maintaining the integrity of the overall schedule.

Section 4: Time Blocking vs. To-Do Lists: A Neuroscientific Comparison

The reliance on traditional to-do lists, while common, fails to adequately support the EF deficits of time blindness and is a primary driver of overwhelm for women with ADHD. Understanding this distinction is key to embracing Time Blocking as the superior visualization tool.

The Failure of the To-Do List

Traditional to-do lists are simply a memory dump, a place to record tasks so they aren't forgotten. However, they fail the ADHD brain in critical ways:

- **Lack of Context:** They list tasks without assigning duration, effort, or location, making all tasks appear equally large and overwhelming. This ambiguity triggers **decision fatigue** and contributes to task paralysis.

- **Poor Prioritization:** A long, undifferentiated list of tasks (e.g., "Email boss," "Buy groceries," "Renew insurance," "Call friend") does not indicate which item is urgent or which requires the most time. The brain struggles to prioritize based on abstract importance, often defaulting to either the easiest / most stimulating task or, conversely, avoiding the list entirely.

- **Fueling Shame:** When a long list inevitably goes unfinished, it acts as a persistent source of shame and negative feedback, reinforcing the inner critic's narrative of failure and incompetence.

The Strength of Time Blocking

Time Blocking transforms the vague list into a functional map of reality, providing the structure and clear boundaries required for the ADHD brain to engage effectively.

- **Enforced Planning:** To create a time block, you *must* estimate duration and identify the steps involved, forcing the brain to engage the crucial **planning and organization** aspects of executive function.

- **Visual Urgency:** By turning the schedule into a visible, color-coded block, time is visually represented as a finite resource. This external pressure creates a necessary sense of urgency that motivates initiation, bypassing the internal dopamine deficit required to start tasks that are not inherently stimulating.

- **Sustained Effort:** Time Blocking supports better transitions and reduces the cognitive load associated with making moment-to-moment decisions. This sustained, lower-friction effort is the key to maintaining momentum and avoiding the burnout caused by constant task-switching and chaotic urgency.

Conclusion: Reclaiming Your Time, Defeating Overwhelm

The journey of defeating overwhelm requires the mastery of time, the resource that is most often compromised by ADHD. Time blindness is a fundamental neurobiological challenge, but it is not an insurmountable one. By strategically externalizing your time perception, you systematically dismantle the planning, organization, and estimation deficits that have plagued your productivity.

The implementation of **visual timers** and the discipline of **Time Blocking** transform time from an abstract source of anxiety into a concrete, manageable, and predictable ally. You are moving past the frustrating cycle of self-blame and chronic lateness, replacing it with a strategic, intentional rhythm that honors your brain's unique need for structure and visible cues.

This new mastery of time is the crucial second pillar of your journey. By creating a reliable time map, you ensure that the mental energy you conserved through external organization (Book 1) is now actively redirected toward high-leverage, sustained focus. This is the foundation upon which true attention mastery, emotional resilience, and integrated success will be built.

Chapter 1 Workbook: Visualize Time: Banish Time Blindness with Concrete Scheduling Tools

Objective: To practice externalizing time and creating visual blocks that counteract the effects of **Time Blindness**.

Scientific Anchor: Time Blocking forces the ADHD brain to estimate task duration, which directly addresses the estimation deficit and provides a clear, non-negotiable external structure that reduces overwhelm.

Activity 1.1: The Estimation Deficit Audit

Instructions: Select three medium-sized, recurring tasks. **Before** you start the task, write down your estimate. **After** completing the task, record the actual time spent. This exercise trains your Executive

Function's estimation skill by providing immediate, factual feedback.

1. **Task: Loading / Unloading Dishwasher & Wiping Counters**
   - *Initial Estimate:*_____ *minutes*
   - *Actual Time Spent:* _____ *minutes*
2. **Task: Processing Email Inbox (Triage 20 messages)**
   - *Initial Estimate:* _____ *minutes*
   - *Actual Time Spent:* _____ *minutes*
3. **Task: Preparing / Assembling Dinner**
   - *Initial Estimate:* _____ *minutes*
   - *Actual Time Spent:* _____ *minutes*

Activity 1.2: The Time Block Conversion Challenge

Instructions: Take your vague to-do list for tomorrow and convert it into a fully time-blocked schedule. Ensure every activity—including breaks, transitions, and personal care—has a fixed duration and time slot.

1. **Vague To-Do List Items:** List three general tasks for tomorrow (e.g., "Work on report," "Errands," "Laundry").

   Vague Tasks: _____

   _____

   _____

   _____

   _____

   _____

   _____

   _____

   _____

   _____

   _____

   _____

   _____

   _____

   _____

2. **Time Block Schedule:** Convert these vague tasks into fixed, timed appointments. **Crucially, include buffers and transitions.**

Time Slot	Activity	Duration	Neuro-Adjustment (Buffer / Cue)
9:00 AM – 10:00 AM	**Deep Work: Report Draft (Pomodoro Sprint)**	60 mins	(Block time for only ONE task; close all other tabs.)
10:00 AM – 10:15 AM	**Transition Block: Walk to Mailbox & Water**	15 mins	(Scheduled break to support smooth transition.)
10:15 AM – 11:30 AM	**Work: Email Triage / Admin**	75 mins	(This is the scheduled **only** time for email.)
Your Block 1:			
Your Block 2:			
Your Block 3:			

Reflection 1.3: Visualizing Urgency and Finitude

Instructions: Reflect on the emotional difference between viewing a long list and viewing a time-blocked schedule.

1. When you look at a traditional to-do list, what is the primary negative emotion that arises (e.g., anxiety, overwhelm, paralysis)? Why?

    Emotion: _____

    _____

    _____

    _____

    _____

2. When you look at your new Time Block Schedule, what positive sense or feeling is created? (Think: clarity, control, confidence, structure, or reduced anxiety).

    Positive Feeling: _____

    _____

    _____

    _____

    _____

    _____

3. How does the act of scheduling a task to end at a specific time (e.g., "Stop at 10:00 AM") make the task feel less daunting and reduce the risk of procrastination? (Hint: Think about **finitude** vs. infinity).

    Reduction in Daunt: _____

    _____

    _____

    _____

    _____

    _____

CHAPTER 2

SCHEDULE SUCCESS: SWITCH FROM ENDLESS TO-DO LISTS TO TIME BLOCKING

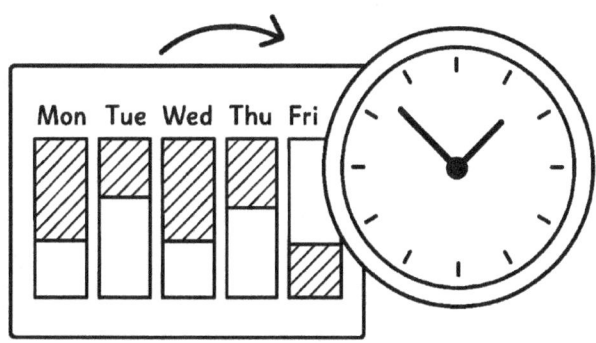

The journey to defeat the chronic, pervasive feeling of overwhelm for a woman with Attention-Deficit / Hyperactivity Disorder (ADHD) requires the establishment of rigorous, external structure. In Chapter 1, we learned that **Time Blindness**, the inability to accurately feel or estimate the passage of time, is a core neurobiological deficit that makes reliable planning nearly impossible. This chapter introduces the strategic solution: the abandonment of traditional, ineffective to-do lists in favor of **Time Blocking**, an evidence-based scheduling method that directly counteracts the planning and estimation deficits of the ADHD brain.

While to-do lists are intuitively appealing, they externalize tasks, preventing memory overload, they are profoundly inadequate for sustaining productivity and reducing anxiety for the time-blind individual. A simple list fails to provide the two elements most critical to the ADHD brain: **context** (when does this happen?) and **duration** (how long will this take?). Without these concrete boundaries, the brain perceives the list as an overwhelming, undifferentiated mass of obligations, leading inevitably to **overload, procrastination, and shame**.

This chapter provides the blueprint for mastering Time Blocking, transforming abstract aspirations into fixed, non-negotiable appointments. By forcing a specific time allocation for every task, break, and transition, you systematically embed external Executive Function (EF) into your schedule, turning your calendar from a mere record of events into a powerful, proactive map of your day. The goal is to replace the chaos of reactive time management with the calm, self-directed rhythm of intentional action.

Section 1: The Neurobiological Failure of the To-Do List

The struggle with the traditional to-do list is not a sign of laziness; it is a measurable cognitive failure rooted in the specific ways ADHD compromises executive functions required for effective planning.

1. The Estimation Deficit and Overwhelm

The core flaw of the traditional to-do list is that it provides no information about time or effort. For the ADHD brain, which struggles acutely with time estimation (**time blindness**), this lack of duration context is devastating. When faced with an undifferentiated list, such as "Work on report," "Call insurance," "Go grocery shopping", the brain registers every item as equally demanding and equally urgent.

This perceived uniformity of effort leads to **cognitive overload** and **paralysis**. The entire list feels amorphous and infinite, triggering the brain's natural shutdown response, a phenomenon often described as **task paralysis**. The psychological cost of facing a long list that inevitably goes unfinished is immense: it acts as a constant source of negative feedback, reinforcing the inner critic's narrative of failure and incompetence, thereby fueling shame and low self-worth.

2. Lack of Context and Priority Ambiguity

The to-do list is simply a **memory dump**, a place to record tasks so they aren't forgotten. However, it fails to engage the crucial EF skills of **planning and prioritization**.

- **Ambiguity:** Because the list lacks context (Where? When? For how long?), the brain must expend significant energy deciding what to do next. This contributes to **decision fatigue**, draining EF reserves before any actual work is done. The brain often defaults to either the easiest / most stimulating task (ignoring priorities) or avoiding the list entirely.

- **The Problem of Vague Tasks:** As research suggests, if a task on a list is too vague (e.g., "Exercise" or "Organize"), the brain tends to skip right over it because it doesn't provide a clear, actionable starting point. Time Blocking, conversely, forces the user to define the action: "Exercise: 30-minute power walk from 5:00 PM to 5:30 PM."

3. The Fuel for Shame

When a woman sees a long list of tasks that remains consistently incomplete, the list becomes a document of personal failure. This persistent external reminder of underperformance amplifies the shame that women with ADHD are already prone to internalizing, damaging self-efficacy and confidence. Time Blocking, by limiting the expectation to what is temporally possible, turns the schedule from a source of judgment into a realistic plan for action.

Section 2: The Neurobiological Power of Time Blocking

Time Blocking is a therapeutic strategy that transforms how the ADHD brain interacts with time and tasks, serving as a powerful **external executive** function tool. It directly addresses the core deficits of time blindness, planning, and prioritization through intentional structure and visualization.

1. Making Time Concrete and Visible

The primary strength of Time Blocking is its ability to take abstract time and render it concrete and visible.

- **Visual Representation:** When time is represented by a physical block of color or space on a calendar, it becomes tangible, something the eye can see and the brain can anchor to. This visualization helps counteract **time blindness**, allowing the brain to better grasp and respect duration, transforming time from an enemy into a predictable resource.
- **Enforced Finitude:** By assigning clear start and end times to every activity, Time Blocking imposes **finitude** on tasks, ensuring they do not feel amorphous or infinite. The brain knows the commitment is limited (e.g., 9:00 AM to 10:30 AM), which significantly reduces the anxiety that triggers **paralysis** and lowers the necessary **activation energy** to begin.

2. Forcing Planning and Estimation

Time Blocking forces the brain to engage the crucial executive functions of planning and estimation *before* the work begins, providing the necessary cognitive scaffolding.

- **Pre-Allocation of Effort:** To create a Time Block, you *must* estimate the task duration and define the steps involved. This intentional pre-allocation of time forces the brain to engage the planning aspect of EF, a skill that is often inconsistent in ADHD.
- **Minimizing Guesswork:** When the entire day is mapped out, the cognitive guesswork of "What should I do next?" is eliminated. The schedule becomes a clear, non-negotiable roadmap, which reduces feelings of overwhelm and conserves EF reserves that would otherwise be wasted on moment-to-moment decision-making, a process that leads to severe fatigue.
- **Better Transitions:** Time Blocking supports smoother transitions between activities, a common sticking point for the neurodivergent brain, which struggles with context switching. By scheduling specific start and end times, you create clear boundaries that help the brain disengage from one task and transition smoothly to the next, conserving mental energy.

3. Leveraging the Dopamine System

The ADHD brain is driven by the immediate reward of a dopamine release. Time Blocking provides structured opportunities for this necessary reinforcement:

- **Immediate Feedback:** When a Time Block is completed, the visible act of checking it off, removing it from the schedule, or moving the focus to the next block provides a tangible sense of accomplishment. This immediate positive feedback generates a small burst of dopamine, reinforcing the productive behavior and building the necessary **momentum** to tackle the next scheduled task.
- **Visual Urgency:** The sight of the scheduled time block marching toward its end creates a constructive sense of urgency. This external pressure provides the necessary **activation energy** that the brain struggles to generate internally for boring tasks.

Section 3: Strategic Implementation for the ADHD Brain

To ensure Time Blocking is sustainable and effective, the system must be customized to accommodate the inherent deficits of ADHD, turning a rigid schedule into a flexible, supportive framework.

1. Compensating for the Estimation Deficit (The Buffer Rule)

People with ADHD consistently **underestimate** how long tasks will take, a phenomenon that fuels rushing, anxiety, and eventual system abandonment. Time Blocking must proactively neutralize this deficit.

- **Schedule with Buffers:** The cardinal rule of ADHD time blocking is to **intentionally schedule more time than you think you need**. Add a time buffer of 25–50% to your initial estimate for every major block of work. If a report should take two hours, schedule 2.5 to 3 hours. This simple adjustment provides crucial breathing room, reducing the stress that comes from unrealistic temporal constraints and preventing the schedule from becoming a source of impossible pressure.

- **Block Transitions:** Do not schedule tasks back-to-back. Intentional transition periods (e.g., "15-Minute Break / Reset" or "Walk to next meeting location") must be blocked between major focus tasks. This supports the smooth mental shift required for the ADHD brain and mitigates the high **cognitive cost of context switching**, which occurs every time the brain changes its focus.

2. Enforcing Boundaries (The Respect Rule)

The most powerful rule of Time Blocking is to **respect the block**— both its beginning and its end.

- **Respect the Start:** When the time block begins, the task is the non-negotiable focus. All distractions (e.g., checking email, answering texts) must be suppressed, mirroring the approach used for Deep Work. This training strengthens **inhibitory control**, the ability to resist temptations, a core EF skill.

- **Respect the End:** When the scheduled time is up, the task **stops**, whether it is finished or not. This protects the integrity of the overall schedule, ensuring that one hyperfocused task does not bleed into and derail the subsequent appointments, which is a major source of chaos for the ADHD brain. If the task is unfinished, schedule a new, finite block for it immediately.

3. Integrating Deep Work and Single-Tasking

Time Blocking naturally integrates the principle of **single-tasking**, the necessary antidote to the inefficient and draining process of rapid task-switching.

- **Anchor One Task:** Within a defined time block (e.g., 9:00 AM–10:30 AM), only **one specific, defined task** should be anchored (e.g., "Draft Introduction to Report," not "Work on Report"). This focus minimizes the cognitive effort required to decide what to do and prevents the brain from engaging in rapid toggling, which drains mental energy.
- **Batch Similar Tasks:** To further reduce the draining cost of **context switching**, schedule similar activities together in the same block (e.g., dedicate one block for "Email Triage / Admin" and a separate block for "Creative Writing / Deep Work"). This allows the brain to stay in one cognitive mode for a longer period, conserving EF resources.

4. Externalizing the Schedule (Visual and Digital Anchors)

The schedule must live in a location that is impossible to ignore, thereby acting as a constant **external working memory cue** that bypasses internal forgetfulness.

- **Visual Prominence:** Your time-blocked schedule must be visually prominent, a large digital calendar view, a color-coded whiteboard, or a physical planner left open on your desk. If the schedule is hidden, the time-blind brain will forget it exists.
- **Color-Coding for Clarity:** Use a simple, consistent color-coding system to visually categorize blocks (e.g., blue for Work / Deep Focus, green for Health / Self-Care, yellow for Administrative / Errands). This visual cue allows the brain to quickly process and prioritize the schedule at a glance, minimizing the cognitive effort required to interpret the schedule.
- **Automated Reminders:** Leverage technology to provide automated, external cues. Use digital calendars that provide multiple, automated reminders for transitions, task completion, and upcoming deadlines. Set alerts for a week before, a day before, and an hour before major deadlines to anchor the abstract future into the urgent present.

Section 4: The Emotional and Economic Payoff: Defeating the ADHD Tax

Mastering Time Blocking is not merely about increasing productivity; it is a vital strategy for emotional stabilization and mitigating the profound economic costs associated with unmanaged ADHD.

1. Reducing Shame and Building Self-Efficacy

The consistent failure of the traditional to-do list fuels a cycle of shame and inadequacy in women with ADHD, reinforcing the narrative that they are incapable of consistent performance. Time Blocking directly interrupts this cycle:

- **Realistic Expectations:** Time Blocking forces the creation of a schedule that is temporally realistic. By building in buffers and limiting the number of tasks, it sets achievable expectations, reducing the likelihood of failure and self-criticism.

- **Evidence of Competence:** Each completed Time Block provides tangible evidence of competence and follow-through, building **self-efficacy**, the belief in one's own ability to succeed. This self-efficacy is a powerful psychological resource that bolsters overall emotional resilience.

- **Neutralizing Emotional Dysregulation:** The structure and predictability of Time Blocking help stabilize the nervous system, reducing the chaotic internal environment that triggers **emotional dysregulation**. When the day is predictable, the brain is less likely to feel overwhelmed, which can prevent small triggers from escalating into a disproportionate emotional storm.

2. Mitigating the Financial and Economic ADHD Tax

Unmanaged ADHD symptoms carry a significant and measurable **"ADHD Tax,"** which includes the cumulative cost, financial, emotional, and mental, of operating in a world designed for neurotypical brains. Time Blocking is a direct weapon against the most costly elements of this tax:

- **Combating Productivity Loss:** The largest component of the societal excess cost of adult ADHD is indirect cost related to work loss and productivity. The total societal excess cost attributable to ADHD in US adults is estimated at **$122.8 billion annually**, with excess costs of unemployment and productivity loss comprising the largest proportion. Time Blocking enhances productivity by enforcing single-task focus and minimizing context switching, directly reducing the waste of time and effort.

- **Addressing the Core Financial Risk:** Time blindness, disorganization, and poor prioritization contribute to financial instability, including late fees and lower earnings. Time Blocking helps enforce vital, non-stimulating administrative tasks, such as "Pay Bills: 4:00 PM–4:30 PM, Friday", by giving them non-negotiable, visible appointments, mitigating the risk of financial penalties caused by forgetfulness and procrastination. Furthermore, improved planning and organization, which are trained through consistent Time Blocking, are linked to better long-term financial outcomes.

3. Reducing Relational Friction

Time Blocking reduces friction in relationships by externalizing planning and ensuring necessary household and relational tasks are addressed.

- **Managing Shared Responsibilities:** By scheduling specific blocks for shared responsibilities (e.g., "Laundry / Chores: 7:00 PM–8:00 PM"), the ADHD partner externalizes their commitment, reducing the neurotypical partner's need to act as a **taskmaster** or reminder.

- **Supporting Communication:** Time Blocking allows for the intentional scheduling of high-leverage relational habits, such as "Weekly Check-in / Roundtable" or "Active Listening Practice." As research suggests, scheduling brief weekly check-ins helps build a routine of open dialogue and lightens the load of daily stress.

Conclusion: The Strategic Path to Control

The journey of defeating overwhelm requires replacing the chaos of reactive living with the strategic structure of intentional scheduling. The traditional to-do list, while useful for memory, fails the ADHD brain because it lacks the context and duration required to overcome time blindness and the activation deficit.

The mastery of **Time Blocking** transforms your relationship with time. By rendering time concrete, enforcing estimation, and embedding buffers and transitions, you systematically build the external EF required for consistent follow-through. This structural stability reduces the pervasive anxiety of chaos, conserves precious mental energy, and mitigates the emotional and economic costs associated with unmanaged attention.

The mental bandwidth conserved by creating this reliable time map is the resource you need for the internal work that follows in this book. You are no longer merely coping; you are proactively commanding your focus and shaping your reality. This commitment to intentional structure is the key to unlocking your full potential and moving toward a life defined by self-efficacy and control.

Chapter 2 Workbook: Schedule Success: Switch from Endless To-Do Lists to Time Blocking

Objective: To practice converting vague to-do items into concrete, time-bound, actionable appointments that compensate for Time Blindness and the Estimation Deficit.

Scientific Anchor: Time Blocking forces the engagement of planning and estimation skills, which are core executive functions challenged by ADHD, while its visual nature counteracts time blindness by making time concrete.

Activity 2.1: The To-Do List Conversion Audit

Instructions: Identify three items from a recent or current vague to-do list that caused you stress or that you procrastinated on. Convert them into Time Block appointments, ensuring you include the necessary boundaries (start / end time) and specific action cues.

Vague To-Do Item (Problematic)	Time Block Appointment (Solution)	Neuro-Adjustment Added (Why it works)
(Example: "Organize files")	**2:00 PM – 2:45 PM: Process Invoices and File (45 min fixed block)**	Enforced duration reduces paralysis and stress.
(Your Item 1)		
(Your Item 2)		
(Your Item 3)		

Activity 2.2: The Buffer and Transition Rule

Instructions: Plan a critical 3-hour work block for tomorrow, intentionally building in two types of crucial buffers: **The Estimation Buffer** (extra time for the core task) and **The Transition Buffer** (a mandatory break between activities).

1. **Core Task:** (E.g., "Draft Client Proposal"). Your honest estimate for this task is 1.5 hours.

2. **Time Block Plan (3 Hours Total):**

Time Slot	Activity	Duration (Fixed)	Neuro-Strategy
9:00 AM – 10:45 AM	**Core Focus Work (Task)**	105 minutes	(1.5 hours + 30 min **Estimation Buffer**)
10:45 AM – 11:00 AM	**Mandatory Transition / Reset**	15 minutes	(Scheduled physical / mental break to mitigate context switching cost)
11:00 AM – 12:00 PM	**Secondary Task (Follow-up calls)**	60 minutes	

Reflection 2.3: Visualizing Control and Finitude

Instructions: Reflect on the emotional difference between the two scheduling methods.

1. When you look at a long, vague to-do list, the item "Draft Client Proposal" feels like it requires **infinite** time. How does seeing the task confined to a **105-minute block** on your calendar reduce the risk of you procrastinating? (Focus on the concept of **finitude**).

   Finitude Effect: _____
   _____
   _____
   _____
   _____
   _____

2. The goal of Time Blocking is to conserve EF. How does pre-scheduling the **Transition Block** (10:45–11:00 AM) reduce the daily cognitive load that would normally be wasted deciding when or how to stop the first task and start the next?

EF Conservation: _____

_____

_____

_____

_____

_____

3. Name one specific way you plan to make your Time Block schedule **visually prominent** (e.g., using a large screen widget, a whiteboard, or color-coding) to counteract the effect of Time Blindness and externalize the schedule.

Visualization Tool: _____

_____

_____

_____

_____

_____

_____

CHAPTER 3
CUSTOMIZE YOUR FOCUS: APPLY THE POMODORO TECHNIQUE TO YOUR ATTENTION SPAN

POMODORO TECHNIQUE

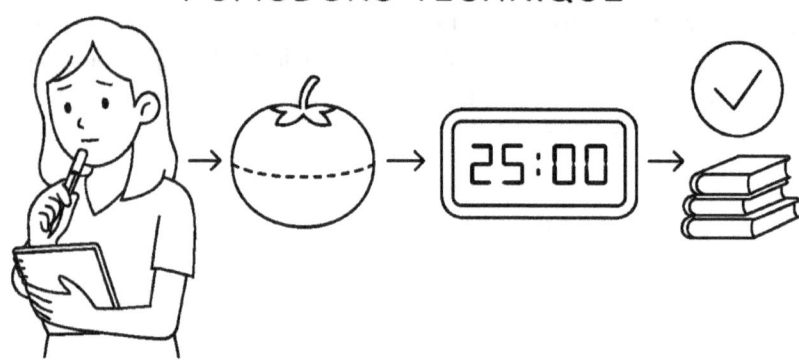

In Chapter 2, you mastered **Time Blocking**, transforming abstract time into a concrete schedule and enforcing the necessary boundaries of duration and transition. This structural discipline, however, still faces a formidable opponent: the difficulty of sustaining focus *within* those blocks, a struggle rooted in the dual paradox of ADHD attention, the unpredictable swing between acute **inattention** and disabling **hyperfocus**.

This chapter provides the tactical solution to this dilemma: the disciplined and customized application of the **Pomodoro Technique**. This evidence-based time management system utilizes short, fixed work sprints followed by mandatory, short breaks. For the ADHD brain, the Pomodoro Technique is more than a productivity hack; it is a neurological strategy that systematically addresses three core executive function deficits:

1. **Task Activation Deficit (Paralysis):** It makes the commitment to start feel short and manageable.
2. **Time Blindness:** It makes time visible, eliminating the feeling of infinite, overwhelming duration.

3. **Attention Dysregulation:** It provides a critical external "circuit-breaker" to prevent burnout from sustained, uncontrolled hyperfocus.

By customizing the duration of your focus sprints to match your current energy levels and attention span, you stop fighting your internal resistance and begin harnessing your inherent bursts of attention with intentional, reliable structure. This is the key to transforming chaotic energy into consistent, high-quality output.

Section 1: The Neurobiology of Finitude: Defeating Paralysis and Time Blindness

The first and most critical function of the Pomodoro Technique is to counteract the anxiety, paralysis, and overwhelm triggered by the perception of an infinite, daunting task. This intervention relies on the powerful psychological effect of **finitude**.

1. The Threat of Infinite Time

Time blindness, the inability to accurately perceive or estimate the flow of time, is a core neurobiological reality of the ADHD brain. When faced with a large, undifferentiated project, the brain perceives the commitment as amorphous, unquantifiable, and potentially unending.

- **Overwhelm Triggers Paralysis:** This perception of infinity instantly triggers **cognitive overload** and the **paralysis response**. The brain attempts to protect itself from the immense, unknown mental effort required, leading to procrastination and avoidance.
- **The Activation Deficit:** The task is too boring or too complex to generate the necessary internal burst of **dopamine** (activation energy) required to start. The commitment of working for an unknown, potentially long period feels too high.

The Pomodoro Technique directly attacks this anxiety by imposing **clear, fixed boundaries**. Committing to a task for only 25 minutes (or less) transforms the project from a paralyzing marathon into a manageable sprint. The visible, ticking timer serves as a constant, non-negotiable external cue, providing the brain with the precise structure it requires to initiate the effort. This dramatically lowers the activation energy, making the organized choice the easiest choice.

2. The Power of Visibility and Momentum

The use of a physical or digital timer as a countdown mechanism serves as a continuous external representation of time passing, which is vital for the time-blind brain.

- **Concrete Time:** The timer translates the abstract concept of duration into a visual or auditory cue, allowing the brain to anchor its attention to the external environment rather than relying on unreliable internal time perception. This makes the time spent feel tangible and measurable.

- **Momentum and Dopamine:** Each completion of a fixed work interval provides an immediate, tangible "win." This sense of success generates a small, but powerful burst of **dopamine** (the brain's reward chemical), reinforcing the productive behavior and building **momentum** for the next sprint. This positive feedback loop is crucial for overcoming the motivation deficit associated with the ADHD brain and is far more reliable than relying on abstract, distant rewards.

Section 2: The Mechanism: Pomodoro as External Regulator

The genius of the Pomodoro structure for ADHD is its symmetrical approach to the problem of attention dysregulation: it effectively manages both **inattention** (difficulty starting / staying on task) and **hyperfocus** (difficulty stopping / transitioning).

1. Managing Inattention and Distraction

The short, fixed work interval is specifically designed to work *with* the ADHD brain's tendency toward novelty-seeking and restlessness, rather than fighting against it.

- **Sustaining Engagement:** The limited duration of the work period (e.g., 25 minutes) is less intimidating than a long, unstructured block. The brain knows the commitment is short, which makes it easier to sustain concentration and reduces the mental fatigue often caused by continuous effort. The timer itself serves as a constant, gentle redirection mechanism, pulling the attention back to the task whenever it wanders.

- **Reducing "Mental Friction":** By committing to a single task within the fixed interval, you enforce the discipline of **single-tasking**, which is the necessary antidote to the inefficient and draining cost of constant **task-switching**. You are telling your brain, "You only need to focus on this one thing until the bell rings." This clear boundary reduces the cognitive load associated with filtering distractions and making constant choices about priority.

2. The Circuit Breaker: Preventing Hyperfocus and Burnout

While hyperfocus can generate impressive productivity, it is ultimately a form of attention dysregulation that can lead to burnout, missed appointments, and relationship friction (e.g., forgetting to eat, neglecting family needs, failing to transition to a critical deadline). The mandated break is the Pomodoro Technique's most critical feature for the hyperfocus-prone ADHD brain.

- **Enforced Disengagement:** The scheduled break acts as an **external circuit-breaker**. The timer going off forces the individual to stop working, even if they feel they are in a productive flow state. This external boundary protects the integrity of the overall schedule and prevents the hyperfocused task from bleeding into and derailing subsequent appointments, which is a major source of chaos for the ADHD brain.

- **Preventing Mental Fatigue:** The **mandatory 5-minute break** provides a regular, guilt-free opportunity for the brain to reset and seek the novelty and low-effort stimulation it craves (e.g., stretching, getting a drink of water, listening to one song, or stepping away from the desk). This strategically scheduled break prevents the deep mental fatigue and burnout often associated with prolonged, continuous concentration, ensuring that the next work interval starts with higher energy reserves.

Section 3: Customization: Tailoring the Sprint to Your Brain

The traditional 25-minute Pomodoro is merely a suggestion. For the ADHD brain, the technique is only effective and sustainable when the duration is **customized** to match the individual's unique attention span and energy cycle. Rigidly adhering to a standard that causes excessive struggle simply creates a new source of shame.

1. Matching Duration to Attention Span

Your focus intervals should be low-friction and achievable. The duration should be challenging enough to facilitate deep work, but short enough to avoid triggering anxiety or burnout.

- **Start Short and Build:** If 25 minutes feels daunting, start with a shorter interval, such as **15 minutes** of focused work followed by a **5-minute break**. Successfully completing three 15-minute sprints builds more confidence and momentum than struggling through one 25-minute block. Over time, you can gradually extend the work interval as your attentional muscle strengthens.

- **The "Energy Matching" Rule:** Match your work duration to your daily energy cycle. Schedule longer Pomodoro sprints (e.g., 45–50 minutes) during your peak mental energy hours (often the morning) and shorter, high-impact sprints (e.g., 10–15 minutes) during your afternoon energy slump or when transitioning between complex tasks.

2. Customizing the Break for Optimal Reset

The break is as important as the work interval, serving as a restorative reset for the brain. The break must be low-stakes and intentionally non-productive.

- **Movement Over Screens:** While the ADHD brain craves the stimulation of a screen (email, social media), engaging with these during the break risks fragmenting attention and increasing context-switching cost, making it harder to return to focus. Prioritize **physical movement** (e.g., stretching, walking, drinking water) during the break to discharge pent-up physical restlessness and stimulate the dopamine system in a healthy way.
- **Sensory Reset:** Use the break to engage in a simple **sensory reset**. For instance, step outside to feel the air, or engage in a quick **grounding technique** (e.g., the 5-4-3-2-1 method) to pull the attention away from internal chatter and into the present environment. This prepares the brain to re-engage with focus.

Section 4: Advanced Implementation and Momentum

Integrating the Pomodoro Technique with other EF strategies ensures that the method becomes a resilient tool for **Deep Work**, not just a timer for busywork.

1. The Pre-Flight Checklist Ritual

Before starting any Pomodoro sprint, the ADHD brain requires a consistent ritual to ensure the environment and mind are prepared for focus, minimizing the cognitive load of initiation.

- **Define the Single Task:** Review the Time Block schedule (Chapter 2) and confirm the **single, specific task** for the next interval (e.g., "Draft the conclusion paragraph," not "Work on report"). This specificity is a direct antidote to the paralysis caused by ambiguity.

- **Minimize Distraction:** As the timer is set, perform a quick **Notification Annihilation** ritual: silence all devices, close unnecessary browser tabs (each is an "open loop" consuming working memory), and clear the immediate desk area of everything not related to the task. This intentional preparation saves valuable executive function during the sprint.

2. Integrating External Accountability

When the internal motivation is low, the Pomodoro timer should be anchored with the external support of **Body Doubling** (Chapter 4, Book 1).

- **Accountability Anchor:** The physical presence or visible virtual presence of a Body Double provides the non-judgmental accountability necessary to ensure the Pomodoro sprint begins on time and continues uninterrupted until the timer rings. The double serves as an external pacer and a stable, non-distracting focal point, which is crucial for maintaining attention during the focused interval.

- **Shared Structure:** If working with a partner or peer, commit to synchronized Pomodoro cycles (e.g., everyone starts their 25-minute timer at the same moment). This shared structure leverages social commitment to enforce the schedule, making the transition back to work easier for all parties.

3. Leveraging Momentum for Larger Projects

The goal of the Pomodoro Technique is to transform large, daunting projects into chains of achievable sprints. This harnesses the power of **momentum** to sustain effort.

- **Chaining Micro-Steps:** Use the Pomodoro intervals to execute the **micro-steps** defined in Chapter 1. A 25-minute sprint should be used to complete two or three small, defined micro-steps, rather than tackling a vague, large chore. The satisfaction of checking off multiple micro-steps during the break provides a powerful burst of dopamine that reinforces the next sprint.

- **Tracking the Sprints:** Visually track the number of Pomodoro sprints completed each day or week (e.g., a simple tally mark on a whiteboard). This externalizes progress and provides a concrete, visible record of effort, which helps the ADHD brain appreciate progress and build confidence in its ability to sustain focus over time.

Section 5: The Emotional Payoff: Self-Compassion and Sustainable Focus

Mastering the Pomodoro Technique yields significant emotional benefits, creating a sustainable foundation that actively protects against shame and burnout, the primary emotional drivers of overwhelm.

1. Reducing Shame and the Inner Critic

The chronic failure to meet deadlines or sustain focus fuels a cycle of shame and self-blame in women with ADHD. The Pomodoro Technique provides tangible proof of competence, directly countering this inner critic.

- **Evidence of Competence:** Each successfully completed 25-minute sprint provides undeniable evidence of focus and follow-through, building **self-efficacy**, the belief in one's own ability to succeed. This steady accumulation of small wins gradually dismantles the pervasive feeling of inadequacy.

- **Guilt-Free Breaks:** The mandated 5-minute break is a built-in act of self-compassion. It legitimizes rest, ensuring that the woman does not feel guilty for pausing her effort. The break becomes an integral, non-negotiable part of the system, not a reward earned through punishing effort. This shifts the focus from rigid self-criticism to compassionate self-management.

2. Preventing Burnout and Protecting Energy Reserves

The cycle of burnout, uncontrolled hyperfocus followed by exhaustion, task avoidance, and crisis management, is a major source of chaos for the ADHD brain.

- **Energy Regulation:** By enforcing regular breaks, the Pomodoro Technique ensures that mental energy is managed proactively, preventing the total depletion of EF reserves that occurs during uncontrolled hyperfocus. This protects the brain from the chronic fatigue and mental sluggishness that define the "ADHD Tax" on energy.

- **Sustainable Effort:** The technique promotes **sustainable effort** rather than sporadic, intense bursts of productivity. By working in short, manageable chunks and recovering frequently, the woman creates a predictable, consistent rhythm that is resilient to the chaos of overwhelm.

Conclusion: Your Focused Edge

The journey through this chapter has provided the tactical mastery necessary to sustain focus within the structure established by Time Blocking. The customized application of the **Pomodoro Technique** systematically addresses the core attentional challenges of the ADHD brain, time blindness, task paralysis, and hyperfocus—by leveraging external cues and fixed boundaries.

You are no longer leaving focus to chance or fighting internal resistance with sheer willpower. Instead, you are using the timer as a reliable external regulator, transforming daunting commitments into manageable, rewarding sprints. This disciplined, yet compassionate, approach empowers you to command your mental spotlight, achieving higher-quality work with less mental fatigue. This cultivated focus is the definitive step toward defeating overwhelm and preparing your entire system for the essential work of strengthening your core Executive Function skills that follows.

Chapter 3 Workbook: Customize Your Focus: Apply the Pomodoro Technique to Your Attention Span

Objective: To customize the Pomodoro Technique to match your unique attention span and energy cycle, transforming work into manageable, timed sprints.

Scientific Anchor: Customizing the Pomodoro interval (e.g., starting shorter) reduces the anxiety that triggers task paralysis, while mandated breaks prevent hyperfocus and burnout, thereby maintaining executive function reserves.

Activity 3.1: Attention Span Customization Audit

Instructions: Identify your current optimal focus interval (Work) and the necessary duration of a true mental break (Rest). This moves beyond the standard 25 / 5 interval.

1. **Work Interval Assessment:** If a task is boring, what is the *shortest* amount of time you can commit to before feeling the urge to check your phone or move? (Select one: 10 min, 15 min, 25 min, 30 min).
   - *My Custom Work Interval (A):* _____ *minutes*
2. **Break Interval Assessment:** How long do you need to stand, stretch, and move your body before you can successfully

re-engage? (Select one: 3 min, 5 min, 10 min).
   o *My Custom Break Interval (B):* _____ *minutes*
3. **My Customized Pomodoro Cycle: A (Work)** minutes / **B (Break)** minutes.

Activity 3.2: The Anti-Hyperfocus Break Protocol

Instructions: The break is mandatory and must be designed to interrupt the flow of hyperfocus and truly reset the brain. Design your three go-to **Break Actions** that are low-friction and actively avoid screens (to prevent context-switching cost).

Break Action	Duration (Fixed)	Neuro-Benefit (Why it works)
Action 1: Physical Movement	(E.g., 2 minutes)	(Example: Standing, 5 jumping jacks, or brisk walk to the window. Discharges physical restlessness)
Action 2: Sensory Reset	(E.g., 1 minute)	(Example: Splash cold water on face, hold ice cube, or use 5-4-3-2-1 grounding technique.)
Action 3: Hydration/ Dopamine Reward	(E.g., 2 minutes)	(Example: Get a specific drink of water / tea. Quick, safe reward that reinforces follow-through.)

Reflection 3.3: Anchoring Focus and Defeating Guilt

Instructions: Reflect on how the structure of this technique supports both your focus and your emotional well-being.

1. **Defeating Paralysis:** You are about to start a task you hate. How does seeing the timer set for your **Custom Work Interval (A)** instantly reduce the anxiety that would otherwise lead to procrastination? (Focus on **finitude**).

   Reduction in Anxiety: _____
   _____
   _____
   _____

2. **Stopping Hyperfocus:** When the timer rings and you are deep in hyperfocus, what is the single biggest challenge you face (e.g., guilt, feeling the loss of momentum, urgency)?

Challenge: _____

_____

_____

_____

3. **Self-Compassion and the Break:** How does knowing the break is **mandatory** (an integral part of the system, not a reward you must earn) reduce the feeling of **guilt** or self-criticism when you pause your work?

Guilt Reduction: _____

_____

_____

_____

CHAPTER 4
FUTURE-PROOF YOUR BRAIN: STRENGTHEN WORKING MEMORY WITH PLANNING ROUTINES

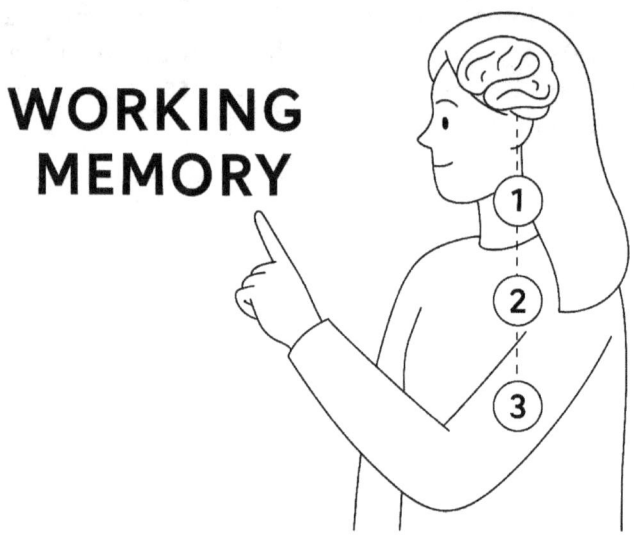

The work completed in the preceding chapters, establishing external organization (Book 1) and mastering time visualization through Time Blocking and Pomodoro sprints (Chapters 1–3), has provided the essential structural scaffolding for your life. You have successfully reduced the chaotic, reactive demands on your attention. Now, the journey shifts to the deepest level of Executive Function (EF) mastery: **internal strengthening and resilience**.

This chapter is dedicated to the core cognitive skills required for sustained adult function: **Working Memory (WM)** and **Inhibitory Control (IC)**. WM is your brain's "mental scratchpad", the ability to hold and manipulate information for short-term use, while IC is your brain's "brakes" , the capacity to resist temptation and think before speaking or acting. Both are crucial EF skills that are often inconsistent in the ADHD brain, leading to forgetfulness, poor follow-through, and impulsive decisions.

This chapter is about building a powerful, long-term cognitive strategy. While external tools compensate for deficits, consistent practice and the establishment of reliable, fixed planning routines are necessary to truly **future-proof your brain** against the stress, inconsistency, and shame that define unmanaged ADHD. By training these skills and reducing the internal friction associated with planning, you create a foundation for resilience that is less susceptible to the chaos of fatigue and distraction.

Section 1: The Neurobiology of Core Executive Function Deficits

To effectively strengthen WM and IC, we must first understand the specific neurobiological deficits that make these processes challenging for women with ADHD. Both WM and IC are highly dependent on the function of the **prefrontal cortex (PFC)**, the brain's command center for higher-level cognitive functions.

1. Working Memory: The Inconsistent "Mental Scratchpad"

Working memory (WM) is the system that allows you to temporarily hold multiple pieces of information in mind and manipulate them simultaneously, such as remembering a multi-step instruction while executing the first step, or keeping track of conversation points while formulating a response. For a woman with ADHD, WM can feel like a sieve.

- **Impact on Multi-Step Tasks:** This deficit makes it difficult to follow lengthy verbal instructions, remember the location of an item moments after placing it down, or retain the steps of a task management plan. When WM fails, follow-through suffers, tasks are often left unfinished, and the brain is quickly overwhelmed by the number of steps required for a goal.

- **The Planning Barrier:** WM is essential for effective **planning**. You must be able to hold the goal, the steps, and the available resources in mind simultaneously to map out a strategy. A compromised WM means this planning stage is taxing, leading to frustration, avoidance, and reliance on spontaneous, often inefficient, action rather than intentional, planned execution.

2. Inhibitory Control: The Weakening of the "Brakes"

Inhibitory control (IC) is the ability to resist an urge or temptation, curb impulsivity, and think before acting or speaking. It is the EF responsible for discipline, perseverance, and delayed gratification.

- **Impulsivity and Regulation:** When IC is inconsistent, it manifests as impulsive interruptions during conversations, difficulty resisting the urge to check a notification, or the inability to stay on task despite boredom or setbacks. For women with ADHD, this can contribute significantly to both **emotional dysregulation** (impulsive outbursts) and **relational friction** (interrupting a partner).

- **Dopamine's Role in Delay:** IC is heavily tied to the **dopamine dysregulation** in the ADHD brain. Because the brain struggles to generate internal motivation for tasks that lack novelty, the impulse to seek immediate stimulation (e.g., procrastination, checking social media) is often prioritized over the long-term, abstract reward of the task at hand. Strengthening IC means strengthening the "brakes" to resist this immediate gratification.

Section 2: Strengthening Inhibitory Control: Training the "Brakes"

Improving any executive function skill, including inhibitory control, requires consistent practice and challenge. The work is similar to physical exercise: the muscle must be challenged to grow. By intentionally engaging in activities that require you to override an automatic response, you strengthen the neural pathways responsible for IC.

1. Intentional Resistance Games

Behavioral therapies and EF training often utilize activities that require the individual to think before acting and to curb impulses, which are essential components of IC.

- **Structured Behavioral Games:** Engaging in structured activities that require suppression of a dominant response helps build IC. Simple games like "Simon Says" (where the command must be filtered before execution) are clinically noted to improve inhibitory control by training the brain to resist the automatic urge. These can be adapted for adults (e.g., intentionally performing the opposite of a simple command).

- **Delayed Gratification Practice:** Actively creating small, intentional opportunities for **delayed gratification** trains the brain to resist immediate reward. This could involve using a specific "Waiting Basket" for non-urgent notifications or committing to a **"Ten-Minute Rule"** before making a non-essential purchase or responding to a heated text message. This crucial pause allows the PFC to engage and override the amygdala's impulsive reaction, which is key to reducing both financial impulsivity and emotional volatility.

2. The Power of Single-Task Focus

The deliberate practice of **single-tasking** (Chapter 4, Book 2) is a form of intensive IC training.

- **Resisting Context Switching:** When committing to a Pomodoro sprint, every time the urge to check email, open a new browser tab, or look at your phone arises, you are engaging and strengthening your IC. The act of resisting the distraction and maintaining focus on the primary task forces the brain to suppress the impulse, building the attentional muscle required for long-term concentration.

- **Managing Internal Distraction:** IC also involves suppressing internal cognitive noise. During a focused block, the appearance of an intrusive thought or a fleeting idea is inevitable. Instead of immediately pursuing the thought, IC trains you to acknowledge the thought without judgment and gently redirect your focus back to the task at hand, reinforcing the discipline of internal self-control.

Section 3: Enhancing Working Memory: Supporting the "Mental Scratchpad"

WM training requires a dual approach: building a reliable external system that compensates for memory deficits and engaging in consistent cognitive challenge to improve retrieval and retention.

1. Externalizing Memory with Fixed Routines

The most effective strategy for managing WM deficits is to consistently offload all essential information onto a reliable **external system**, preventing the mental scratchpad from becoming overloaded. The Time Blocking structure (Chapter 2) and organizational systems (Book 1) are already serving this function. This section focuses on the **routine** of using those tools.

- **Fixed Planning Rituals:** WM is strengthened when the need for it is reduced. Establishing a daily, non-negotiable planning ritual ensures all necessary instructions and objectives are externalized and placed in a visible, predictable location (e.g., your Time Block schedule). This ritual should involve:
  - **The Daily Prep:** At the start of the workday, visually review the day's schedule and mentally rehearse the first two transition points. This loads the instructions into short-term memory with minimal effort.

- o **The End-of-Day Review:** Before shutting down, capture all new tasks and ideas (the **Brain Dump**) and immediately process them into the planner for future scheduling. This prevents "open loops" from consuming WM overnight and causing sleep anxiety.
- **Creating Checklists and Templates:** To compensate for forgetting steps or instructions, create visual **checklists and templates** for repetitive tasks (e.g., "The Meeting Prep Checklist," "The Morning Routine Checklist"). These external scaffolds ensure consistency without requiring the brain to expend WM energy recalling multi-step sequences.

2. Cognitive Challenge and Practice

While systems are essential for daily function, consistent, targeted cognitive practice challenges the underlying WM capacity.

- **Cognitive Exercises:** Engaging in brain training exercises designed to stress working memory, such as dual N-back tasks, memory games, or structured puzzles that require multi-step recall, can strengthen the neural connections associated with WM function over time. This intentional practice challenges the EF muscle to adapt and improve its capacity for sustained information processing.
- **Verbalizing Steps:** When faced with a multi-step project, verbalize the steps aloud (or write them down immediately). This externalization reinforces the instruction and aids the process of encoding information into memory, improving the likelihood of retention and follow-through.

Section 4: Future-Proofing through Routine: The Fixed Planning Rituals

For the ADHD brain, the greatest enemy is inconsistency. The intentional, fixed planning rituals outlined below are the mechanism for translating the skills of WM and IC into resilient, long-term habits.

1. The Weekly Review (The Strategy Session)

The Weekly Review is a non-negotiable appointment (scheduled and time-blocked) designed to proactively engage the planning aspect of EF, ensuring the abstract future is made concrete and manageable.

- **Goal Setting and Prioritization:** Dedicate 60–90 minutes each week (e.g., Sunday afternoon) to review the past week's progress and the upcoming week's commitments. This process forces engagement with **goal setting** and **prioritization**, identifying the few high-leverage tasks that must be accomplished, rather than allowing a massive to-do list to create overwhelm.

- **Scheduling the "Boring" Tasks:** Use the review to specifically time-block tasks that lack intrinsic reward and are prone to avoidance (e.g., administrative tasks, bill paying, follow-up calls). By scheduling them into the Time Block as non-negotiable appointments, you bypass the reliance on future internal motivation, which is often inconsistent.
- **Resource Management:** This review is used to ensure you have the necessary materials and resources for the upcoming week, mitigating the risk of starting a task only to discover a key item is missing, a common frustration that triggers task abandonment.

2. The Daily Execution Prep (The Launch Sequence)

The Daily Execution Prep is the launch sequence that ensures the WM is loaded with the necessary instructions for the day, minimizing morning chaos and uncertainty.

- **The Nightly Offload:** The most critical step occurs the night before: reviewing the Time Block schedule for the next day, collecting all materials needed for the first task (e.g., reports, specific pens, water bottle), and performing the **Digital Reset** (clearing the desktop / closing tabs) to ensure a clean start. This prevents "open loops" from disrupting sleep and minimizes decision fatigue in the morning.
- **The Morning Activation:** Upon waking, immediately check the Time Block for the first appointment and the corresponding materials. This intentional, structured beginning activates the Task Positive Network (TPN) and ensures the WM is loaded with the immediate instructions, transitioning the brain smoothly from the Default Mode Network (DMN) (rest / mind-wandering) to focused effort.

Section 5: The Holistic Context: Sustaining Cognitive Growth

The PFC's capacity for WM and IC is highly vulnerable to impairment from internal psychological states. Sustaining cognitive growth requires actively minimizing the things that impair EF and enhancing the things that support it.

1. Reducing the Impact of Stress and Sadness

Research is clear: EF skills **blossom most when we lessen things that impair them (like stress or sadness) and enhance the things that support them (like joy or feelings of belonging)**. This means the intentional emotional regulation and self-compassion work (to be addressed in Book 4) is a non-negotiable part of improving focus and WM.

- **Emotional Resilience is Cognitive Resilience:** Stress, anxiety, and feelings of shame consume immense EF resources, making focus and planning exponentially harder. By utilizing the external structures of Time Blocking and Pomodoro sprints, you reduce the systemic stress of daily chaos, thereby providing the necessary emotional buffer for your cognitive skills to flourish.

- **Mindfulness and Re-Entry:** Mindfulness practices (Chapter 3, Book 2) are crucial for strengthening attention regulation. They train the brain to gently observe internal chaos without judgment and return to the chosen focus, reinforcing the IC muscle required for sustained effort.

2. Physiological Support for the Prefrontal Cortex

The PFC requires optimal fuel for peak function. Sustaining cognitive growth requires prioritizing the physiological factors that directly support neurotransmitter regulation.

- **Sleep Hygiene:** Quality sleep is non-negotiable for WM and IC. Sleep deprivation can be as impairing as the core symptoms of ADHD themselves. Consistent, prioritized sleep hygiene is essential for restoring the PFC's capacity and mitigating the chronic mental fatigue that drains EF reserves.

- **Nutrition and Movement:** Consistent protein and complex carbohydrates maintain stable energy and blood sugar, preventing the crashes that exacerbate WM / IC deficits. Regular physical exercise is a powerful, evidence-based tool that promotes dopamine release, improving attention and inhibitory control, acting as a natural cognitive enhancement.

Conclusion: Your Future-Proofed Mind

The work of this chapter moves beyond mere compensation into true cognitive enhancement. By establishing fixed planning rituals, intentionally training your Inhibitory Control to resist distraction, and supporting your Working Memory through external offloading, you are actively increasing your long-term resilience.

You have transformed WM and IC from unreliable, internal deficits into skills supported by a robust, predictable system. This intentional, disciplined practice is the definitive step toward conquering the fragmented mind and replacing chronic overwhelm with the quiet confidence of self-mastery. The mental energy conserved by this internal structure is the final resource you need to ensure that the effort of focus is not only powerful but also sustainable, preparing you for the final stage of Executive Function mastery: ruthlessly protecting your cognitive space from digital and mental noise.

Chapter 4 Workbook: Future-Proof Your Brain: Strengthen Working Memory with Planning Routines

Objective: To practice strengthening **Working Memory (WM)** and **Inhibitory Control (IC)** using fixed planning routines and targeted exercises.

Scientific Anchor: Executive Function (EF) skills, including WM and IC, improve through continuous challenge and consistent practice. Fixed planning rituals externalize the cognitive burden, allowing the core skills to stabilize.

Activity 4.1: The Weekly Review: Future-Proofing Your Plan

Instructions: Schedule a 60-minute appointment this week for a **Weekly Review**. This process proactively engages WM and planning EFs.

1. **Identify Three High-Leverage Tasks:** What are the three **most important, non-urgent** tasks for the upcoming week? (These are the items most likely to be forgotten or avoided).

   Task 1: _____

   Task 2: _____

   Task 3: _____

2. **Externalize Resources:** For your first task, list every resource, material, and contact you need. (This offloads instructions from WM).

   Resources Needed: _____

   _____

   _____

   _____

   _____

   _____

3. **Time Block Commitment:** Commit these three tasks to your Time Block schedule for the upcoming week (Chapter 2), ensuring you add a **25% Estimation Buffer** to each block.

Task 1 Block: (Time / Duration): _____

_____

_____

Activity 4.2: Training Inhibitory Control (IC)

Instructions: Practice intentionally resisting an urge for 10 minutes, strengthening your brain's "brakes" (IC).

1. **Identify Your #1 Impulse:** What is the most common, low-stakes impulse that derails your focus? (E.g., Checking your phone, opening a social media tab, getting a snack, interrupting a conversation).

Impulse: _____

_____

_____

2. **The 10-Minute IC Sprint:** Set a timer for 10 minutes. During this time, commit to working on an existing task while actively, mindfully **resisting** the identified Impulse whenever it arises. Each resistance is a "rep" for your IC muscle.

IC Practice: _____

Start time: _____

End time: _____

Reflection 4.3: Analyzing Executive Function Gain

Instructions: Reflect on how your consistent routine supports your focus and conserves EF energy.

1. **WM Conservation:** How does performing the **Nightly Offload** (capturing tasks for the next day) reduce your brain's tendency to ruminate or worry before sleep? (Focus on how the external system manages the "open loops").

Sleep / WM Benefit: _____

_____

_____

_____

2. **EF and Emotional Load:** The PFC's ability to plan and focus is impaired by stress and sadness. How does the structure of a predictable Time Block schedule, which reduces rushing and late penalties, act as a psychological buffer that supports your EF?

   Emotional / EF Support: _____

   _____

   _____

   _____

   _____

3. **The Strength of Routine:** What is one checklist or template (e.g., "The Meeting Prep Checklist," "The Morning Routine") you can create this week to offload a multi-step instruction from your Working Memory?

   Checklist to Create: _____

   _____

   _____

   _____

   _____

CHAPTER 5

PROTECT YOUR ENERGY: REDUCE COGNITIVE LOAD BY ELIMINATING DIGITAL NOISE

The mastery of focus, achieved through Time Blocking, customized Pomodoro sprints, and the strengthening of Working Memory (WM) and Inhibitory Control (IC), is not solely about increasing output; it is fundamentally about the intelligent management and **protection of your finite mental energy**. The entire effort of setting up structural scaffolding (Book 1) and time discipline (Chapters 1–4) can be instantly negated by one insidious, pervasive threat: **Digital Noise** and the neurological drain caused by **Context Switching**.

For the woman with Attention-Deficit / Hyperactivity Disorder (ADHD), the modern world, a hyper-stimulating landscape of flashing notifications, open browser tabs, and constantly refreshing inboxes, is perfectly designed to dismantle sustained concentration. Each digital "ping" is a siren call for the novelty-seeking, dopamine-driven brain, forcing a taxing shift in attention that rapidly depletes the finite resources of the Executive Functions (EFs).

This chapter provides the final, essential stage of focus mastery: the strategy of **Cognitive Load Annihilation**. It details how to ruthlessly eliminate the digital and environmental friction that fragments attention, thereby protecting the mental energy necessary for consistent follow-through and preventing the descent into profound **mental fatigue** and burnout. By minimizing context switching and eliminating digital noise, you systematically reduce the chronic effort required to fight distraction, allowing your newly strengthened EF skills to operate at their most efficient, sustainable level. This is the difference between sporadic productivity and enduring, integrated self-mastery.

Section 1: The Neurobiology of Noise: Why Digital Distraction is Draining

The core challenge in sustaining focus for the ADHD brain is its impaired ability to filter out irrelevant stimuli, leading to a state of perpetually high mental effort, the **Cognitive Load (CL)**.

1. Cognitive Load and the Filtering Deficit

Cognitive load refers to the total amount of mental effort consumed by your working memory during a task. For a neurotypical individual, the brain effortlessly filters out background stimuli, prioritizing the central task. However, for a woman with ADHD, the brain's filtering mechanism is often less efficient, registering all incoming information, internal thoughts, external noise, and digital cues, with nearly equal significance.

- **Disproportionate Impact:** This inefficient filtering means that a stray notification or a distracting sound does not simply divert attention; it forces the brain to expend immense, measurable energy processing and suppressing that irrelevant stimulus. Research indicates that as CL increases, individuals with ADHD experience reduced performance and increased reaction time variability compared to their neurotypical peers.

- **The "Open Loop" Drain:** Every unread email, every ignored text message, and every open browser tab represents an "open loop", an unresolved task or piece of information that the brain is subconsciously tracking. These open loops consume valuable WM resources, placing a constant, low-level demand on EF reserves and contributing significantly to the feeling of being perpetually "frenzied, frazzled, and overwhelmed." The goal of energy protection is to systematically close these loops and reduce the background noise that consumes CL.

2. The Cost of Context Switching: Debunking the Multitasking Myth

The pervasive myth that one can efficiently multitask is the single greatest drain on the ADHD brain's energy. Multitasking is scientifically inaccurate; what it describes is rapid **Context Switching**, the act of quickly shifting attention between two or more cognitively demanding tasks (e.g., drafting a report while responding to instant messages).

- **The Task Switch Penalty:** Each time the brain switches tasks, it incurs a measurable **cognitive penalty**. This penalty involves the mental effort required to disengage from the first task, reorient attention, and load the new set of information and rules into the compromised Working Memory. This process is highly inefficient, leading to increased errors, slower overall completion time, and significant mental exhaustion.

- **Dopamine's Role in the Switch:** The ADHD brain is highly susceptible to this switching because the act of checking a new notification provides an immediate, low-effort burst of dopamine (novelty / reward), while resisting it requires the challenging, high-effort function of Inhibitory Control (IC). The brain favors the path of least resistance, leading to constant toggling that fragments focus and rapidly depletes the finite EF reserves. By minimizing context switching, we protect the brain's energy from this continuous, self-imposed tax.

Section 2: The Strategy of Annihilation: Eliminating Digital Friction

Protecting your focus begins with a ruthless, strategic annihilation of the digital cues that are actively pulling your attention and demanding context switches. This must be a systematic, environment-wide commitment.

1. Notification Annihilation: Silence as Self-Care

Notifications are the primary culprit in fragmentation, turning devices from tools into demanding masters. The strategy must be absolute and uncompromising: turn off all non-essential pings.

- **The Rule of Essential Only:** Go through every app on your phone, tablet, and computer and turn off all alerts for social media, news applications, and non-critical email accounts. Only notifications that signal an **immediate, non-deferrable emergency** (e.g., calendar reminder for a critical meeting, high-priority work alert) should remain active.

- **Creating the Digital "Do Not Disturb" Zone:** Commit to using your device's "Do Not Disturb" or "Focus Mode" feature during all scheduled **Time Blocks** (Chapter 2) and **Pomodoro Sprints** (Chapter 3). This creates a clear, non-negotiable external boundary that physically and digitally protects your concentration and reduces the temptation to check a new ping.

- **The Cost of the Vibrate:** Even a silent vibration or a flashing light should be managed, as these subtle cues still register in the background, consuming a fraction of CL and tempting a context switch. Placing your phone out of immediate sight (e.g., in a drawer or face-down across the room) during deep work intervals is crucial for reinforcing IC.

2. Browser Management: Closing Open Loops

The modern desktop, with its multitude of open browser tabs, is a perfect visual representation of the ADHD brain's tendency toward accumulation and cognitive overwhelm. Each open tab is a subtle demand on Working Memory (WM) and a potential distraction for IC.

- **The Three-Tab Rule:** Implement a strict rule: you may only have **three browser tabs open** at any given time, one for the current task, one for immediate reference, and one for your planner / timer. This physically limits the number of cognitive "open loops" your brain is tracking.

- **The "Later" Parking Lot:** When a thought or distraction related to a new, non-essential website arises during a focus sprint, use a dedicated external system (e.g., a "Brain Dump" note, a digital bookmark folder) as a "parking lot" for the idea. Write down the thought immediately and return to the main task. This offloads the thought from WM without allowing the brain to reward the distraction impulse.

- **Digital Triage:** Perform a **Digital Reset** (Chapter 5, Book 1) at the end of every work session or day. This includes closing all unnecessary tabs and moving all temporary files from the desktop into a single, designated "To File" folder. A clean, quiet desktop is the necessary environmental cue for a successful launch into the next day's focused effort.

3. Email and Communication Batching

Managing the constant influx of digital communication as it arrives is a guaranteed path to continuous context switching and mental exhaustion. The brain must be trained to engage with communication on its own terms, not the sender's.

- **Scheduled Triage:** Dedicate specific, **Time Blocked** intervals (e.g., 9:00 AM–9:30 AM and 3:00 PM–3:30 PM) solely for checking and processing emails and messages. Turn off the email client entirely outside of these designated blocks. This intentional "email batching" minimizes context switching and allows the brain to remain in a "Deep Work" mode for longer, conserving EF resources.

- **The "Two-Minute Rule":** When engaging with communication during a scheduled triage block, implement the classic "Two-Minute Rule": if an email or message can be dealt with in two minutes or less (delete, respond briefly, or schedule a Time Block appointment), do it immediately. Otherwise, defer it by moving it to a **"To Do"** folder or scheduling an appointment for the necessary work. This low-friction triage system prevents the inbox from becoming an ambiguous, overwhelming to-do list that triggers paralysis.

Section 3: Sustaining Energy: Proactive Burnout Prevention

The persistent struggle with filtering, context switching, and sustained effort makes women with ADHD significantly more susceptible to **Mental Fatigue and Burnout** than their neurotypical peers. This chronic exhaustion is the culmination of the **ADHD Tax** on energy. Sustaining focus requires proactive strategies that protect the brain's overall physiological and cognitive reserves.

1. Managing Mental Fatigue as a Core Symptom

Mental fatigue is not merely feeling tired; it is a temporary physiological sluggishness and slowdown of thinking abilities caused by the chronic, high cognitive demands placed on the ADHD brain. This state directly impairs Working Memory and Inhibitory Control, making focus and emotional regulation exponentially harder.

- **Scheduled Recovery:** Schedule mandatory, non-negotiable **rest and recovery blocks** into your weekly Time Block schedule (Chapter 2). These are not blocks for chores or errands; they are for genuine passive rest, such as reading for pleasure, intentional relaxation, or quiet time without digital stimuli. This scheduled recovery is essential for restoring the prefrontal cortex's capacity.

- **The Power of Movement:** Regular physical movement is a powerful, evidence-based tool for combating mental fatigue, promoting dopamine release, and enhancing focus. Utilize the **Pomodoro Break** (Chapter 3) to enforce short bursts of movement (e.g., stretching, brisk walk to the water cooler). This proactive physical reset is crucial for discharging pent-up restlessness and stimulating the neurochemistry required for renewed attention.

2. Physiological Foundations for Cognitive Health

Sustaining focus requires protecting the physiological systems that directly support EF and neurotransmitter regulation.

- **Sleep Hygiene as EF Protection:** Quality sleep is non-negotiable for EF and WM function. Sleep deprivation can be as impairing as the core symptoms of ADHD themselves. Consistent, prioritized sleep hygiene is essential for restoring the prefrontal cortex's capacity and mitigating the chronic mental fatigue that drains EF reserves. The **Nightly Offload** routine (Chapter 4) should be performed to externalize worries and clear the mental space required for restorative sleep.

- **Fueling the PFC:** The brain relies on stable fuel for peak performance. Consistent consumption of lean protein and complex carbohydrates prevents the blood sugar crashes that exacerbate WM and IC deficits. Intentional hydration is also crucial for maintaining optimal brain function and mental clarity. By stabilizing your physiological environment, you provide the necessary, steady foundation for sustained attention.

Section 4: The Emotional and Economic Payoff of Annihilation

The commitment to ruthless distraction elimination yields profound benefits that extend beyond a few extra hours of productivity, directly addressing the shame and economic costs associated with unmanaged attention.

1. Economic Gains: Mitigating the Cost of Work Loss

Unmanaged attention and context switching are direct causes of reduced productivity and work loss—the largest components of the overall societal **ADHD Tax**.

- **Quantified Cost:** The excess costs associated with ADHD in US adults are estimated at **$122.8 billion annually**, with costs of unemployment ($66.8 billion) and productivity loss ($28.8 billion) comprising the largest proportion.

- **Protecting Income:** By enforcing single-task focus and minimizing context switching through Cognitive Load Annihilation, you are directly increasing your efficiency and quality of work. This strategic focus is an active measure against productivity loss, providing a measurable economic gain by supporting career stability and performance.

2. Emotional Liberation: Defeating Shame and Overwhelm

The constant failure to maintain focus and follow through, often caused by digital distraction, is a significant driver of shame and the pervasive feeling of being overwhelmed for women with ADHD.

- **Building Self-Efficacy:** Successfully completing a focused Pomodoro sprint (Chapter 3) without being derailed by notifications provides tangible evidence of **competence and control**. This consistent success builds **self-efficacy**, the belief in your ability to manage your focus, which is the direct antidote to the shame and inadequacy that characterize unmanaged attention.
- **Sustained Calm:** By eliminating the sources of fragmented attention, you reduce the chronic internal turmoil and anxiety that arises from fighting digital noise. This creates a state of sustained calm, allowing you to operate from a place of intentional control rather than frantic, reactive chaos.

Conclusion: Your Focused Sanctuary

The work of **Protecting Your Energy** is the final, non-negotiable step in mastering focus. By ruthlessly applying the strategy of Cognitive Load Annihilation, you move beyond merely coping with distraction and actively design an environment that compels focus.

You have transformed your relationship with your attention: it is no longer a fragile, easily fragmented resource, but a powerful, sustained tool, supported by the external structure of Time Blocking and protected by the boundaries of digital silence. This systematic effort conserves the mental energy needed for sustained self-mastery.

This cultivated internal stability, the quiet confidence of a mind no longer fragmented by noise, is the essential prerequisite for the next stage of your journey. You are now equipped to manage your attention, making you resilient against the profound **hormonal fluctuations** that can destabilize focus and emotions. The mastery of your mental energy is the critical bridge to managing your body's rhythm and achieving true integrated success.

Objective: To identify and eliminate key sources of digital noise and unnecessary context switching, thereby protecting finite Executive Function resources.

Scientific Anchor: Digital notifications and open browser tabs create "open loops" that consume Working Memory and increase Cognitive Load, disproportionately impacting performance for individuals with ADHD. Strategic elimination of these distractions conserves EF energy.

Activity 5.1: The Digital Noise Annihilation Audit

Instructions: Audit your primary work device (phone or computer) and immediately turn off notifications for non-essential apps. Use the three categories below to guide your decision.

1. **Phone Notification Audit (Be Ruthless):**
   o *Apps You Silence Immediately (Non-Essential):* (Example: Social Media, News, Games, Most Shopping Alerts)
   o *Apps You Keep ON (Critical):* (Example: Calendar Alerts, Emergency Calls Only)

2. **Browser / Desktop Audit:** How many browser tabs do you currently have open? Commit to closing all but the three most essential tabs and turning off all pop-up notifications for non-essential websites.

   Current Open Tabs:; _____

   Cognitive Benefit of Closing Tabs: (How does this feel, or what mental benefit do you anticipate?)

Activity 5.2: Measuring the Cost of Context Switching

Instructions: Select a focused work block (e.g., a Pomodoro sprint) and intentionally track how often you switch tasks or succumb to digital temptation.

1. **Task:** (Select a specific, single task, e.g., "Draft the summary paragraph.")
2. **Duration:** Set a timer for 25 minutes.
3. **Context Switch Tally:** Every time you switch away from your designated task (e.g., check phone, open a new browser tab, start a different chore), place a tally mark below.

Tally: _____

_____

_____

_____

_____

_____

4. **Analysis:** Each tally mark represents a cognitive penalty, a drain on EF. If you had zero context switches, what would be the most important task you could accomplish with that conserved energy?

Conserved Energy Use: _____

_____

_____

_____

_____

_____

Reflection 5.3: Energy Gain and Resilience

Instructions: Reflect on how eliminating digital noise creates a foundation for sustained energy and emotional resilience.

1. **EF Conservation:** How does intentionally closing all notifications and tabs *before* starting work reduce the mental energy (Cognitive Load) required for your brain to engage the task, compared to trying to filter them out *while* you work?

Mental Energy Reduction: _____

_____

_____

_____

2. **Burnout Prevention:** The constant fight against distraction leads to mental fatigue. How does the discipline of **Batching Email** (only checking at fixed times) help prevent the chronic sense of being "frenzied" and "frazzled" throughout the day? (Think about the neurological shift from **reactive** to **proactive**).

Proactive Calm: _____

_____

_____

_____

_____

3. **Bridge to Hormones:** Stress, anxiety, and mental fatigue severely impair Executive Functions, and hormonal shifts exacerbate these symptoms. How does the reduction of digital noise and cognitive load provide a stable, protected mental baseline that prepares you to better manage the **hormonal fluctuations** that can destabilize focus and mood?

Hormonal Resilience: _____

_____

_____

_____

CHAPTER 6
REFLECT AND INTEGRATE:
YOUR FOCUS JOURNEY SO FAR

You have reached a pivotal moment in your journey toward integrated self-mastery. The work of Book 2 has been dedicated to the deepest, most taxing internal struggle of the ADHD brain: the mastery of **attention dysregulation** and the pervasive chaos of **Time Blindness**. You have moved beyond simply coping with distraction to actively commanding your focus, transforming your mind from a source of perpetual fragmentation into a powerful, reliable tool.

This chapter is a moment of necessary pause, a time to **reflect and integrate** the profound cognitive and emotional gains achieved through the disciplined practice of the strategies you have mastered: **Time Blocking**, **Pomodoro sprints**, and **Cognitive Load Annihilation**. The aim is to solidify the foundational shift from a life defined by **reactive chaos** and **overwhelm** to a state of **proactive, intentional action**.

The core insight of this book is that consistent focus is not a matter of willpower; it is a measurable, neurobiological function directly tied to **energy management** and **strategic structure**. You have learned that the struggle was never laziness, but a challenge of **Executive Function (EF)** that required an evidence-based toolkit to compensate for deficits in time perception, task initiation, and filtering capacity. By systematically reducing the external noise and structuring your time to work *with* your brain's need for novelty and finitude, you have reclaimed precious mental bandwidth, creating the stability required to manage the complex emotional and physiological challenges addressed in the books that follow.

Section 1: The Cognitive Transformation: Conquering Time and Load

The most powerful outcome of mastering the EF strategies in this book is the mitigation of two core, debilitating deficits: the inability to perceive time accurately and the chronic drain of high cognitive load. This transformation of the cognitive landscape is the tangible benefit of replacing inconsistent internal effort with predictable external structure.

1. The Banishment of Time Blindness and the Estimation Deficit

The feeling of being perpetually behind, rushing deadlines, and being surprised by the sudden emergence of appointments is the emotional reality of **Time Blindness**, the inability to feel or accurately estimate the passage of time. This neurobiological deficit makes effective long-term planning virtually impossible, leading to the financial and relational penalties of chronic lateness and poor prioritization. The strategies in this book directly counteract this deficit by making time concrete and visible, thereby reducing the anxiety and overwhelm that triggers **task paralysis**.

- **Time Blocking as an External Clock:** By enforcing the practice of **Time Blocking** (Chapter 2), you replaced the abstract, amorphous nature of time with a tangible, visual map of your day. This technique directly addresses the **estimation deficit** by forcing you to pre-allocate duration for every task, break, and transition. The visible schedule minimizes the cognitive guesswork of "What to do next?", conserving EF resources that were previously wasted on moment-to-moment decisions and providing the necessary external context that the time-blind brain lacks. This methodical approach ensures that even tasks that lack intrinsic interest are assigned a fixed, non-negotiable temporal slot, circumventing the dopamine deficit that fuels procrastination.
- **The Power of Finitude and Momentum:** The customized application of the **Pomodoro Technique** (Chapter 3) strategically attacks the paralysis triggered by the perception of

an infinite, daunting task. By committing to short, fixed sprints, you impose **finitude** on the task, lowering the psychological barrier to initiation. The visible timer provides a constant, external cue, anchoring attention and generating the necessary **momentum** through the immediate reward of completing a structured sprint. This systematic approach transforms work from an overwhelming marathon into a chain of manageable, dopamine-rewarding sprints, allowing you to sustain attention over periods that were previously impossible to command.

2. Cognitive Load Annihilation and EF Conservation

The chronic state of overwhelm in the ADHD experience is rooted in the high **Cognitive Load (CL)**, the relentless mental effort consumed by an overstimulated mind that struggles to filter stimuli. The mastery of **Cognitive Load Annihilation** (Chapter 5) is the most direct defense against this drain.

- **Defeating Context Switching:** By enforcing **single-tasking** and **email / notification batching** (Chapter 5), you systematically eliminated the draining cost of **Context Switching**—the rapid shifting of attention between different cognitive demands. This practice is crucial because each switch, particularly for the ADHD brain with its inefficient filtering, incurs a measurable cognitive penalty, rapidly depleting EF resources (like Working Memory and Inhibitory Control) and leading to significant mental exhaustion. By reducing digital noise and minimizing "open loops" (e.g., closing unnecessary browser tabs), you conserved the mental energy that was once consumed by fighting internal and external distractions.

- **Strengthening Internal Resilience:** The consistent practice of **Inhibitory Control (IC)** and **Working Memory (WM)** training within fixed planning routines (Chapter 4) created a powerful internal structure. IC was strengthened by intentionally resisting the urge to check notifications during Pomodoro sprints, and WM was supported by externalizing all task instructions onto fixed checklists and planners. This dual approach, externalizing the burden while strengthening the internal "brakes", builds a long-term cognitive resilience that is less susceptible to collapse under stress. Furthermore, this deliberate training of IC (thinking before acting) is the very muscle needed for emotional regulation (resisting impulsive emotional reactions), a key component for future mastery (Book 4).

The structured focus achieved in this book yields profound benefits beyond mere mental clarity; it actively reduces the quantifiable **"ADHD Tax"**, the cumulative financial, emotional, and mental cost of navigating life with unmanaged executive function deficits. This mitigation leads directly to increased self-efficacy and emotional stability.

1. Mitigating the Economic Cost of Work Loss and Financial Strain

Unmanaged attention dysregulation is a direct cause of work loss and reduced productivity, the largest components of the societal economic burden associated with ADHD. The commitment to Time Blocking and sustained focus is a fundamental economic defense strategy.

- **Addressing Productivity Loss:** The total societal excess cost attributable to ADHD in US adults is estimated at **$122.8 billion annually**, with excess costs of unemployment ($66.8 billion) and productivity loss ($28.8 billion) comprising the largest proportion. Time Blocking and Pomodoro sprints directly counteract this economic drain by enforcing single-task focus and consistent follow-through, increasing efficiency and quality of work. This stability is a proactive measure against the financial toll that includes lower savings and earnings that affect adults with a history of ADHD.

- **Reducing Penalties:** The banishment of time blindness ensures that crucial administrative tasks (like bill payment, follow-up calls, or administrative work) are scheduled as non-negotiable appointments (Time Blocks), mitigating the risk of financial penalties, late fees, and lost opportunities that stem from inattention and poor prioritization. The systematic scheduling enforces the kind of reliable behavior that protects credit and financial standing, areas often compromised by ADHD impulsivity and poor memory.

2. Defeating Shame and Building Self-Efficacy

The chronic failure to maintain focus and follow through, a frequent result of digital distraction and time blindness, is a significant driver of shame and the pervasive feeling of overwhelm for women with ADHD.

- **The Antidote to the Inner Critic:** The mastery of Time Blocking replaces the long, overwhelming to-do list (a document of perceived failure) with a realistic, manageable schedule, thereby setting **achievable expectations** and reducing the likelihood of failure and self-criticism. The fact that you are setting a realistic schedule, complete with buffers and recovery time, is an act of **self-compassion** that actively disarms the "all-or-nothing" perfectionism trap.

- **Evidence of Competence:** Each successfully completed Time Block or Pomodoro sprint provides tangible, undeniable evidence of competence and follow-through. This consistent success builds **self-efficacy**, the belief in one's ability to manage their focus and time, which is the direct psychological antidote to the inadequacy that characterizes unmanaged attention. The power lies in realizing that success is due to a deliberate, effective strategy, not inconsistent willpower.

3. Protecting the Emotional Baseline and Relationships

The continuous fight against distraction and chaos creates a state of chronically elevated stress and anxiety, which directly triggers or exacerbates **emotional dysregulation**, the sudden, intense emotional surges common in ADHD.

- **Stress Reduction:** The structural predictability of a Time Blocked schedule, coupled with the digital silence of the focus sprints, stabilizes the nervous system by reducing the chaotic inputs that trigger anxiety. This conserved emotional bandwidth creates a more stable baseline, reducing the likelihood of minor triggers escalating into disproportionate emotional storms (the "green-to-red" phenomenon).

- **Reducing Relational Friction:** By clearly blocking time for necessary tasks and reducing chronic lateness (Time Blindness), the focus skills directly reduce friction in relationships. Consistent follow-through, supported by the scheduled Time Blocks, lessens the neurotypical partner's need to act as a **taskmaster** or reminder, mitigating the resentment and the unhealthy "parent-child" dynamic that often develops in neurodiverse couples.

Section 3: The Bridge to Resilience: Preparing for Hormonal and Emotional Challenges

The structural stability of focus achieved in Book 2 is not an end goal; it is the essential **prerequisite** for engaging with the complex internal work of the upcoming books. The Executive Functions you have strengthened are necessary to build resilience against the profound physical and emotional volatility that characterizes the female ADHD experience.

1. EF Stability as a Buffer Against Hormonal Chaos (Book 3)

The brain's Executive Function skills, particularly Working Memory and attention, are known to be highly sensitive to hormonal fluctuations. Research suggests that the decline in **estrogen** during the low-estrogen phases of the menstrual cycle (e.g., the luteal phase) can exacerbate core ADHD symptoms like inattention and disorganization.

- **The Problem of Hormonal Fluctuation:** Preliminary pilot data suggests that within-person declines in estrogen, particularly in the context of rising levels of progesterone just post-ovulation, are associated with meaningful increases in ADHD symptoms (e.g., inattention and hyperactive-impulsive features). These fluctuations, which are unique to the female lifespan (puberty, menstrual cycle, perimenopause), act as a "double whammy" on an already dysregulated system.

- **Neutralizing the Effect:** By maintaining a robust, external EF system (Time Blocking, predictable Pomodoro routines), you create a functional buffer against these inevitable internal shifts. When hormonal changes inevitably cause an internal drop in dopamine-linked focus, the external system (the schedule, the timer, the task boundaries) remains intact, preventing the system from collapsing into chaos. This stability ensures that the impact of the hormonal fluctuation is absorbed by the structure, rather than leading to a complete functional failure.

- **Data Collection for Advocacy:** The disciplined use of the scheduled Pomodoro sprints and Time Blocks provides objective **data** on performance consistency (e.g., how many sprints were completed, how accurate were the time estimates). This data becomes the essential tool for tracking the impact of hormonal cycles on your productivity, enabling you to advocate for personalized treatment approaches (like "cycle dosing") with your healthcare professional, a practice that is necessary given the established **gender health gap** in ADHD research.

2. Focus as the Foundation for Emotional Mastery (Book 4)

Emotional dysregulation is the most impairing symptom for many women with ADHD, and its effective management relies heavily on the EF skills you have practiced.

- **Activating the "Brakes":** The practice of **Inhibitory Control (IC)**, resisting the urge to check a notification or interrupt a conversation (Chapter 4), is the very same EF muscle required for **emotional regulation**, resisting the urge to react impulsively during an intense emotional surge. You are training the brain's "brakes" (the PFC) to successfully override the emotional accelerator (the amygdala).
- **Mindfulness and Attention:** The capacity for sustained attention, honed through the Pomodoro Technique, is the prerequisite for effective **Mindfulness** (a cornerstone of DBT). Mindfulness is the ability to gently anchor attention to the present moment without judgment. This EF skill creates the critical **"pause"** between feeling an intense emotion and reacting to it, allowing the cognitive strategies of CBT (challenging the thought) to engage before the emotional storm takes over. By stabilizing focus, you build the internal toolkit necessary to navigate the complexities of intense feelings and Rejection Sensitive Dysphoria (RSD), which is often exacerbated by emotional volatility.

Section 4: The Laws of Sustained Attention

To ensure the focus gained is resilient, we must integrate the key principles of Book 2 into a set of non-negotiable laws that govern your attention. These laws solidify the shift from chaos to command.

Law 1: Time is Visible, Finite, and Blocked

- **Principle:** Never leave time or task duration vague. Every activity must be scheduled as a fixed appointment with a clear start and end time (Time Blocking).
- **Rule:** Always apply an **Estimation Buffer** (25–50% extra time) and schedule mandatory **Transition Blocks** between activities to compensate for the estimation deficit and the cognitive cost of context switching.

Law 2: Attention is Anchored by Finitude and Structure

- **Principle:** Sustain focus by structuring effort into small, manageable sprints that reduce the psychological cost of commitment.
- **Rule:** Use the **Customized Pomodoro Cycle** to match work periods to your current attention span, and always enforce the **mandatory break** to prevent burnout and interrupt hyperfocus.

Law 3: Energy is Conserved by Annihilation, Not Effort

- **Principle:** The best way to create focus is to ruthlessly eliminate the sources of distraction and cognitive load that consume Working Memory.
- **Rule:** Enforce **Cognitive Load Annihilation** by minimizing context switching (single-tasking), strictly implementing **Notification Annihilation** across all devices, and maintaining a clean **Digital Desktop** to protect your limited EF reserves.

Conclusion: Your Empowered Attention

The journey through Book 2 marks the completion of the structural foundation required for integrated self-mastery. You have systematically defeated Time Blindness, conquered the paradox of focus, and reclaimed valuable mental bandwidth from the chaos of digital noise and fragmented attention.

The stability achieved here is your most valuable asset. The mental energy that was once consumed by fighting your own brain is now a conserved resource, a stable platform upon which you can build emotional resilience and navigate the complex, dynamic landscape of your hormonal health.

You are no longer a passive victim of your neurobiology, but an active, strategic commander of your attention. This powerful new sense of competence and control is the definitive antidote to the shame and overwhelm that has characterized your struggle, equipping you for the profound work of self-mastery that lies ahead.

Chapter 6 Workbook: Reflect and Integrate: Your Focus Journey So Far

Objective: To synthesize the cognitive and emotional gains achieved in Book 2, solidifying the shift from reliance on willpower to resilient system design.

Scientific Anchor: Reflective practice reduces the impact of stress and sadness on Executive Functions, allowing the functional systems built to flourish. Acknowledging neurobiological reality counters the shame cycle.

Activity 6.1: The Time Blindness & Load Reduction Scorecard

Instructions: Rate the severity of your challenges **before** Book 2 and **now**, focusing on the impact of the new time and focus strategies. (Scale: 1 = Minimal Challenge, 5 = Severe Challenge)

Challenge Area	Before Book 2 (Initial)	After Book 2 (Current)	Reflection: The Tool That Helped Most
Chronic Lateness/ Time Estimation			(Example: Estimation Buffer / Time Block)
Task Paralysis / Starting Boring Work			(Example: Pomodoro Finitude)
Distraction from Digital Notifications			(Example: Notification Annihilation)
Mental Fatigue / Brain Fog			(Example: Scheduled Recovery / IC Practice)

Reflection 6.2: Shifting from Shame to Strategy

Instructions: Use this space to integrate the core concept that struggles with focus are neurological, not moral, and assess your progress in building self-efficacy.

1. **The Overwhelm to Control Shift:** Identify one specific moment this week where you felt an urge to procrastinate or switch tasks. How did remembering a specific tool (**IC Practice** or the **Customized Pomodoro**) create a crucial pause that allowed you to choose a strategic action?

   The Intervention: _____

   _____

   _____

   _____

   _____

2. **The Shame Antidote:** Identify one self-critical thought you had about your focus (e.g., "I'm lazy for losing focus after 30 minutes"). Rephrase this thought using the compassionate, neurobiological reality you learned (e.g., "My brain is wired for novelty and needs a mandated break after 30 minutes to reset. I am managing my energy strategically.")

   New, Empowered Narrative: _____

   _____

   _____

   _____

3. **Building Self-Efficacy:** What is the most important piece of **evidence of competence** you created this week (e.g., sticking to a Time Block, ignoring a notification, completing three Pomodoros)? How does this tangible "win" counteract a previous feeling of inadequacy?

   Evidence of Competence: _____

   _____

   _____

   _____

Activity 6.3: Bridge to Hormonal Resilience (Book 3 Prep)

Instructions: The capacity for focus (EF) is highly vulnerable to hormonal fluctuations, stress, and anxiety. Use this activity to analyze your current EF stability.

1. **Vulnerability Audit:** Thinking about the week before your menstrual cycle (the low-estrogen phase) or a period of high stress, what three EF skills are most likely to fail first? (e.g., Working Memory, Inhibitory Control, Time Estimation).

   Vulnerable Skill 1: _____

   Vulnerable Skill 2: _____

   Vulnerable Skill 3: _____

2. **External Buffer Plan:** For the three vulnerable skills you identified, name the specific **external system** from Book 2 that you will use to compensate for that weakness when your focus dips due to hormonal shifts or stress.

   External Buffer 1 (System): _____

   External Buffer 2 (System): _____

   External Buffer 3 (System): _____

CHAPTER 7
PRACTICE AND APPLY:
YOUR EXECUTIVE FUNCTION ACTION TOOLKIT

You have mastered the core neurobiological strategies for managing attention, time blindness, and chronic overwhelm. This chapter provides the final **Action Toolkit** for Book 2, designed to transform these concepts into consistent, low-friction habits that build lasting Executive Function (EF) resilience. The consistent use of these tools ensures that the mental bandwidth you reclaimed from fighting external chaos is now actively utilized for intentional, sustained focus.

Toolkit 1: Time Blocking and Buffer Application

Objective: To systematically defeat **Time Blindness** by creating fixed, time-bound appointments that include estimation and transition buffers.

Scientific Anchor: Time Blocking forces the engagement of planning and estimation skills, which are core executive functions challenged by ADHD, while mandatory buffers reduce the stress caused by the Estimation Deficit.

1.   **Select a Task:** Choose one specific, demanding task for tomorrow (e.g., "Draft the summary," not "Work on report").

2. **Estimate:** Write your honest, quick estimate for how long it will take: minutes.

3. **Schedule the Block:** Create a fixed Time Block, adding a **25% Estimation Buffer** to your original time (e.g., if you estimated 60 min, block 75 min).

Time Slot	Activity	Fixed Duration (Includes Buffer)
(Example: 9:00 AM)	**Focus Sprint: Your Task**	____ minutes
(Time after Task)	**Mandatory Transition Block**	**15** minutes

Commitment: Commit to respecting the **Transition Block**. When your work time is up, physically move away from your desk for the 15 minutes to clear your mind and prevent the cognitive cost of context switching.

Toolkit 2: Inhibitory Control (IC) Training

Objective: To actively strengthen your brain's "brakes" (Inhibitory Control) by resisting a common, low-stakes digital distraction during a short work sprint.

Scientific Anchor: Resisting immediate gratification strengthens the neural pathways responsible for self-control (IC), which is essential for sustained focus and emotional regulation.

Activity 7.2: The Digital Resistance Sprint

1. **Identify Your #1 Impulse:** Name the primary, non-essential impulse that derails your focus (e.g., Checking text messages, opening the news app, grabbing a snack).

   Impulse: _____

   _____

   _____

2. **The Sprint:** Set a timer for **10 minutes**. Work on your most boring task. Every time the urge to act on your Impulse arises, perform a **micro-pause**: acknowledge the urge without judgment, take one deep breath, and gently redirect your focus back to the task.

3. **Tally:** Record how many times you successfully resisted the impulse in 10 minutes.

   Successful Resistances: _____

   _____

   _____

   _____

   _____

   _____

   (Each resistance is a "rep" for your IC muscle.)

Toolkit 3: Cognitive Load Annihilation

Objective: To reduce **Cognitive Load** and free up Working Memory by systematically eliminating digital "open loops."

Scientific Anchor: Unresolved tasks (open tabs, unchecked notifications) consume Working Memory. Closing these "open loops" conserves mental energy and prevents fragmentation of attention.

Activity 7.3: The Digital Reset

1. **Browser Cleanup:** How many browser tabs do you have open right now?

   Current Tab Count: _____

   Action: Immediately close all but the **three most essential tabs**.

2. **Notification Audit:** Check your phone's notification settings for three non-essential apps (e.g., social media, shopping, non-critical news).

   Action: Immediately set these three apps to **silent** or **turn off all alerts**. This is **Notification Annihilation**, silence as self-care.

3. **Email Batching Commitment:** Commit to checking your email only during two fixed, Time Blocked windows tomorrow.

   Email Block 1 (Start / End Time): _____

   Email Block 2 (Start / End Time): _____

Reflection 7.4: Focus System Assessment

1. **Pomodoro Efficacy:** The core benefit of the Pomodoro Technique is **finitude**. How does knowing a work session is limited to 25 minutes reduce the feeling of **overwhelm** that often leads to procrastination?

    Finitude Effect: _____

    _____

    _____

    _____

2. **Relational Benefit:** How does consistently using **Time Blocking** to schedule fixed time for non-work tasks (e.g., "6:00 PM–7:30 PM: Dinner / Family Time") reduce the internal guilt or external pressure that often arises when the ADHD brain is hyperfocused on work?

    Guilt Reduction: _____

    _____

    _____

    _____

CONCLUSION
SUMMARY: YOUR EMPOWERED ATTENTION

You have reached a definitive inflection point in your journey toward self-mastery. The work of Book 2 has been a disciplined, sustained assault on the internal chaos that defines unmanaged Attention-Deficit / Hyperactivity Disorder (ADHD): the systemic fragmentation of attention, the tyranny of **Time Blindness**, and the profound exhaustion of **Cognitive Load (CL)**. You have successfully moved beyond the reactive struggle, where your focus was a victim of distraction, to a state of **proactive, intentional command**.

The core insight solidified here is that consistent focus is not a mysterious gift of willpower; it is the measurable result of disciplined **Executive Function (EF) management** and the strategic application of **external scaffolding**. By systematically reducing the external noise and structuring your time to work *with* your brain's need for novelty and finitude, you have reclaimed precious mental bandwidth. This stability is the necessary foundation for managing the complex emotional and physiological challenges addressed in the books that follow. You have not just managed your focus; you have successfully future-proofed your capacity for consistent follow-through, providing the ultimate antidote to the pervasive feeling of being "frenzied, frazzled, and overwhelmed."

Section 1: The Victory Over Time and Load (Cognitive Synthesis)

The most powerful outcome of mastering the EF strategies in this book is the mitigation of two core, debilitating deficits: the inability to perceive time accurately and the chronic drain of high cognitive load. This transformation of the cognitive landscape is the tangible benefit of replacing inconsistent internal effort with predictable external structure.

1. The Banishment of Time Blindness: Finitude and Planning

Time blindness, the inability to accurately perceive or estimate time, is the primary driver of chronic lateness, poor prioritization, and the anxiety that triggers task paralysis. The strategies in this book directly counteract this neurobiological deficit by making time concrete and measurable.

- **Time Blocking as an External Clock:** The discipline of **Time Blocking** (Chapter 2) replaced the amorphous chaos of the to-do list with a tangible, visual map of your day. By forcing the allocation of fixed duration for every task and transition, you directly addressed the **estimation deficit** (the tendency to underestimate time), ensuring that your schedule is temporally realistic and includes the necessary **Estimation Buffers** (25–50% extra time). This enforced planning minimized the cognitive guesswork of "What to do next?", conserving EF resources.

- **The Power of Pomodoro Finitude:** The customized application of the **Pomodoro Technique** (Chapter 3) strategically attacks the paralysis triggered by the perception of an infinite, daunting task. By committing to short, fixed sprints (e.g., 25 minutes), you impose **finitude** on the task, lowering the psychological barrier to initiation. The timer serves as a constant, non-negotiable external cue, anchoring attention and generating the necessary **momentum** through the immediate reward of completing a structured sprint, systematically bypassing the internal dopamine deficit.

- **Strengthening Working Memory:** The practice of utilizing **fixed planning rituals** and external scaffolds (Chapter 4), such as reviewing your plan nightly, actively offloaded instruction-following and multi-step tasks from your unreliable **Working Memory (WM)**. This systematic offloading ensured that your WM was not overloaded, which is crucial for preventing the "brain fog" and forgetfulness that accompany high cognitive load.

2. Cognitive Load Annihilation: Conserving Energy from Digital Noise

The chronic state of overwhelm is rooted in the high **Cognitive Load (CL)** caused by an overstimulated mind that struggles to filter stimuli and manage multiple **"open loops."** The mastery of **Cognitive Load Annihilation** (Chapter 5) is the most direct defense against this drain.

- **Defeating Context Switching:** By enforcing **single-tasking** and **email / notification batching**, you systematically eliminated the draining cost of **Context Switching**, the rapid shifting of attention between different cognitive demands. Each switch incurs a measurable cognitive penalty, rapidly depleting EF resources and leading to severe mental fatigue.

- **Digital Sanctuary:** The strict implementation of **Notification Annihilation** and the maintenance of a clean **Digital Desktop** (closing open tabs) systematically closed digital "open loops," conserving the mental energy that was once consumed by fighting internal and external digital distractions. This intentional environment management protected your **Inhibitory Control (IC)**, your brain's "brakes", from the constant temptation of novelty, ensuring those resources are conserved for higher-leverage tasks, such as sustained focus and emotional regulation.

Section 2: The Emotional and Economic Payoff: Mitigating the ADHD Tax

The structured focus achieved in this book yields profound benefits beyond mere mental clarity, actively reducing the quantifiable **"ADHD Tax"**, the cumulative financial, emotional, and mental cost of navigating life with unmanaged EF deficits.

1. Mitigating the Economic Cost of Work Loss

Unmanaged attention dysregulation is a direct cause of work loss, reduced productivity, and financial instability, the largest components of the societal economic burden associated with ADHD.

- **Quantified Cost Reduction:** The total societal excess cost attributable to ADHD in US adults is estimated at **$122.8 billion annually** ($14,092 per adult), with excess costs of unemployment and productivity loss comprising the largest proportion. Time Blocking and Pomodoro sprints directly counteract this drain by enforcing single-task focus and consistent follow-through, actively increasing efficiency and the quality of work. This stability serves as a crucial defense against the financial consequences, such as lower earnings and savings, that affect adults with a history of childhood ADHD, even in adulthood.

- **Reducing Penalties:** The banishment of time blindness ensures that crucial administrative tasks (like bill payment or scheduling) are scheduled as non-negotiable appointments, mitigating the risk of financial penalties, late fees, and lost opportunities that stem from inattention and poor prioritization.

2. Defeating Shame and Building Self-Efficacy

The chronic failure to maintain focus and follow through, a frequent result of digital distraction and time blindness, is a significant driver of shame and the pervasive feeling of overwhelm for women with ADHD.

- **The Antidote to the Inner Critic:** The mastery of Time Blocking replaces the long, overwhelming to-do list (a document of perceived failure) with a realistic, manageable schedule, thereby setting **achievable expectations** and reducing the likelihood of failure and self-criticism. The fact that your schedule is realistic, complete with buffers and recovery time, is an inherent act of **self-compassion** that disarms the "all-or-nothing" perfectionism trap.

- **Evidence of Competence:** Each successfully completed Time Block or Pomodoro sprint provides tangible, undeniable evidence of competence and follow-through. This consistent success builds **self-efficacy**, the belief in one's ability to manage their focus and time, which is the direct psychological antidote to the inadequacy that characterizes unmanaged attention.

Section 3: The Bridge to Resilience: Preparing for Hormonal and Emotional Challenges

The structural stability of focus achieved in Book 2 is the essential **prerequisite** for engaging with the complex internal work of the upcoming books. The Executive Functions you have strengthened are necessary to build resilience against the profound physical and emotional volatility that characterizes the female ADHD experience.

1. EF Stability as a Buffer Against Hormonal Chaos

The brain's Executive Function skills, particularly Working Memory and attention, are known to be highly sensitive to hormonal fluctuations.

This link is critical, as estrogen directly influences the dopamine system that governs focus.

- **The Vulnerability:** Research suggests that the decline in **estrogen** during the low-estrogen phases of the menstrual cycle (e.g., the luteal phase and perimenstrual periods) can exacerbate core ADHD symptoms, including inattention and poor organization, due to the corresponding dip in dopamine support. Furthermore, progesterone's influence can increase anxiety and emotional reactivity. These fluctuations impose a "double whammy" on an already vulnerable system.

- **Neutralizing the Effect:** By maintaining a robust, external EF system (Time Blocking, predictable routines), you create a functional buffer against these inevitable internal shifts. When hormonal changes inevitably cause an internal drop in focus, the external system (the clear schedule, the mandatory breaks, the strict task boundaries) remains intact, preventing the entire system from collapsing into chaos. This stability ensures that the impact of the hormonal fluctuation is absorbed by the structure, rather than leading to a complete functional failure.

- **Data Collection for Advocacy:** The disciplined use of the scheduled Pomodoro sprints and Time Blocks provides objective **data** on performance consistency. This data becomes the essential tool for tracking the impact of hormonal cycles on your productivity, enabling you to advocate for personalized treatment approaches (like "cycle dosing") with your healthcare professional, a necessary step given the established **gender health gap** in ADHD research.

2. Focus as the Foundation for Emotional Mastery

Emotional dysregulation, the most impairing symptom for many women with ADHD, is profoundly linked to the EF skills you have practiced. Effective emotional management relies on the ability to pause and redirect attention, skills honed in Book 2.

- **Activating the "Brakes":** The practice of **Inhibitory Control (IC)**, resisting the urge to check a notification or interrupt a conversation (Chapter 4), is the very same EF muscle required for **emotional regulation**, resisting the urge to react impulsively during an intense emotional surge. You are training the brain's "brakes" (the PFC) to successfully override the emotional accelerator (the amygdala).

- **Mindfulness and the "Pause":** The capacity for sustained attention, honed through the Pomodoro Technique, is the prerequisite for effective **Mindfulness** (a cornerstone of DBT). Mindfulness is the ability to gently anchor attention to the present moment without judgment. This EF skill creates the critical **"pause"** between feeling an intense emotion and reacting to it, allowing the cognitive strategies of CBT (challenging the thought) to engage before the emotional storm takes over. By stabilizing focus, you build the internal toolkit necessary to navigate the complexities of intense feelings and **Rejection Sensitive Dysphoria (RSD)**.

Section 4: The Laws of Sustained Attention

To ensure the focus gained is resilient, we must integrate the key principles of Book 2 into a set of non-negotiable laws that govern your attention. These laws solidify the shift from chaos to command, allowing you to sustain focus indefinitely.

Law 1: Time is Visible, Finite, and Blocked

- **Principle:** Never leave time or task duration vague. Every activity must be scheduled as a fixed appointment with a clear start and end time (Time Blocking).
- **Rule:** Always apply an **Estimation Buffer** (25–50% extra time) and schedule mandatory **Transition Blocks** between activities to compensate for the estimation deficit and the cognitive cost of context switching.

Law 2: Attention is Anchored by Finitude and Structure

- **Principle:** Sustain focus by structuring effort into small, manageable sprints that reduce the psychological cost of commitment.
- **Rule:** Utilize the **Customized Pomodoro Cycle** to match work periods to your current attention span, and always enforce the **mandatory break** to prevent burnout and interrupt hyperfocus.

Law 3: Energy is Conserved by Annihilation, Not Effort

- **Principle:** The best way to create focus is to ruthlessly eliminate the sources of distraction and cognitive load that consume Working Memory.

- **Rule:** Enforce **Cognitive Load Annihilation** by minimizing context switching (single-tasking), strictly implementing **Notification Annihilation** across all devices, and maintaining a clean **Digital Desktop** to protect your limited EF reserves.

The journey through Book 2 marks the completion of the structural foundation required for integrated self-mastery. You have systematically defeated Time Blindness, conquered the paradox of focus, and reclaimed valuable mental bandwidth from the chaos of digital noise and fragmented attention.

You are no longer a passive victim of your neurobiology, but an active, strategic commander of your attention. This powerful new sense of competence and control is the definitive antidote to the shame and overwhelm that has characterized your struggle, equipping you for the profound work of self-mastery that lies ahead.

BOOK THREE

SHARPEN EXECUTIVE FUNCTION IN WOMEN WITH ADHD

INTRODUCTION

The structural discipline initiated in the foundational work, clearing the external chaos of disorganization and creating predictable physical systems, has successfully established a crucial sanctuary in your life. This hard-won stability reduced the debilitating, reactive pressure on your attention and conserved mental energy that was previously consumed by fighting clutter. Now, this book marks the transition to the most demanding phase of self-mastery: the conquest of **Time Blindness** and the intensive, systematic sharpening of the core cognitive engine of the brain. This volume is dedicated to mastering the internal landscape of the ADHD brain, focusing relentlessly on regulating attention, prioritizing complexity, and sharpening **Executive Function (EF)** skills, the very "mental toolkit for success" required for long-term productivity and emotional self-regulation.

For many women with Attention-Deficit / Hyperactivity Disorder (ADHD), the concept of "focus" is a profound paradox, often presenting as a debilitating struggle rather than a steady capacity. This experience is defined by the dual extremes of attention dysregulation: the chaotic fragmentation of the mind and the intense, often uncontrolled absorption known as **hyperfocus**. On one hand, a woman's attention can be so fragmented that she experiences a "thousand-yard stare," mind-wandering, or "zoning out" during essential conversations or tasks, which leads to forgetfulness, missed details, and a pervasive, anxious sense of being perpetually in a fog. On the other hand, when a task is intensely stimulating, novel, or provides immediate reward, the ADHD brain can lock into the state of hyperfocus. While this state can lead to incredible bursts of creativity and productivity, where hours vanish without notice, it is often uncontrolled, leading a woman to neglect critical responsibilities, miss scheduled appointments, or disregard basic physiological needs, thereby creating significant friction and imbalance in her life.

The fundamental challenge is not a lack of ability to pay attention, but rather a profound **difficulty in regulating and directing it**. The issue lies in the brain's struggle to control its "on / off" switch, preventing it from consistently sustaining its mental spotlight on mundane, but necessary, tasks. This inherent **dysregulation of attention** is a primary, internal driver of the chronic overwhelm that defines the female ADHD experience, leading to a profound sense of mental fatigue, inadequacy, and the feeling of being perpetually "frenzied, frazzled, and overwhelmed."

This book provides the strategic, evidence-based roadmap to move beyond this paradox. It is built on the understanding that conquering overwhelm requires the systematic strengthening of EF skills, allowing you to proactively harness your attention, manage your time effectively, and achieve a state of intentional, sustained focus rather than reactive distraction. The goal is to replace the chaotic demands of an easily fragmented mind with the calm, self-directed structure of cognitive command.

The Neurobiological Reality: Executive Function and the Cognitive Tax

To achieve mastery over focus and productivity, we must first confront the neurological roots of these challenges. The difficulties with planning, sustained attention, prioritization, and impulse control are not signs of poor intelligence or laziness; they are direct consequences of neurobiological differences in how the ADHD brain processes information and regulates itself.

1. Executive Function (EF) Deficits: The Command Center

Executive functions (EFs) are the high-level mental processes that allow us to organize, plan, regulate behavior, meet new challenges with flexibility, and stay focused and concentrate. These functions, which include planning, goal setting, **working memory**, **inhibitory control**, and time management, are essential for success in adult life, proving highly predictive of academic and career outcomes. EFs have been described as the **"mental toolkit for success."**

For individuals with ADHD, these EF skills are prone to inconsistency and functional impairment. The brain's **prefrontal cortex (PFC)**, the "command center" for these skills, is often less developed or less active than in neurotypical individuals. This deficit leads to measurable difficulties in nearly every aspect of organization and productivity, from struggling to hold multi-step instructions in mind (poor working memory) to the difficulty initiating a boring task (task activation deficit). Research consistently highlights the essential nature of these executive skills to success, noting that problems with EFs are among the core ways ADHD affects a person. This constant struggle to execute intentions creates a feeling of profound functional inadequacy, contributing directly to the shame, self-blame, and anxiety so common in women with ADHD.

2. The Dopamine-Driven Dysregulation

The ADHD brain's relationship with attention is distinct and deeply rooted in its **dopamine system**. Dopamine, the key neurotransmitter for motivation, reward, and activation, is thought to be dysregulated in the ADHD brain, often resulting in lower effective signaling in the synapses.

This deficit creates a powerful, persistent craving for **novelty and immediate stimulation**. When a task is under-stimulating (boring, repetitive, or requiring sustained, effortful attention), the brain struggles to produce enough dopamine to find it interesting, leading to distraction, mind-wandering, and task avoidance. The strategies in this book are designed to strategically introduce external structure, like fixed time limits and immediate feedback, to supply the necessary cues and reward required to sustain attention on necessary tasks, thereby effectively bypassing the internal dopamine deficit.

3. Time Blindness: The Invisible Barrier to Planning

Perhaps the most disruptive deficit for productivity and life management is **Time Blindness**, the inability to accurately perceive or estimate the flow of time. Time does not feel like a consistent, measurable resource; instead, the ADHD brain lives predominantly in the "now," making the future feel abstract, distant, and less urgent.

This profound difficulty in feeling the passage of time creates several critical challenges:

- **Estimation Deficit:** You consistently underestimate how long tasks will take, leading to chronic rushing, missed deadlines, and the inevitable stress that results from constant lateness.
- **Overwhelm by Infinity:** When faced with a large task, the time needed to complete it feels amorphous and infinite, which instantly triggers an overload response and **paralysis**. This neurobiological shutdown against overwhelming mental effort is a frequent cause of procrastination.

The comprehensive solution explored in this book is to stop relying on inconsistent internal time perception and instead use **concrete, visual tools** and **intentional scheduling** to make time palpable, measurable, and manageable. This involves mastering techniques like **Time Blocking** to enforce duration and utilizing **Timers** to make abstract time visible.

The Emotional and Cognitive Toll of a Fragmented Mind

The daily struggle with attention dysregulation and EF deficits takes a significant toll on a woman's emotional and cognitive well-being, leading directly to the pervasive sense of overwhelm that this book is designed to defeat.

1. High Cognitive Load and Mental Fatigue

The ADHD brain often struggles with an impaired **filtering mechanism**, meaning it registers all incoming stimuli, a flickering light, a phone notification, a fleeting thought, with almost equal importance. This results in a constant, effortful struggle to filter distractions, creating a state of chronically high **Cognitive Load (CL)**, the mental effort consumed by working memory. Research consistently shows that high cognitive load disproportionately impairs performance for people with ADHD, reducing brain network efficiency.

This continuous mental fight leads to profound **mental fatigue**, a temporary sluggishness and slowdown of thinking abilities that results in poor focus, forgetfulness, and exhaustion. This chronic effort to manage an overstimulated mind is the **"ADHD Tax"** on energy reserves, a measurable cumulative cost that depletes mental capacity and leads to burnout and a diminished capacity for sustained effort. The entire strategy of focus mastery is designed to dramatically lower this baseline cognitive load, reserving mental energy for high-leverage tasks.

2. Shame, Masking, and the Loss of Self-Worth

The persistent difficulties with focus, time management, and follow-through often lead a woman with ADHD to internalize her struggles and blame herself, interpreting her symptoms as moral or character failings. This internalized struggle is amplified by the intense societal pressure on women to be organized, calm, and effortlessly competent.

This conflict drives **masking**, the exhausting practice of developing sophisticated compensatory behaviors to hide the internal chaos and appear "neurotypical" to the outside world. This continuous performance is an invisible burden that leads to a lifetime of internalized shame, anxiety, and a shattered sense of self-worth. Studies confirm that girls are more likely to mask their symptoms than boys, and this practice prevents authentic connection and reinforces feelings of inadequacy.

The Strategic Roadmap for Sustained Focus

The path to defeating overwhelm involves strategically creating external and internal structures that compensate for EF deficits. This book guides you through a process of learning to work *with* your brain's unique wiring, not against it, through evidence-based practices drawn from specialized ADHD coaching and therapeutic principles.

The upcoming chapters will provide you with a comprehensive toolkit to sharpen your cognitive command:

- **You will master the schedule:** You will move beyond vague deadlines by learning the **Reverse Timeline** method, transforming overwhelming projects into sequential, manageable **Milestones**. This strategic method systematically minimizes the **Task Activation Deficit** that triggers paralysis, anchoring the project to the immediate present.

- **You will prioritize effectively:** You will gain techniques to identify high-leverage tasks and allocate resources with intention, countering the brain's tendency to get bogged down in an undifferentiated mass of obligations and achieving clarity in decision-making.

- **You will harness attention:** You will utilize structured time management techniques, including the **Pomodoro Technique**, to break work into short, focused sprints. This provides the necessary **finitude** to reduce overwhelm and prevents burnout from uncontrolled hyperfocus, transforming chaotic energy into reliable output.

- **You will strengthen resilience:** You will build the internal mental muscles responsible for planning and recall by mastering fixed planning routines and engaging in cognitive exercises designed to improve **working memory** and **inhibitory control** (thinking before acting).
- **You will protect your sanctuary:** You will learn to recognize and ruthlessly eliminate the sources of **digital noise** and unnecessary **context switching** that fragment your attention and increase cognitive load (CL). This involves implementing strategies like **Notification Annihilation** to protect your precious mental energy reserves.

This book provides the strategic roadmap for replacing the chaotic demands of an easily fragmented mind with the calm, self-directed structure of cognitive command. This cultivated focus and sense of control are not only vital for career and productivity but are the foundation upon which emotional resilience and strong relationships are built, preparing you for true integrated success.

CHAPTER 1

MASTER YOUR SCHEDULE: TRANSFORM DEADLINES INTO MANAGEABLE MILESTONES

The greatest internal hurdle for women with Attention-Deficit / Hyperactivity Disorder (ADHD) is the mastery of time. The experience of **Time Blindness**, the inability to accurately perceive or estimate the flow of time, is the core neurobiological deficit that makes reliable planning impossible and fuels chronic stress. Deadlines always feel abstract until they become immediate crises, triggering the adrenaline-fueled cycle of last-minute overwhelm and shame.

This chapter provides the strategic toolkit to dismantle this chaos by transforming daunting deadlines into concrete, manageable **Milestones**. By proactively converting vague future requirements into visible, tangible steps anchored to the present, you systematically counteract the symptoms of time blindness, turning time from a source of anxiety into a predictable, functional ally. The shift is from relying on inconsistent internal urgency to utilizing strategic, external structure.

Section 1: The Neurobiology of the Crisis Cycle

The chronic cycle of procrastination, crisis, and last-minute rushing is not a character flaw; it is a neurobiological consequence of how the ADHD brain processes time and motivation, directly impacting Executive Function (EF) skills like planning and initiation.

1. Time Blindness and the Estimation Deficit

The inability to accurately gauge the passage of time creates the **Estimation Deficit**, the tendency to consistently and severely underestimate how long tasks will take. When faced with a multi-day project, the time-blind brain may incorrectly allocate only a fraction of the necessary hours, leading to predictable failure and frustration.

- **Abstract Future, Urgent Present:** Because the future feels abstract to the ADHD brain, tasks scheduled far away carry little **dopamine reward** or internal sense of urgency, making them impossible to initiate. Action is delayed until the deadline becomes an imminent threat, which finally generates the intense adrenaline / dopamine response required for task activation (the crisis cycle).

- **Overwhelm and Paralysis:** The perception of a large, complex deadline (e.g., "Finish the entire report") feels amorphous and infinite, which instantly triggers **cognitive overload** and the **paralysis response**. The complexity overwhelms the brain's filtering mechanisms, leading to a neurobiological shutdown against overwhelming mental effort.

The solution is to eliminate the concept of one giant deadline and replace it with a series of small, low-friction, rewarding Milestones that anchor the project to the immediate present.

2. The Power of Finitude and Visibility

To counteract the feeling of infinite, overwhelming duration, time management must impose **finitude**, a clear, visible end point, on tasks.

- **Milestones as Finitude:** Breaking a long project into **Milestones** (e.g., "Milestone 1: Outline complete by Tuesday morning") transforms the commitment from a marathon into a manageable sprint. This dramatically lowers the **activation energy** required to start, making the initial step psychologically approachable.

- **Visible Anchors:** Visual tools, such as calendars, planners, and timers, are essential for anchoring the project to the present. The visual display of a project's timeline bypasses reliance on inconsistent internal memory, acting as a reliable **external Executive Function** cue. This intentional structuring helps the brain manage the complexity often associated with EF challenges like planning, goal setting, and time management.

Section 2: The Strategic Milestone Framework

This framework provides a systematic approach to converting any large deadline into a series of predictable, manageable, and rewarding actions, leveraging the planning and organizational executive skills that are compromised by ADHD.

1. Deconstruct the Deadline (The Reverse Timeline)

Instead of planning forward from the start date, the ADHD brain benefits from planning backward from the final deadline. This process forces the abstract deadline into the immediate present, generating necessary urgency.

- **Define the Finish Line:** Start with the **Final Deadline** (e.g., Report Due: Friday, 5 PM).
- **Identify Critical Milestones:** Work backward, listing 3–5 non-negotiable **Milestones** (Mini-Deadlines) that must be completed to meet the final goal. These should be 20–30% of the overall project.
  - *Example Milestone 1:* Final Draft to Editor: Wednesday, 10 AM.
  - *Example Milestone 2:* Data Analysis / Outline Complete: Monday, 3 PM.
- **Establish Actionable Steps:** For the very first Milestone (Milestone 2, due Monday), break it down into the smallest possible **Actionable Steps** (micro-steps). This micro-commitment reduces the cognitive load and is essential for task initiation, ensuring the first step is low-friction (e.g., "Task #1: Collect dishes from the living room and place them in the kitchen sink" is easier than "Clean the entire living room").

2. Time Block and Buffer Application

Every Actionable Step and Milestone must be immediately scheduled into your calendar as a non-negotiable appointment using **Time Blocking** (introduced in Book 2). This ensures the task has the necessary

context and duration that the traditional to-do list lacks, a significant failure point of vague to-do lists for the ADHD brain.

- **Forced Estimation and Buffers:** For each time block, intentionally schedule **more time than you think you need** (the Estimation Buffer) to compensate for the Estimation Deficit. This prevents the stress of constant rushing, a common trigger for emotional dysregulation, and provides crucial breathing room, reducing the likelihood of failure and self-criticism.
- **Block Transitions:** Schedule **Transition Blocks** (e.g., 15 minutes) between Milestones and major work periods. This is crucial as it supports better transitions between activities, which is often a sticking point for ADHD brains, mitigating the draining **context switching cost**.

3. Anchor with Visual Cues and Alerts

The schedule must live in a location that is visually prominent and supported by automated cues to overcome internal forgetfulness and the abstract nature of future time.

- **Visual Prominence:** Use a calendar or planner that is visible on your wall or desktop. Use **Color-Coding** and clear labels to categorize the project and its Milestones to minimize the cognitive effort required to interpret the schedule.
- **Automated Urgency:** Set multiple, automated digital reminders for Milestones: one **two days before** (to check progress) and one **one hour before** the scheduled Time Block (to generate activation energy). This anchors the abstract future into the urgent present, supplying the necessary external cue to act, bypassing the internal motivation deficit.

Section 3: The Emotional and Cognitive Payoff

Transforming deadlines into manageable Milestones is profoundly effective because it addresses the emotional and cognitive barriers that fuel overwhelm, leading to increased self-efficacy and resilience.

1. Reducing Paralysis and Overwhelm

By breaking down the project into defined Milestones, you reduce the perceived complexity that triggers **task paralysis**. This strategic reduction in complexity systematically lowers the cognitive load, allowing the brain to engage without immediate shutdown. This contrasts with traditional to-do lists, which often contribute to disappointment because the items are too large or vague to be actionable.

2. Building Self-Efficacy and Momentum

Each completed Milestone, a fixed, tangible win, generates an immediate **dopamine hit** that reinforces productive behavior and builds **momentum**. This steady accumulation of small, visible successes builds **self-efficacy** (the belief in one's ability to succeed), which is the direct psychological antidote to the shame and inadequacy that characterize unmanaged ADHD. This proof of competence replaces the reliance on inconsistent willpower with a strategic system you can trust, empowering clients to build lasting improvements in both personal and professional domains.

3. Mitigating the ADHD Tax on Time

The disciplined use of this Milestones framework directly combats the financial and time cost of the **ADHD Tax**, the cumulative cost, emotional, mental, and financial, of navigating life with the condition. By systematically prioritizing and meeting deadlines, you reduce the likelihood of late fees, lost opportunities, and the excess time spent compensating for mistakes, all measurable consequences of unmanaged time blindness and poor organization.

Chapter 1 Workbook: Master Your Schedule: Transform Deadlines into Manageable Milestones

Objective: To practice converting one complex deadline into a fixed, manageable series of Milestones and Actionable Steps.

Scientific Anchor: Breaking deadlines into Milestones reduces cognitive load and task paralysis by imposing finitude and structure on an otherwise overwhelming project, which is critical for the ADHD brain.

Activity 1.1: The Reverse Timeline Deconstruction

Instructions: Identify one complex project or deadline you are currently facing (work, school, or personal).

1. **The Final Deadline (Fixed Date):** _____
2. **Milestone Mapping (Work Backward):** List 3 non-negotiable Milestones that must be achieved on fixed days *before* the Final Deadline.

   - **Milestone 1 (First Step)**
     - Date Due _____

- Action (What must be 100% complete?)

  _____
  _____
  _____

- ○ **Milestone 2 (Mid-Point Check)**
  - Date Due _____
  - Action (What must be 100% complete?)

    _____
    _____
    _____

- ○ **Milestone 3 (Final Review / Prep)**
  - Date Due _____
  - Action (What must be 100% complete?)

    _____
    _____
    _____

3. **Actionable Steps:** Take **Milestone 1** (your first step) and break it down into the smallest possible actions that take less than 15 minutes each (Micro-Steps).
   - ○ **Step 1:** (Example: Open the correct folder / document)
     - Micro-Step _____
     - Time Estimate (Actual Effort) _____
     - Neuro-Strategy (Low Friction) _____
   - ○ **Step 2:**
     - Micro-Step _____
     - Time Estimate (Actual Effort) _____
     - Neuro-Strategy (Low Friction) _____
   - ○ **Step 3:**
     - Micro-Step _____
     - Time Estimate (Actual Effort) _____
     - Neuro-Strategy (Low Friction) _____

Activity 1.2: Time Block and Buffer Commitment

Instructions: Take the Actionable Steps from Activity 1.1 and schedule them into your calendar for tomorrow, applying the necessary EF buffers.

1. **Time Block Commitment:** Select the time slot you will use tomorrow for this task.

Time Slot	Scheduled Activity	Duration (with 25% Buffer)
10:00 AM (example)	Focus Sprint: Actionable Steps 1 & 2	_____ minutes

2. **Anchor Commitment:** What **external alert** will you set one hour before this Time Block to ensure you initiate the task?

   Alarm / Reminder Text: _____

   _____

   _____

   _____

   _____

   _____

Reflection 1.3: The Shame / Paralysis Antidote

Instructions: Reflect on how this strategic framework impacts the emotional challenges of the ADHD brain.

1. **Paralysis to Momentum:** When you first thought of the Final Deadline, on a scale of 1 to 10 (10 = Total Paralysis), what was your resistance level? How did breaking it into Actionable Steps reduce that feeling?

   Initial Resistance: _____

   Reduction in Paralysis: _____

2. **Defeating the Inner Critic:** The inner critic often says, "You're going to miss that deadline, you always do." How does looking at your Time Blocked Milestones provide **tangible, visual evidence** to counter that thought?

   Visual Evidence: _____

   _____

   _____

   _____

   _____

   _____

   _____

CHAPTER 2

PRIORITIZE LIKE A PRO: TECHNIQUES TO IDENTIFY WHAT TRULY MATTERS

In Chapter 1, you mastered the critical first step in managing Executive Function (EF) deficits: transforming paralyzing deadlines into actionable Milestones, imposing structure on the chaos of **Time Blindness**. This intentional scheduling provided the necessary external scaffolding. Now, the challenge moves from mastering *when* tasks happen to mastering *which* tasks should happen at all.

For the woman with Attention-Deficit / Hyperactivity Disorder (ADHD), the inability to effectively prioritize is a core symptom of EF dysfunction that fuels chronic overwhelm. When faced with an undifferentiated mass of obligations, a long to-do list, competing demands from work and family, and an avalanche of new ideas, the brain registers every item as equally urgent and equally demanding. This ambiguity triggers **cognitive overload**, leading to ineffective prioritization where the brain often defaults to the path of least resistance: either tackling the most stimulating, low-leverage task, or avoiding the entire list altogether in a state of **paralysis**.

This chapter provides the strategic toolkit to conquer this ambiguity. By implementing clear mental frameworks, you will learn to systematically identify your high-leverage tasks, allocate your finite energy reserves with intention, and simplify the daunting process of decision-making. The goal is to replace the chaotic demands of an overstuffed schedule with a calm, self-directed focus on activities that truly drive your goals and reduce overall stress.

Section 1: The Neurobiological Roots of Prioritization Failure

Effective prioritization requires the sustained, simultaneous engagement of several complex Executive Function skills, all of which are inconsistent in the ADHD brain.

1. Cognitive Overload and the Filtering Deficit

Prioritization relies on the ability to filter out non-essential information and hold the importance of tasks in **Working Memory (WM)**. However, the ADHD brain struggles with an impaired filtering mechanism, meaning every task, notification, and demand consumes measurable mental energy, the **Cognitive Load (CL)**.

- **Ambiguity is Energy Drain:** When the brain is unable to quickly determine if a task is important (high reward) or urgent (high deadline), it expends valuable CL resources on continuous internal debate. This ambiguity, inherent in a long, undifferentiated list, is draining. Research shows that as CL increases, the ADHD brain's performance and efficiency decrease disproportionately compared to neurotypical peers.

- **The Paradox of Urgency:** Because the brain struggles to generate internal urgency for future rewards, it often falls into the trap of prioritizing "crisis-of-the-moment" tasks or small, trivial, high-dopamine tasks (e.g., answering easy emails) over complex, high-leverage work (e.g., report drafting). This pattern leaves the woman perpetually busy but ineffective, increasing the overall sense of stress and inadequacy.

2. Planning Deficits and the Fear of Choice

Prioritization is fundamentally an act of planning and choice, both of which trigger anxiety when EF skills are compromised.

- **Lack of Goal Coherence:** Effective prioritization requires holding long-term goals and their necessary sub-steps in WM. When planning skills are inconsistent, the connection between a small daily task and a large future goal is weak, making it difficult to allocate energy correctly. The ADHD brain loses sight of the long-term payoff, making the immediate, easy task more appealing.

- **Decision Paralysis:** Prioritization involves making difficult decisions about what to *not* do. For the ADHD brain, which already struggles with the decision process, the immense volume of choices presented by an unprioritized to-do list (e.g., 50 tasks) triggers **decision paralysis**, a state of mental shutdown caused by overload, leading to task avoidance and immobilization.

Section 2: Strategic Prioritization Frameworks

The solution to prioritization failure is to introduce external mental frameworks that bypass cognitive ambiguity, forcing the brain to analyze tasks based on clear, visual boundaries rather than subjective feeling or internal debate.

1. The Eisenhower Matrix: The Essential Filter

The Eisenhower Matrix (Urgent / Important Matrix) is a powerful, visually simple tool that forces the brain to categorize tasks based on two critical criteria, eliminating the ambiguity that triggers overload.

- **The Quadrants:** Tasks are categorized into four quadrants:

Quadrant	Priority	Action (EF Strategy)	ADHD Neuro-Benefit
Q1: Urgent & Important	Crisis	DO NOW. Firefighting, immediate deadlines.	Reserves energy for true emergencies; minimizes impulse to delay.
Q2: Not Urgent & Important	Goal	SCHEDULE (Time Block). Strategy, planning, health.	Forces attention onto long-term rewards, countering dopamine deficit.
Q3: Urgent & Not Important	Delegation / Minimize	DELEGATE or REJECT. Interruptions, others' priorities.	Protects boundaries and reduces time wasted on low-leverage demands.
Q4: Not Urgent & Not Important	Eliminate	DELETE. Distractions, time-wasters, digital noise.	Ruthlessly reduces Cognitive Load (CL) by closing "open loops."

- **Applying the Matrix:** When using a long to-do list, the woman must physically move each item into one of the four quadrants. This simple, forced categorization prevents the brain from treating all tasks as equally demanding, reducing CL and focusing effort on the high-leverage **Q2 (Goal) tasks**, the ones most critical for long-term EF mastery and success.

2. The Rule of Three: Limiting Cognitive Scope

The greatest antidote to decision paralysis is severely limiting the scope of choice. The "Rule of Three" limits the brain's focus to the absolute essentials, preventing the overwhelm associated with a massive to-do list.

- **Defining Daily Success:** At the start of the day (during your scheduled planning routine), review your entire list and select **only three high-leverage tasks** (ideally pulled from the Q2 / Goal quadrant) that, if completed, would make the day feel successful.
- **Benefits:** This technique bypasses the complexity of having 50 choices. The brain receives a clear, finite signal: "These three items are the only things that matter." This drastically reduces the ambient anxiety and frees up WM to concentrate solely on the primary goals, reserving remaining mental energy for unexpected interruptions or lower-priority maintenance tasks.

3. Energy Matching and Allocation

Traditional prioritization often ignores the brain's internal energy state, leading to scheduling failures. The ADHD brain's EF performance fluctuates throughout the day due to energy cycles and medication timing. **Energy Matching** aligns task difficulty with mental resource availability.

- **Identify Energy Peaks:** Schedule your most cognitively demanding tasks (Q2 work, planning, writing, problem-solving) for your **peak energy window** (e.g., morning, post-medication peak).
- **Allocate Low-Energy Tasks:** Reserve low-stakes, routine, or repetitive work (e.g., email batching, filing, chores, passive learning) for **trough periods** (e.g., late afternoon, pre-meal slump). Scheduling low-demand work during low-energy times prevents the collapse of EF performance and reduces the stress of trying to force focus when resources are depleted.

Section 3: Simplifying Decision-Making (The Cognitive Offload)

The goal of prioritization is not just to decide what to do, but to systematically reduce the need for constant, taxing decision-making throughout the day, ensuring EF reserves are conserved for truly important choices.

1. The Power of Routines and Checklists

Prioritization failure often happens when routine tasks (e.g., morning prep, bill paying) require spontaneous decision-making. Fixed routines eliminate this cognitive drain.

- **Routines as Automation:** Establishing fixed routines (e.g., the **Daily Reset** from Book 1) automates sequences of behavior, shifting control from the inconsistent PFC to reliable habit loops. This eliminates the need to expend mental energy deciding *when* or *how* to start a chore, saving EF for complex problem-solving.

- **Checklists for WM Offload:** For complex or multi-step routine processes (e.g., travel preparation, weekly grocery list, meeting setup), create permanent, external **Checklists**. These checklists offload instructions and sequences from your unreliable WM, ensuring consistency and accuracy without requiring mental effort, thereby reserving WM for immediate task execution.

2. The Decision Matrix for Financial and Digital Clarity

Prioritization frameworks can be applied to digital life and financial management—areas where ADHD-related impulsivity and inattention create significant chaos and economic cost.

- **Digital Triage:** When processing an email inbox or digital files, the decision should be instant, based on the Eisenhower Matrix: **Delete** (Q4 / Q3), **Do Now** (Q1, if < 2 min), or **Time Block** (Q2 / Q3, if complex). This structured triage eliminates the ambiguity that causes many with ADHD to leave emails open, creating an unmanaged "open loop" that drains CL.

- **Financial Pause:** Impulsive buying is a form of prioritization failure (prioritizing immediate dopamine reward over long-term financial health). Implementing a mandatory **"24-Hour Rule"** for non-essential purchases, forcing a delay between impulse and action, allows the PFC's Inhibitory Control to engage, changing the priority from immediate novelty to long-term value.

Mastering prioritization frameworks is a crucial psychological intervention that directly addresses the shame and emotional volatility that define overwhelm for women with ADHD.

1. Reducing Shame and Building Self-Efficacy

The consistent failure to prioritize correctly leads to missed deadlines and the sense of constant rushing, reinforcing the inner critic's narrative of inadequacy.

- **Realistic Expectations:** The use of the **Rule of Three** and **Time Blocking** enforces a schedule that is temporally realistic. By consciously limiting daily expectations, you set achievable goals, reducing the likelihood of failure and self-criticism. This is a crucial practice of **self-compassion**, honoring your capacity rather than fighting against it.

- **Evidence of Competence:** Successfully completing the three daily prioritized tasks provides tangible evidence of competence and follow-through, directly countering shame and building **self-efficacy** (the belief in one's ability to execute a plan).

2. Protecting Emotional Resilience

Overwhelm is often the precursor to **emotional dysregulation** (the sudden shift from calm to intense emotion). Prioritization acts as a psychological buffer against this emotional trigger.

- **Stress Management:** When the schedule is prioritized, the brain experiences less background anxiety. Reducing the chaotic inputs that trigger stress conserves the emotional bandwidth required for resilience, preventing minor setbacks from escalating into disproportionate emotional storms.

- **Clear Boundaries:** Prioritization provides a rational framework for setting boundaries (Q3 / Delegate / Reject), allowing a woman to decline external demands that would overwhelm her schedule, thereby protecting her finite EF reserves and overall well-being. This assertive self-protection is vital for sustainable emotional health.

Conclusion: Prioritization as Cognitive Command

The mastery of prioritization frameworks is the definitive step in moving beyond the reactive chaos of overwhelm. By applying tools like the **Eisenhower Matrix** and the **Rule of Three**, you transform your to-do list from an ambiguous source of anxiety into a clear, actionable map of intentions.

You have now learned to not only control *when* you work (Milestones) but also *where* to direct your finite energy (Prioritization). This dual mastery, of time and task allocation, is the ultimate expression of Executive Function command. This structure conserves the mental energy needed for the sustained concentration, memory enhancement, and decision simplification techniques that will follow, setting the stage for true cognitive resilience.

Chapter 2 Workbook: Prioritize Like a Pro: Techniques to Identify What Truly Matters

Objective: To practice using external frameworks to systematically analyze and prioritize tasks, thereby reducing cognitive overload and decision paralysis.

Scientific Anchor: Categorizing tasks into matrices or limited scopes (e.g., Rule of Three) reduces the ambiguity that consumes Working Memory and triggers ADHD paralysis.

Activity 2.1: The Eisenhower Matrix Filter

Instructions: List 10 tasks currently weighing on your mind (work, home, personal). Use the Eisenhower Matrix below to categorize them based on **Urgency** (requires immediate attention) and **Importance** (moves you toward a major life goal).

1. **List of 10 Tasks:** (e.g., A. Pay electricity bill, B. Plan next vacation, C. Answer low-priority emails, D. Buy groceries, E. Outline new project, F. Call partner's doctor, G. Clean kitchen counter, H. Research new hobby, I. Organize old files, J. Call insurance company).

2. **Categorization:** Place each letter (A–J) into the most appropriate quadrant.

Quadrant	Tasks (A–J)	Action Commitment	Neuro-Benefit
Q1: Urgent & Important	(Crisis - Do Now)		Reserve for true emergencies.
Q2: Not Urgent & Important	(Goal - Time Block)		Forces focus onto long-term goals.
Q3: Urgent & Not Important	(Delegation/ Minimize)		Reduces time wasted on others' demands.
Q4: Not Urgent & Not Important	(Eliminate / Delete)		Reduces Cognitive Load (CL).

Activity 2.2: The Rule of Three Commitment

Instructions: Take the tasks you placed in the **Q2 (Not Urgent & Important)** and **Q1 (Urgent & Important)** quadrants and select **only three** high-leverage tasks to prioritize for tomorrow. This limits the cognitive scope to the essential.

1. **High-Leverage Task 1 (Must Do):** -------------------------------
2. **High-Leverage Task 2 (Should Do):** ----------------------------
3. **High-Leverage Task 3 (Could Do):** -----------------------------

Time Block Commitment: Immediately schedule these three tasks into your Time Block calendar for tomorrow, ensuring they have fixed start / end times and buffers (Chapter 1).

Reflection 2.3: Analyzing Paralysis and Energy Allocation

Instructions: Reflect on how these frameworks impact the emotional and cognitive challenges of the ADHD brain.

1. **Defeating Decision Paralysis:** How does forcing every task into one of the four boxes (Activity 2.1) reduce the feeling of **paralysis** that often occurs when looking at a long, undifferentiated list?

Reduction in Ambiguity: _____

_____

_____

_____

_____

_____

2. **Energy Matching:** Identify your **peak energy window** tomorrow (e.g., 9:00 AM–11:00 AM). Which of the three prioritized tasks will you intentionally schedule during this peak window to maximize your focus?

   Task and Time Slot: _____

   _____

   _____

   _____

   _____

   _____

3. **Shame and Self-Efficacy:** If you only complete the **three** high-leverage tasks tomorrow (and ignore the rest of the list), how does that outcome feel compared to the shame of completing 10 random, low-value tasks?

   Feeling of Efficacy: _____

   _____

   _____

   _____

   _____

   _____

CHAPTER 3
HARNESS YOUR ATTENTION:
STRATEGIES TO BUILD LASTING FOCUS

You have successfully established external order by converting deadlines into manageable Milestones (Chapter 1) and proactively prioritizing tasks (Chapter 2), ensuring your efforts are directed toward high-leverage goals. Now, the challenge moves to the micro-level: sustaining **attention** during the actual work block, systematically defeating the neurobiological forces of distraction, impulsivity, and the dual paradox of inattention and **hyperfocus**.

For the woman with Attention-Deficit / Hyperactivity Disorder (ADHD), the difficulty lies not in a lack of intelligence, but in a profound inability to **regulate** attention. The brain struggles to control its "on / off" switch, making it difficult to maintain focus on mundane tasks and challenging to disengage from stimulating ones. This struggle is fueled by the ADHD brain's craving for novelty and immediate reward, often leading to rapid **task-switching**, a drain on Executive Function (EF) reserves that results in significant mental fatigue and chronic overwhelm.

This chapter provides the tactical toolkit to anchor your focus. You will learn to utilize structured time management techniques, such as the **Pomodoro Technique**, to impose **finitude** on tasks, leverage **external accountability** to bypass motivation deficits, and embrace **single-tasking** to transform fragmented effort into consistent, high-quality output. The goal is to move beyond wishing for focus to proactively commanding your attention with strategic, evidence-based structure.

Section 1: The Neurobiological Foundations of Attention Failure

To harness attention effectively, we must first understand the core neurobiological mechanisms that fragment it, particularly the role of motivation and the cost of task-switching.

1. The Dopamine Deficit and the Craving for Novelty

The ADHD brain's relationship with attention is deeply rooted in the dysregulation of **dopamine**, the neurotransmitter critical for motivation, reward, and sustained engagement.

- **Low Activation Energy:** When a task is under-stimulating (boring, repetitive, or complex), the brain struggles to produce enough dopamine to find it interesting, leading to a constant search for novelty, distraction, or mind-wandering. This deficit is the core reason why initiating and sustaining focus on necessary, non-stimulating tasks is so difficult.

- **Hyperfocus as Uncontrolled Flow:** Conversely, a task that is intensely stimulating or provides immediate, satisfying feedback can cause a dopamine surge, leading to the state of **hyperfocus**. While productive, this state is uncontrolled, consuming time and energy at the expense of other critical responsibilities.

The strategy must provide consistent, external cues and frequent, small rewards to compensate for the inconsistent internal dopamine system, making sustained, mundane effort neurologically palatable.

2. The Cognitive Cost of Task-Switching

The single greatest threat to sustained attention is the illusion of **multitasking**, which is actually rapid **task-switching**, a process highly inefficient and mentally exhausting for the ADHD brain.

- **Executive Function Drain:** Each time the brain switches tasks (e.g., from drafting a report to checking an email notification), it incurs a measurable **cognitive penalty**, the effort required to disengage from the first task, reload new rules and information into **Working Memory (WM)**, and reorient attention. This switching rapidly depletes the finite resources of the Prefrontal Cortex (PFC), leading to increased errors, slower pace, and severe **mental fatigue**.

- **The Impulse Trap:** The brain favors the path of least resistance, often preferring the low-effort dopamine hit of checking a notification (novelty) over the high-effort task of resisting it (Inhibitory Control). This leads to chronic toggling that fragments focus and prevents the attainment of *deep work*, the focused effort needed for high-quality output.

Section 2: The Pomodoro Technique: Anchoring Attention with Finitude

The **Pomodoro Technique**, breaking work into short, fixed work sprints followed by mandatory breaks, is the foundational tactical tool for anchoring attention in the ADHD brain. It works by imposing **finitude** and structure on work, neutralizing the anxiety that triggers procrastination and hyperfocus.

1. Finitude: Defeating Paralysis and Overwhelm

The core strength of Pomodoro is its ability to transform an overwhelming, amorphous project into a manageable sprint by providing a clear, fixed boundary for effort.

- **Lowering Activation Energy:** Committing to a task for only 25 minutes (or a customized shorter duration) dramatically reduces the commitment cost, which is essential for bypassing the **Task Activation Deficit**. The visible, ticking timer acts as a non-negotiable external cue, providing the brain with the precise structure it requires to initiate the effort.

- **Making Time Concrete:** For the time-blind brain, the timer translates the abstract concept of duration into a tangible, visual cue, anchoring attention to the external environment rather than relying on unreliable internal perception. This makes the time spent feel measurable and manageable, systematically reducing the mental stress caused by the Estimation Deficit (Chapter 1).

2. Breaks: The External Circuit-Breaker

The mandatory break is the most critical feature for sustaining attention in the ADHD brain.

- **Preventing Hyperfocus and Burnout:** The scheduled break acts as an **external circuit-breaker**, forcing the individual to stop working even if they are deep in hyperfocus. This protects the integrity of the overall Time Block schedule and prevents the task from consuming energy reserves and leading to exhaustion or missed appointments.

- **Restorative Reset:** The **mandatory 5-minute break** provides a regular, guilt-free opportunity for the brain to reset and seek the novelty and low-effort stimulation it craves (e.g., stretching, getting water). This strategically scheduled recovery prevents the deep mental fatigue associated with prolonged, continuous concentration, ensuring the next work interval starts with higher energy reserves.

3. Customization: Tailoring the Sprint to Your Brain

The Pomodoro Technique is only sustainable when the duration is **customized** to match the individual's unique attention span and energy cycle.

- **Matching Duration to Flow:** If a 25-minute sprint feels daunting, shorten it to **10 or 15 minutes** (e.g., 10 minutes of work, 5 minutes of rest). Successfully completing multiple shorter sprints builds more confidence and momentum than struggling through one long block.

- **Intentional Breaks:** Ensure your break is low-friction and actively restorative (e.g., physical movement, sensory reset, or grabbing a drink of water). Avoid engaging in distracting activities like checking email or social media during the break, as this increases the draining cost of context switching.

Section 3: Leveraging External Accountability and Single-Tasking

The structured sprint must be supported by external accountability and the discipline of single-tasking to maximize efficiency and minimize the drain from fragmentation.

1. External Accountability: The Body Double Anchor

For tasks that are particularly difficult to initiate or sustain, **Body Doubling**, working alongside another person (in-person or virtually) who is focused on their own work, provides an essential source of external Executive Function.

- **Anchoring Attention:** The physical presence of a Body Double, even a silent one, acts as a consistent, non-judgmental anchor for the ADHD brain, pulling attention back to the task and reducing the risk of being pulled away by internal or external distractions.

- **Bypassing Motivation Deficits:** The mere act of committing to work in the presence of another person provides a subtle yet powerful source of **social accountability**, supplying the necessary external cue to overcome procrastination and initiate the work.

2. Embracing Single-Tasking: The Antidote to Chaos

The discipline of single-tasking is the necessary antidote to the inefficient and draining cost of constant task-switching.

- **Single Focus, Fixed Block:** Within a Time Block (Chapter 1) and a Pomodoro sprint, commit to focusing on **one specific, defined task** (e.g., "Draft the outline," not "Work on the project"). This clear boundary minimizes the cognitive effort required to decide what to do and prevents the brain from engaging in rapid toggling.
- **Batching Similar Tasks:** To further reduce context switching cost, schedule similar activities together in the same work session (e.g., dedicating a block for "Email / Admin" separate from "Deep Work"). This allows the brain to stay in one cognitive mode for longer, conserving precious EF resources.

Section 4: The Emotional and Cognitive Payoff

Mastering attention through structure yields immediate emotional and cognitive dividends, reinforcing the positive feedback loop necessary for long-term consistency.

1. Building Self-Efficacy and Momentum

Each successfully completed Pomodoro sprint provides tangible, immediate evidence of **competence and follow-through**. This steady accumulation of small wins generates a positive burst of dopamine, systematically dismantling the pervasive feeling of inadequacy and building **self-efficacy** (the belief in one's ability to succeed) that is the direct psychological antidote to shame.

2. Preventing Mental Fatigue and Burnout

The constant effort required to manage attention is the primary cause of chronic mental fatigue. By enforcing regular, restorative breaks and structured work intervals, you are proactively managing your energy, preventing the total depletion of EF reserves that leads to burnout. This controlled rhythm promotes **sustainable effort** rather than sporadic, intense bursts of productivity, creating a resilient foundation for the rest of your life.

Chapter 3 Workbook: Harness Your Attention: Strategies to Build Lasting Focus

Objective: To customize the Pomodoro Technique to match your unique attention span and utilize external accountability to anchor focus.

Scientific Anchor: Customizing the Pomodoro interval reduces the anxiety that triggers task paralysis, while mandated breaks prevent hyperfocus and burnout, thereby maintaining executive function reserves.

Activity 3.1: Attention Span Customization Audit

Instructions: Identify your current optimal focus interval (Work) and the necessary duration of a true mental break (Rest). This moves beyond the standard 25 / 5 interval.

1. **Work Interval Assessment:** If a task is boring, what is the *shortest* amount of time you can commit to before feeling the urge to check your phone or move? (Select one: 10 min, 15 min, 25 min, 30 min).

   o *My Custom Work Interval (A):* _____ *minutes*

2. **Break Interval Assessment:** How long do you need to stand, stretch, and reset your mind before you can successfully re-engage? (Select one: 3 min, 5 min, 10 min).

   o *My Custom Break Interval (B):* _____ *minutes*

3. **My Customized Pomodoro Cycle: A (Work)** minutes / **B (Break)** minutes.

Activity 3.2: The External Accountability Anchor

Instructions: Commit to using external accountability for one difficult task this week to leverage the momentum generated by social anchoring.

1. **Target Task (High Resistance):** Select one task that you consistently procrastinate on (e.g., administrative paperwork, detailed planning).

   Task: _____

   _____

   _____

2. **Accountability Anchor:** Commit to using either **Body Doubling** (working on a video call or in person with a friend) or **Public Accountability** (telling a trusted person a fixed time you will finish).

   Anchor Method: _____

   _____

   _____

   _____

3. **The Finitude Commitment:** Schedule the task using **3 cycles** of your Customized Pomodoro Cycle (from Activity 3.1).

   Total Time Block: _____*minutes*

Reflection 3.3: Analyzing Focus and Shame

Instructions: Reflect on how the structure of this technique supports both your focus and your emotional well-being.

1. **Defeating Paralysis:** You are about to start a task you hate. How does seeing the timer set for your **Custom Work Interval (A)** instantly reduce the anxiety that would otherwise lead to procrastination? (Focus on **finitude**).

   Reduction in Anxiety: _____

   _____

   _____

2. **Stopping the Switch:** During your last Pomodoro sprint, what was the biggest distraction you successfully resisted (e.g., checking email, opening a new tab)? How did the simple act of resisting that temptation conserve mental energy?

   Distraction Resisted: _____

   _____

   _____

3. **Shame Reduction:** How does the frequent, tangible reward of completing a Pomodoro sprint counteract the feeling that you are "lazy" or "unproductive?"

   Self-Efficacy Gain: _____

   _____

   _____

CHAPTER 4

STRENGTHEN YOUR MEMORY:
TOOLS TO BOOST WORKING MEMORY POWER

You have established structural command over your schedule (Chapter 1) and mastered intentional prioritization and focused work sprints (Chapters 2 and 3). These external strategies are highly effective compensations for the challenges of attention and initiation. Now, the journey shifts to the core internal cognitive skills required for sustained adult function: **Working Memory (WM)** and **Inhibitory Control (IC)**.

For the woman with Attention-Deficit / Hyperactivity Disorder (ADHD), **Working Memory (WM)**, the brain's "mental scratchpad", can feel like an inconsistent sieve. WM is the essential ability to hold and manipulate transient information for short-term use, such as remembering a multi-step instruction while executing the first step, or keeping track of conversation points while formulating a response. When WM is compromised, tasks are often left unfinished, instructions are forgotten, and the brain is quickly overwhelmed by the number of details required for a goal, leading to the pervasive anxiety of forgetfulness and the constant need to double-check information.

This chapter provides the strategic toolkit to actively strengthen your WM and, critically, to reduce the cognitive burden on this vital resource. We will explore how to build reliable **external memory systems** that compensate for internal inconsistency and integrate targeted cognitive practice to build long-term resilience, ensuring your EF reserves are conserved for high-leverage tasks.

Section 1: The Neurobiological Reality of Working Memory Deficits

The struggle with memory in ADHD is a measurable cognitive reality rooted in the function of the **prefrontal cortex (PFC)**, the brain's command center for Executive Functions (EFs).

1. WM and the Inconsistent "Mental Scratchpad"

WM deficits are a core characteristic of ADHD, often resulting in difficulties that are mistakenly attributed to carelessness or lack of effort.

- **Impact on Multi-Step Tasks:** A compromised WM makes it difficult to follow multi-step verbal instructions (e.g., in a recipe or meeting), retain the location of an item moments after placing it down, or hold the necessary data in mind to complete a complex calculation. This functional difficulty is a major contributor to poor follow-through and the feeling of being perpetually overwhelmed by detail.

- **The Planning Barrier:** WM is essential for effective **planning and prioritization** (Chapters 1 and 2). You must be able to hold the overall goal, the necessary resources, and the immediate steps in mind simultaneously to map out a strategic approach. When WM is taxed, this planning stage collapses, leading the brain to rely on spontaneous, often inefficient, action rather than intentional, planned execution.

2. Inhibitory Control (IC): The "Brakes" for Focus

Strengthening WM is intrinsically linked to strengthening **Inhibitory Control (IC)**, your brain's capacity to resist distraction and suppress impulsive responses. IC is vital for protecting WM from being hijacked by irrelevant stimuli.

- **Protecting WM from Noise:** The ADHD brain's filtering deficit means that internal thoughts and external stimuli constantly compete for WM resources. IC provides the "brakes" necessary to suppress these distractions, ensuring WM remains focused on the primary task. Without strong IC, WM is continuously overloaded, leading to fragmentation and mental fatigue.

- **Resisting Impulsivity:** IC governs discipline and perseverance, resisting the urge to procrastinate, check a notification, or interrupt a conversation. Strengthening IC means strengthening the capacity to override the brain's preference for immediate reward (a dopamine hit from novelty) and prioritize the sustained, focused effort that WM requires.

Section 2: Externalizing Memory: Building Reliable Systems

The most effective strategy for managing WM deficits is to consistently and aggressively offload all essential information onto a reliable **external system** that does not rely on inconsistent internal memory. This frees the WM from the taxing burden of constant recall.

1. The Power of Fixed, External Routines

WM is strengthened when the need for it is reduced. Fixed planning and execution routines ensure that all necessary instructions and objectives are externalized and placed in a visible, predictable location.

- **Checklists for WM Offload:** To compensate for forgetting steps or instructions, create visual **Checklists and Templates** for repetitive or multi-step tasks (e.g., "The Morning Routine Checklist," "Meeting Prep Checklist," or "Bill Payment Checklist"). These external scaffolds ensure consistency and accuracy without requiring the brain to expend energy recalling complex sequences, thereby reserving WM for immediate execution.

- **Visualizing Instructions:** For complex tasks, use physical visual cues. Instead of trying to hold the steps in your mind, physically lay out the tools and materials in sequential order. This environmental cue serves as a tangible reminder of the task sequence, offloading the memory burden onto the external world.

- **The Power of Writing:** The simple act of writing down instructions, commitments, or deadlines, even if you use a digital planner, reinforces encoding into memory. Commit to writing down any important information immediately, preventing it from being lost in the sieve of your WM.

2. The Nightly Offload and Morning Activation Ritual

WM is significantly impacted by anxiety and sleep quality. Establishing fixed rituals around transitions conserves WM and prevents "open loops" from consuming resources.

- **The Nightly Offload (Closing Open Loops):** The most critical step occurs the night before. Before bed, perform a **Brain Dump** (externalizing all new thoughts and worries) and process them into your Time Block schedule (Chapter 1). This intentional act of closing all "open loops" prevents them from consuming WM overnight and disrupting sleep, which is non-negotiable for EF restoration.
- **The Morning Activation:** Upon waking, immediately check your **Time Block schedule** and verbally rehearse the first two transition points of the day. This intentional, structured beginning activates the brain's **Task Positive Network (TPN)** and loads the immediate instructions into WM with minimal effort, ensuring a smooth transition into focused effort.

Section 3: Targeted Training: Strengthening the Memory Muscle

While systems compensate for deficits, consistent, targeted cognitive practice challenges the underlying WM capacity, similar to physical exercise.

1. Practice Inhibitory Control (IC) through Resistance

IC training is crucial because it protects WM. The goal is to strengthen the "brakes" so you can choose to suppress distraction and maintain focus.

- **Intentional Resistance:** During focused work sprints (Pomodoro, Chapter 3), use the urge to check a notification or open a new browser tab as a deliberate training opportunity. The act of resisting the distraction and maintaining focus on the primary task forces the brain to suppress the impulse, strengthening the IC muscle required for sustained effort.
- **The "Ten-Minute Rule":** For non-urgent impulses (e.g., an interesting but irrelevant thought, a desire to buy something), commit to a mandatory **"Ten-Minute Rule."** Write down the impulse immediately, and then force yourself to wait ten minutes before acting on it. This crucial pause allows the PFC to engage and override the amygdala's impulsive reaction, which is key to reducing both financial impulsivity and emotional volatility.

2. Cognitive Challenge and Dual-Task Practice

Consistent, low-stakes practice is essential for improving WM retrieval and retention over time.

- **Sequential Recall:** Practice activities that require you to hold multiple pieces of information in sequence (e.g., complex instructions, grocery lists, or phone numbers). Verbalizing the sequence out loud or writing it down immediately reinforces encoding.

- **Dual-Tasking (Controlled):** Engage in tasks that force you to hold focus on one item while simultaneously resisting the pull of a competing stimulus. For example, listen to an informative podcast while performing a simple, routine physical task (e.g., washing dishes). This controlled, low-stakes dual-tasking challenges WM to filter background information while maintaining a primary focus.

Section 4: The Holistic Context: Sustaining Cognitive Health

The PFC's capacity for WM and IC is highly vulnerable to impairment from internal psychological and physiological states. Sustaining cognitive growth requires actively minimizing the things that impair EF.

1. Sleep Hygiene and Physiological Support

Quality sleep and stable physical health are non-negotiable foundations for robust EF.

- **Sleep as Restoration:** Quality sleep is critical for WM and IC restoration. Sleep deprivation is as impairing as the core symptoms of ADHD themselves. Consistent, prioritized sleep hygiene is essential for restoring the PFC's capacity and mitigating the chronic mental fatigue that drains EF reserves.

- **Movement for Neurochemistry:** Regular physical exercise is a powerful, evidence-based tool that promotes dopamine release, improving attention and inhibitory control, acting as a natural cognitive enhancement. Use short bursts of movement during Pomodoro breaks (Chapter 3) to discharge restlessness and enhance focus.

2. Minimizing Stress and Sadness

Research is clear: EF skills **blossom most when we lessen things that impair them (like stress or sadness)** and enhance the things that support them.

- **Stress Reduction:** The structural predictability of Time Blocking and Milestone planning (Chapter 1) reduces the systemic stress of daily chaos, providing the necessary emotional buffer for your cognitive skills to flourish.

- **Self-Compassion:** Embracing self-compassion (to be addressed in Book 5) is essential. Self-criticism and shame consume immense EF resources. By replacing the inner critic with a supportive inner dialogue, you conserve mental energy, allowing your WM and IC to operate efficiently.

Conclusion: Your Resilient Internal Command

You have transformed Working Memory and Inhibitory Control from unreliable, internal deficits into skills supported by a robust, predictable system. By establishing fixed planning rituals, intentionally training your IC to resist distraction, and supporting your WM through external offloading, you are actively increasing your long-term resilience.

This intentional, disciplined practice is the definitive step toward conquering the fragmented mind and replacing chronic overwhelm with the quiet confidence of self-mastery. The mental energy conserved by this internal structure is the final resource you need to ensure that the effort of focus is not only powerful but also sustainable, preparing you for the final stage of Executive Function mastery: ruthlessly protecting your cognitive space from digital and mental noise.

Chapter 4 Workbook: Strengthen Your Memory: Tools to Boost Working Memory Power

Objective: To practice strengthening **Working Memory (WM)** and **Inhibitory Control (IC)** using fixed planning routines and targeted exercises.

Scientific Anchor: Executive Function (EF) skills, including WM and IC, improve through consistent challenge and practice. Fixed planning rituals externalize the cognitive burden, allowing the core skills to stabilize.

Activity 4.1: The WM Offload Checklist

Instructions: Identify one repetitive task you frequently forget steps for (e.g., getting ready for work, preparing a specific meal, sending a weekly report). Create an external WM Offload Checklist for it.

1. **Target Task:** _____
2. **External Checklist:** List 5 sequential non-negotiable steps for this task. Commit to referencing this physical or digital list every time you start the task.

Step	Action (Keep it simple)	WM Offload Benefit
1.		(Example: Reduces cognitive burden of recall)
2.		
3.		
4.		
5.		

Activity 4.2: Training Inhibitory Control (IC)

Instructions: Practice intentionally resisting an urge for 10 minutes, strengthening your brain's "brakes" (IC).

1. **Identify Your #1 Impulse:** What is the most common, low-stakes impulse that derails your focus? (E.g., Checking phone, opening new browser tab, getting a snack, interrupting).

   Impulse: _____

2. **The 10-Minute IC Sprint:** Set a timer for 10 minutes. Work on an existing task while actively, mindfully **resisting** the identified Impulse whenever it arises. Each successful resistance is a "rep" for your IC muscle.

IC Practice: _____

Start time:_____

End time: _____

Reflection 4.3: Analyzing Executive Function Gain

Instructions: Reflect on how your consistent routine supports your focus and conserves EF energy.

1. **WM Conservation:** How does performing the **Nightly Offload** (writing down tomorrow's plan / worries) reduce your brain's tendency to ruminate or worry before sleep? (Focus on how the external system manages the "open loops").

   Sleep / WM Benefit: _____

2. **EF and Emotional Load:** The PFC's capacity to focus is impaired by stress and self-criticism. How does the structure of a predictable schedule, which reduces rushing and late penalties, act as a psychological buffer that supports your EF?

   Emotional / EF Support: _____

   _____

   _____

   _____

   _____

   _____

3. **Future-Proofing:** Name one activity or task you will commit to resisting tomorrow (using your IC strength) that will save you at least 30 minutes of time.

   Time-Saving Resistance: _____

   _____

   _____

   _____

   _____

   _____

CHAPTER 5
SIMPLIFY DECISIONS: REDUCE OVERWHELM WITH CLEAR MENTAL FRAMEWORKS

You have successfully established external command over your schedule (Chapter 1), mastered prioritization (Chapter 2), harnessed your attention (Chapter 3), and strengthened your memory (Chapter 4). This cumulative effort has created a structural and cognitive foundation that conserves vast amounts of mental energy. Now, this chapter targets one of the most critical, yet subtle, drains on Executive Function (EF) reserves: **Decision Fatigue**.

For the woman with Attention-Deficit / Hyperactivity Disorder (ADHD), the constant barrage of choices, from mundane (e.g., *Which laundry detergent to buy?*) to profound (e.g., *Which task to start next?*), rapidly depletes the finite resources of the prefrontal cortex (PFC). This neurological exhaustion leads directly to feelings of **overwhelm, anxiety**, and, critically, **Task Paralysis**, as the brain shuts down to avoid the pain of continuous negotiation. Decision-making is inherently taxing, but for the ADHD brain, the effort is disproportionately high due to deficits in Working Memory (WM) and Inhibitory Control (IC).

This chapter provides the strategic toolkit to systematically **annihilate decision points** wherever possible. By implementing clear mental frameworks, routines, and external automation, you will eliminate the need for constant negotiation, ensuring your EF is conserved solely for high-leverage, important choices. The goal is to make the simplest, most effective choices automatic, reducing the daily friction that fuels chronic overwhelm.

Section 1: The Neurobiological Cost of Decision Fatigue

Decision fatigue is a state of mental exhaustion that arises from having to make a high volume of choices over a sustained period. For the ADHD brain, this exhaustion has immediate and measurable consequences on focus, mood, and productivity.

1. WM Overload and the Paralysis Trigger

Prioritization and choice require holding multiple options, goals, and consequences in **Working Memory** simultaneously. When a woman with ADHD faces a mountain of undifferentiated choices (e.g., a chaotic to-do list, a cluttered desk, a busy email inbox), her WM rapidly overloads.

- **Ambiguity is Painful:** Every ambiguous choice (e.g., *Where does this go? Do I need this?*) forces the brain to expend energy. This constant internal debate, a taxing form of **Cognitive Load (CL)**, drains the PFC.

- **The Shutdown Response:** When CL reaches a critical threshold, the brain defaults to avoidance. This is the physiological mechanism behind **Task Paralysis** and **Decision Paralysis**, the brain shuts down to avoid the pain of continuous negotiation, leading to procrastination and immobilization.

2. Impulsivity and the Breakdown of Inhibitory Control (IC)

Decision fatigue directly compromises **Inhibitory Control (IC)**, the ability to resist temptation and think before acting.

- **Weakened Brakes:** As EF resources are depleted, the brain's "brakes" weaken, making it harder to resist immediate gratification or make rational, long-term choices. This manifests as:

    o **Impulsive Buying:** Susceptibility to spontaneous purchases and going over credit limits (financial ADHD tax).

- **Emotional Outbursts:** Reduced capacity to manage frustration, leading to impulsive words or emotional volatility (compromised IC for emotional regulation).
- **Avoidance:** Impulsively choosing a low-effort, stimulating distraction (e.g., social media) over a high-effort, important task.

The strategies in this chapter are designed to automate or eliminate choices, thereby preserving IC for the moments when rational self-control is truly needed.

Section 2: Frameworks for Eliminating Decision Points

The solution is to introduce simple, external rules that force the brain to execute a choice without expending energy on deliberation. This shifts choice from an internal debate to an automatic system execution.

1. The Power of Default Settings and Automation

The most effective way to eliminate choice is to make the desired choice the **default setting** for your life. This bypasses the need for the PFC to engage entirely.

- **Financial Automation:** Automate all repetitive financial tasks, such as bill payments, savings transfers, and investment contributions, to occur immediately after payday. This eliminates the monthly decision (and risk of forgetting) associated with these high-stakes tasks, directly mitigating the financial **ADHD Tax** caused by poor working memory and time blindness.

- **The Digital Default:** Set your computer and phone environments to default to **Focus Mode** or "Do Not Disturb" (Chapter 5, Book 2) during peak working hours. This eliminates the daily choice to turn off notifications, which would otherwise rely on inconsistent IC. Similarly, automate backups and file saving to eliminate the decision of *where* and *when* to save files.

2. The Binary Rule: The "Two-Minute Rule" and "One-Touch Rule"

For processing inputs like email, mail, or small organizational tasks, the decision must be reduced to a binary (two-choice) system that requires zero deliberation.

- **The Two-Minute Rule (for Digital / Admin):** If an incoming item (email, physical mail, small task on a list) can be dealt with in **two minutes or less**, do it immediately. Otherwise, it is deferred

(Time Blocked or delegated). This rule instantly eliminates the ambiguity of deferral vs. action, reducing the item's burden on WM.

- **The One-Touch Rule (for Physical Items):** When you pick up a piece of physical clutter (e.g., mail, a dish, an article of clothing), you must act on it immediately—either put it in its **Designated Home** (Book 1), or put it in the **Trash / Junk Drawer** (the low-friction containment zone). It cannot be set down elsewhere. This simple rule prevents "piles" from forming, which are the visible manifestation of accumulated decision fatigue.

3. The Constraint Principle: Limiting Choice for Energy

The decision-making process is simplified when the number of available options is intentionally limited, the **Constraint Principle**.

- **The Capsule Wardrobe:** Reduce decision fatigue related to clothing by intentionally limiting your wardrobe to a cohesive "capsule" collection of items that mix and match easily. This eliminates the daily energy expenditure of choosing an outfit, reserving morning WM for high-leverage tasks.

- **Routine Meal Planning:** Establish a **Meal Rotation Schedule** or use a fixed set of recipes for weeknights. This eliminates the agonizing daily decision of "What's for dinner?", which is a classic source of executive fatigue for women managing family responsibilities.

Section 3: Leveraging Structure for Complex Choices

For unavoidable, complex choices (e.g., project strategies, financial investments), the goal is to use clear frameworks to externalize the pros and cons, minimizing internal cognitive negotiation.

1. The Externalized Pros and Cons List

The ADHD brain often struggles to hold and weigh multiple variables in WM simultaneously, leading to impulsive or delayed decisions. The solution is to externalize the variables.

- **The T-Chart Method:** For any non-urgent, high-stakes decision, create a simple, visible T-Chart that externalizes the variables. Title one column "Pros / Goals" (Q2, long-term payoff) and the other "Cons / Costs" (Q4, immediate friction). Visually comparing the lists reduces the reliance on inconsistent WM and allows the logical PFC to engage effectively.

- **The "Ten-Minute Rule" for Impulses:** For high-stakes, tempting impulses (e.g., impulsive spending or committing to a new project), enforce a mandatory **Ten-Minute Wait** (Chapter 4). Write down the impulse and the **Pros / Cons** immediately, then wait. This pause allows the PFC's **Inhibitory Control** to kick in, reducing the emotional urgency that drives poor decisions.

2. The Prioritization Filter (Review of Chapter 2)

Prioritization frameworks mastered in Chapter 2 must be used as the ultimate mental filter for simplifying demands.

- **The Eisenhower Matrix (Q2 Check):** When a new commitment arises (e.g., joining a committee, starting a new project), filter it immediately through the **Q2 (Important / Goal)** matrix. If it does not actively move you toward a major goal, the automatic decision is to **Delegate or Reject** (Q3 / Q4), eliminating the need for deliberation. This protects your time and energy from commitments that don't serve your purpose.

Section 4: The Emotional and Cognitive Liberation

The systematic annihilation of decision points yields a profound emotional and cognitive payoff, reinforcing self-efficacy and reducing the pervasive anxiety of overwhelm.

1. Conservation of Executive Function (EF)

The most direct benefit is the significant conservation of EF resources. By automating or eliminating dozens of micro-decisions daily, you free up mental bandwidth that was previously consumed by fighting ambiguity.

- **Fueling Focus:** This conserved EF is the resource you need to fuel sustained concentration (Pomodoro sprints) and engage in challenging cognitive practice (WM training). The mind is quieter, less cluttered, and more capable of engaging in **Deep Work** (high-leverage, non-fragmented focus).
- **Reduced Mental Fatigue:** Eliminating the chronic effort required for decision-making directly combats the **Mental Fatigue and Brain Fog** that characterize chronic overwhelm, creating a more stable internal environment that promotes clarity and motivation.

2. The Antidote to Shame and Paralysis

Decision fatigue fuels the negative emotional cycle of the ADHD experience, leading to shame over missed opportunities and an inability to act.

- **Building Trust:** Relying on robust, automatic systems builds **trust** in your ability to manage your life (self-efficacy). When high-stakes tasks (bills, savings) are executed reliably by automation, you no longer feel the shame associated with poor memory or inconsistent follow-through.
- **Self-Compassion:** The conscious use of the **Constraint Principle** (e.g., limiting wardrobe, fixed meal plans) is an act of self-compassion. You are acknowledging your neurobiological limits and designing a supportive system, replacing the impossible demand for perfection with a realistic, low-friction framework for success.

Conclusion: Your Automated Life

The journey through this chapter marks the final strategic step in maximizing your Executive Function. By systematically applying frameworks like the **Two-Minute Rule** and **Financial Automation**, you have eliminated the chaotic friction of endless micro-decisions.

You have transformed your daily experience from one defined by decision paralysis and exhaustion to one rooted in clarity and automaticity. This mastery of simplicity is the final, essential foundation for long-term self-mastery, ensuring that your conserved mental energy is now fully available for the crucial emotional regulation work (Book 4) and relational connection (Book 5) that builds a truly resilient and fulfilling life.

Chapter 5 Workbook: Simplify Decisions: Reduce Overwhelm with Clear Mental Frameworks

Objective: To practice using external frameworks to automate decisions and reduce the cognitive burden associated with choice and ambiguity.

Scientific Anchor: Reducing the volume of daily micro-decisions conserves Working Memory and Inhibitory Control, mitigating Decision Fatigue and Task Paralysis.

Activity 5.1: The Binary Rule Audit

Instructions: Identify one area where daily decision-making consistently creates friction (e.g., laundry, dish management, email). Apply a binary rule to eliminate ambiguity.

1. **Friction Area:** _____

2. **The Rule (Yes / No Action):** Create a clear, two-choice action plan for items encountered in this area.
    ○ *Example (Email):* If < 2 minutes, DO NOW. If > 2 minutes, **TIME BLOCK or DELETE**.
    ○ *Your Binary Rule:* If Item is picked up, it must be _____ OR _____ (e.g., Put in Home OR Put in Junk Drawer).

Activity 5.2: Decision Automation Commitment

Instructions: Commit to implementing three automated systems to bypass reliance on inconsistent Working Memory and follow-through.

1. **Financial Automation:** What is one high-stakes bill or savings transfer you will automate this week?

    Automated Action: _____

    _____

2. **Routine Automation (Constraint Principle):** What is one area you will reduce choice in to eliminate morning energy drain? (e.g., Lunch Prep, Outfit Choice).

    Constraint: _____

    _____

    (e.g., "I will only choose from three work outfits on Monday morning.")

3. **Digital Automation (IC Protection):** What will you set your phone / computer to automatically do during your main Time Block hours to eliminate the choice of checking notifications?

    Default Setting: _____

    _____

    (e.g., "Set to Do Not Disturb / Focus Mode automatically 9 AM-12 PM.")

Reflection 5.3: Analyzing Freedom from Choice

Instructions: Reflect on how eliminating small choices impacts your emotional and cognitive energy.

1. **Paralysis to Action:** How does the mere existence of the **Binary Rule** (Activity 5.1) reduce the anxiety that leads to task paralysis? (Focus on the elimination of internal debate).

Reduction in Debate: _____

_____

_____

_____

_____

2. **IC Conservation:** How will the automation of high-stakes financial tasks (Activity 5.2, #1) free up mental energy that was previously consumed by worry, fear of late fees, or guilt?

Worry / Guilt Reduction: _____

_____

_____

_____

_____

3. **The New Priority:** If you save 30 minutes of decision time each day, where will you intentionally re-invest that conserved Executive Function (e.g., starting a Pomodoro sprint, engaging in mindful relaxation)?

Re-investment Plan: _____

_____

_____

_____

_____

_____

CHAPTER 6
REFLECT AND INTEGRATE: INSIGHTS AND GROWTH IN YOUR EXECUTIVE FUNCTION JOURNEY

You have reached a significant milestone in your journey toward self-mastery. The preceding chapters of this book have been a disciplined, sustained campaign against the core internal chaos of the ADHD brain: the systemic fragmentation of attention, the tyranny of **Time Blindness**, and the pervasive exhaustion of **Cognitive Load (CL)**. You have moved beyond the reactive struggle, where your focus was a victim of distraction and procrastination, to a state of **proactive, intentional command** over your mental resources.

This chapter marks a critical moment of pause, a dedicated space to **reflect and integrate** the profound cognitive and emotional gains achieved through the disciplined practice of the strategies you have mastered: **Milestone Planning**, **Prioritization Frameworks**, **Attention Anchoring**, and **Decision Simplification**. The aim is to solidify the foundational shift from a life defined by **reactive chaos** and **overwhelm** to a state of **proactive, intentional action**.

The core insight solidified here is that consistent focus is not a mysterious gift of willpower; it is the measurable result of disciplined **Executive Function (EF) management** and the strategic application of

external scaffolding. You have learned that the struggle was never laziness, but a profound neurobiological challenge that required an evidence-based toolkit to compensate for deficits in time perception, task initiation, and filtering capacity. By systematically structuring your time, ruthlessly prioritizing your energy, and training your cognitive functions, you have established the resilient internal command necessary to manage the complex emotional and physiological challenges that lie ahead.

Section 1: The Cognitive Victory: Annihilating Time Blindness and Overload

The most powerful outcome of mastering the EF strategies in this book is the mitigation of two core, debilitating deficits: the inability to perceive time accurately and the chronic drain of high cognitive load. This transformation of the cognitive landscape is the tangible benefit of replacing inconsistent internal effort with predictable external structure.

1. The Banishment of Time Blindness: Finitude and Planning

Time blindness, the inability to accurately perceive or estimate the flow of time, is the primary driver of chronic lateness, poor prioritization, and the anxiety that triggers task paralysis. The Milestones framework directly counteracted this deficit by making time concrete and visible.

- **Milestones as an External Map:** You replaced the overwhelming abstract nature of deadlines with a series of sequential, manageable **Milestones** (Chapter 1). This technique directly addressed the **estimation deficit** (the tendency to underestimate time) by forcing you to apply the **Reverse Timeline** method and intentionally schedule **Estimation Buffers** (25–50% extra time), ensuring your schedule is temporally realistic. This structured approach minimized the cognitive guesswork of "What to do next?", conserving EF resources.

- **The Power of Finitude and Pomodoro:** The implementation of **Time Blocking** (Chapter 1) and the customized application of the **Pomodoro Technique** (Chapter 3) strategically attacks the paralysis triggered by the perception of an infinite, daunting task. By committing to short, fixed sprints, you impose **finitude** on the task, lowering the psychological barrier to initiation. The visible timer provides a constant, external cue, anchoring attention and generating the necessary **momentum** through the immediate reward of completing a structured sprint, systematically bypassing the internal dopamine deficit.

2. Cognitive Load Annihilation and WM Conservation

The chronic state of overwhelm in the ADHD experience is rooted in the high **Cognitive Load (CL)** caused by an overstimulated mind that struggles to filter stimuli and manage multiple "open loops." The mastery of **Decision Simplification** (Chapter 5) and **Prioritization** (Chapter 2) provided the defense against this drain.

- **Annihilating Decision Fatigue:** By implementing binary frameworks like the **Eisenhower Matrix** (Chapter 2) and **The Rule of Three**, you eliminated the chaotic friction of endless micro-decisions (e.g., *Which task should I start?*). The systematic annihilation of decision points, achieved through automation and the **One-Touch Rule** (Chapter 5), conserved EF resources that were previously consumed by continuous internal negotiation.

- **Strengthening Internal Resilience:** The consistent practice of **Inhibitory Control (IC)** training (Chapter 4)—intentionally resisting the urge to check a notification or interrupt a task—actively protected your limited **Working Memory (WM)** from being fragmented by distraction. Furthermore, utilizing **fixed planning rituals** and external checklists actively offloaded multi-step instructions from your unreliable WM, ensuring that your cognitive resources are available for high-leverage thinking, not constant recall.

Section 2: The Emotional and Psychological Liberation

The EF mastery achieved in this book yields profound emotional dividends, reinforcing the positive feedback loop necessary for long-term consistency and challenging a lifetime of internalized shame.

1. Defeating Shame and Building Self-Efficacy

The chronic failure to maintain focus and follow through—a frequent result of time blindness and fragmentation—is a significant driver of shame and the pervasive feeling of inadequacy for women with ADHD.

- **The Antidote to the Inner Critic:** The mastery of EF strategies replaces the long, overwhelming to-do list (a document of perceived failure) with a realistic, manageable schedule, thereby setting **achievable expectations** and reducing the likelihood of failure and self-criticism. The fact that your schedule includes **Estimation Buffers** is an inherent act of **self-compassion** that disarms the "all-or-nothing" perfectionism trap.

- **Evidence of Competence:** Each successfully completed Milestone or Pomodoro sprint provides tangible, undeniable evidence of competence and follow-through. This consistent success builds **self-efficacy** (the belief in one's ability to execute a plan), which is the direct psychological antidote to the inadequacy that characterizes unmanaged attention. The realization that success is due to a deliberate, effective strategy, a system, replaces the reliance on inconsistent willpower.

2. Mitigating the ADHD Tax and Chronic Fatigue

The chronic, high effort required to manage attention is the primary cause of severe **Mental Fatigue** and burnout. This continuous cognitive effort is the **"ADHD Tax"** on energy reserves, a measurable cumulative cost that depletes mental capacity.

- **Energy Conservation:** By eliminating unnecessary **Context Switching** (Chapter 3) and automating decisions (Chapter 5), you directly conserved the mental energy that was previously consumed by fighting internal friction. This conserved energy directly combats the chronic fatigue and brain fog that characterize overwhelm, leading to a more stable emotional and cognitive baseline.

- **Sustaining Effort:** The structured use of the **Pomodoro Technique**, with its mandated restorative breaks, ensures that mental energy is managed proactively. This disciplined rhythm promotes **sustainable effort** rather than sporadic, exhausting bursts of productivity, which is crucial for the long-term health of the prefrontal cortex.

3. The Economic and Relational Dividend

The EF mastery achieved here translates into measurable improvements in the outside world, directly mitigating the financial and relational costs of the condition.

- **Economic Stability:** The use of the Milestones framework and Decision Simplification (automation) directly combats the financial costs associated with unmanaged time blindness (late fees, financial instability) and impulsivity (impulsive buying). By systematically prioritizing and meeting deadlines, you reduce the time and money wasted on compensation and mistakes.

- **Relational Predictability:** The predictability established through structured scheduling reduces the friction caused by forgetfulness and lateness. Furthermore, the practice of

Inhibitory Control (Chapter 4) provides the internal capacity needed to pause before responding impulsively in relationships, which is a foundational skill for constructive communication (Book 5).

Section 3: The Bridge to Future Mastery: Preparing for Emotional Regulation

The structural stability of focus achieved in this book is the essential **prerequisite** for engaging with the complex internal work of emotional mastery (Book 4). A brain that is constantly battling chaos and cognitive fatigue lacks the resources necessary to manage intense feelings.

1. EF as the Foundation for Emotional Control

Emotional dysregulation, the most impairing symptom for many women with ADHD, relies heavily on the EF skills you have practiced.

- **Activating the "Brakes":** The muscle of **Inhibitory Control (IC)**, honed through resistance practice (Chapter 4), is the very same EF required for **emotional regulation**, resisting the urge to react impulsively during an intense emotional surge. You are training the brain's "brakes" (the PFC) to successfully override the emotional accelerator (the amygdala).

- **Mindfulness and the "Pause":** The capacity for sustained, anchored attention (Pomodoro / Single-Tasking) is the prerequisite for effective **Mindfulness** (a cornerstone of DBT / CBT). This EF skill creates the critical **"pause"** between feeling an intense emotion and reacting to it, allowing the cognitive strategies (challenging thoughts, etc.) to engage before the emotional storm takes over. Without the focus you have cultivated, the "pause" is impossible.

2. The Command Shift

You have transformed from a reactive participant in your life to a strategic commander of your time and attention. Your new system is governed by the following laws of sustained EF:

- **Law of Finitude:** You conquer paralysis by breaking all large projects into small, finite, manageable Milestones and Pomodoro sprints.

- **Law of Conservation:** You conserve energy by ruthlessly eliminating distractions (CL Annihilation) and automating decisions, preserving WM and IC for high-leverage tasks.

- **Law of Proactive Structure:** You replaced vague intentions with predictable, scheduled action, ensuring that your motivation is anchored to the external calendar, not inconsistent internal dopamine.

This powerful new sense of competence and control is the definitive antidote to the shame and overwhelm that has characterized your struggle, equipping you for the profound work of self-mastery that lies ahead.

Chapter 6 Workbook: Reflect and Integrate: Insights and Growth in Your Executive Function Journey

Objective: To synthesize the cognitive and emotional gains achieved in Book 3, solidifying the shift from reliance on inconsistent willpower to resilient system design.

Scientific Anchor: Reflective practice reduces the impact of stress and sadness on Executive Functions, allowing the functional systems built to flourish. Acknowledging neurobiological reality counters the shame cycle.

Activity 6.1: The Executive Function Gain Scorecard

Instructions: Rate the severity of your challenges **before** Book 3 and **now**, focusing on the impact of the new time and focus strategies. (Scale: 1 = Minimal Challenge, 5 = Severe Challenge)

Challenge Area	Before Book 3 (Initial)	After Book 3 (Current)	Reflection: The Tool That Helped Most
Task Paralysis (Starting Projects)			(Example: Milestones/ Micro-Steps)
Chronic Underestimation of Time			(Example: Estimation Buffer / Time Block)
Distraction / Context Switching			(Example: Single-Tasking / CL Annihilation)
Daily Decision Overwhelm			(Example: Rule of Three / Automation)

Reflection 6.2: Shifting from Shame to Strategy

Instructions: Use this space to integrate the core concept that struggles with EF are neurological, not moral, and assess your progress in building self-efficacy.

1. **The Overwhelm to Control Shift:** Identify one specific moment this week where you felt the pressure of **Decision Fatigue**. How did using a specific tool (e.g., **The Binary Rule** or **The Constraint Principle**) create an immediate sense of relief and simplification?

   The Intervention: _____

   _____

   _____

   _____

   _____

   _____

2. **The Shame Antidote:** Identify one self-critical thought you had about your productivity (e.g., "I'm lazy for procrastinating on that report"). Rephrase this thought using the compassionate, neurobiological reality you learned (e.g., "The task lacked clear Milestones, triggering a Task Activation Deficit. My brain needs finitude to start.")

   New, Empowered Narrative: _____

   _____

   _____

   _____

   _____

   _____

3. **Evidence of Self-Efficacy:** What is the most important piece of **evidence of competence** you created this week (e.g., sticking to a Time Block, completing a full Pomodoro without switching, meeting a Milestone)?

   Evidence of Competence: _____

   _____

   _____

   _____

   _____

Activity 6.3: Bridge to Emotional Mastery (Book 4 Prep)

Instructions: The capacity for emotional regulation (Book 4) relies on the EF skills (IC / Attention) you have strengthened.

1. **IC and the Emotional Surge:** When you feel an intense emotion (e.g., frustration, anger) that threatens to trigger an impulsive reaction, you need a **"Circuit-Breaker"** (IC in action). What single tool from Book 3 (e.g., The 10-Minute IC Rule, a physical Pomodoro break) will you commit to using as your first line of defense to create a **pause**?

   Circuit-Breaker Commitment: _____

   _____
   _____
   _____
   _____
   _____

2. **CL and Stress:** How does the reduction in daily background noise (CL Annihilation / Digital Silence) provide more **emotional bandwidth** to handle a sudden conflict or intense feeling without immediately escalating to overwhelm?

   Emotional Bandwidth Gained: _____

   _____
   _____
   _____
   _____
   _____

CHAPTER 7

PRACTICE AND APPLY:
YOUR EXECUTIVE FUNCTION ACTION TOOLKIT

You have completed the intensive work of Book 3, systematically defeating the core internal challenges of the ADHD brain, **Time Blindness**, **Prioritization Failure**, and **Memory Inconsistency**. This final chapter provides the essential **Action Toolkit**, designed to transform the neurobiological strategies mastered in the preceding six chapters into resilient, low-friction habits that automate Executive Function (EF).

The goal of this Practice and Apply chapter is to move beyond theory and solidify the crucial shift from a life governed by inconsistent **willpower** to one governed by reliable **systems**. For the woman with ADHD, sustained success is achieved not by trying harder, but by strategically creating external structures that compensate for neurological deficits in Working Memory (WM) and Inhibitory Control (IC).

This toolkit consolidates the highest-leverage strategies into a single, cohesive daily ritual, ensuring that the mental bandwidth you reclaimed from fighting chaos is now actively utilized for intentional, high-quality focus. Consistency in applying these tools is the key to building long-term EF resilience.

Section 1: The Neurobiological Mandate: Automating Executive Function

The chronic feeling of overwhelm experienced by women with ADHD is rooted in the constant effort required to manage fundamental Executive Functions that are inconsistent. This chapter's strategies aim to automate these functions:

1. **Automating Planning (Time Blindness):** We must externalize time management, using visual cues and fixed schedules (Time Blocking) to anchor the present and make the future predictable, neutralizing the **Estimation Deficit**.

2. **Automating Prioritization (Cognitive Load):** We must impose frameworks (Eisenhower, Rule of Three) to eliminate ambiguity and conserve **CL** (Cognitive Load) and **WM**, ensuring energy is directed only toward high-leverage tasks.

3. **Automating Initiation (Task Paralysis):** We must use structures that impose **finitude** (Pomodoro, Milestones) to lower the **Activation Energy** required to start difficult tasks, leveraging momentum and dopamine reward for follow-through.

The exercises below are designed as your daily EF launch sequence, systematically checking these three boxes every morning.

Toolkit 1: The Time and Task Command Center

Objective: To master the initial planning and scheduling phase by converting abstract deadlines into actionable, time-bound Milestones, directly counteracting **Time Blindness** and **Estimation Deficits** (Chapters 1 & 2).

Scientific Anchor: Time Blocking and Milestones impose **finitude** on tasks, which lowers the cognitive resistance associated with paralyzing, open-ended work. Scheduling buffers compensates for the tendency to underestimate duration, reducing daily stress.

Activity 7.1: The Daily Planning Ritual (Morning / Nightly Prep)

Instructions: Commit 15 minutes each day to this structured planning routine, which externalizes your entire day's agenda.

1. **The Reverse Timeline Check (Chapter 1):** Review your **Weekly Milestones** and identify the single most critical, actionable step required today to move that project forward. This focuses your morning intention on a high-leverage task.

Today's Primary Milestone Action: _____

_____

2. **The Eisenhower / Rule of Three Filter (Chapter 2):** Review your digital inbox / list and select **only three** high-leverage tasks (one Q1 / Urgent, two Q2 / Goal) that define a successful day. All others are deferred, delegated, or deleted (Q3 / Q4). This protects against **Cognitive Overload**.

   High-Leverage Task 1 (Must Do / Q1 or Q2): _____

   High-Leverage Task 2 (Goal / Q2): _____

   High-Leverage Task 3 (Goal / Q2): _____

3. **Time Block with Buffer Application:** Schedule your three tasks into your calendar using fixed time slots, applying the **Estimation Buffer** (add 25% more time than you think you need) and the **Transition Block** (10-15 minutes of scheduled rest) between sessions.

   Task 1 Time Block (Start / End): _____

   Task 1 Buffer / Transition: _____

Reflective Commitment: If I only complete these three tasks today, my day will be (Successful / Productive / Calm).

Toolkit 2: Focus and Resistance Anchors

Objective: To proactively manage attention dysregulation by anchoring focus to structure (Pomodoro) and training **Inhibitory Control (IC)** against distraction (Chapter 3 & 4).

Scientific Anchor: The Pomodoro Technique provides the necessary **finitude** and frequent reward that the dopamine-dysregulated brain needs to sustain effort. IC training directly strengthens the prefrontal cortex's ability to resist the impulse to switch tasks or seek novelty.

Activity 7.2: The Focused Sprint and IC Training

Instructions: For your first scheduled **Time Block** of the day, commit to a focused sprint supported by external structures.

1. **Set the Stage for Single-Tasking:** Before you start the timer, perform a **Cognitive Load Annihilation** ritual:
   - Close all browser tabs except the one needed for Task 1.
   - Silence ALL notifications on all devices (Notification Annihilation).

- Clear your immediate desk area of physical clutter (Visual Noise Reduction).

2. **The Custom Pomodoro Sprint:** Set a timer for your optimal work interval (e.g., 25 minutes).
   - *Work Interval:* _____ *minutes.*
   - *Mandatory Break:* _____ *minutes.*

3. **IC Resistance Practice:** During the work sprint, actively practice **Inhibitory Control**. Every time the urge to check your phone or switch tasks arises, take one deep breath and place a tally mark below (A "rep" for your IC muscle).

   IC Resistance Tally: _____

   _____

   _____

   (The goal is not zero, but to track and acknowledge the effort).

4. **The Restorative Break:** When the timer rings, honor the break immediately. Use a **Sensory Reset** technique to calm the nervous system (e.g., 5 deep breaths, walk to get water, light stretch). Avoid consuming digital media during this time to prevent **Context Switching Cost**.

Toolkit 3: Cognitive Offload and Automation

Objective: To simplify daily existence by automating decisions and reducing the mental effort required for constant recall, conserving Working Memory (WM) (Chapters 4 & 5).

Scientific Anchor: Automating routine tasks and implementing binary rules eliminates ambiguity that consumes WM and triggers Decision Fatigue, preserving EF for high-leverage thinking.

Activity 7.3: The Automation and Offload Ritual

Instructions: Focus on eliminating unnecessary mental friction by implementing external systems for memory and decision-making.

1. **The Binary Decision Rule (Chapter 5):** Apply the **Two-Minute Rule** to your email triage. For every email / small task:
   - If it takes < 2 minutes: **DO NOW.**
   - If it takes > 2 minutes: **TIME BLOCK or DELETE.**
   - *Commitment:* I will not leave any email in my inbox to "decide later."

2. **The WM Offload Checklist (Chapter 4):** Identify one repetitive, multi-step task you constantly forget or rush (e.g., leaving the house, shutting down the kitchen). Create a **permanent, visible checklist** to externalize the steps from your unreliable WM.

   Target Task Checklist: _____

   _____

   _____

   (Commit to reviewing it tonight).

3. **The Decision Simplification Commitment (Chapter 5):** Identify one area where you will apply the **Constraint Principle** this week (e.g., meals, clothing, exercise).

   Constraint: I will only wear _____

   _____

   _____

   (pre-selected outfits this week to conserve morning decision energy.)

4. **The Nightly Offload (Closing Open Loops):** Before turning off your lights, perform this two-step ritual to clear your mind and conserve WM overnight:

   ○ **Step A:** Process any new tasks / worries from the day into your **Time Block Schedule** for future scheduling (Milestone planning).

   ○ **Step B:** Place your **Landing Strip Items** (keys, wallet, phone) in their designated home.

Section 2: Integration and Long-Term Resilience (Reflective Summary)

The consistent, simultaneous application of these five toolkits, Milestones, Prioritization, Pomodoro, Memory Strengthening, and Simplification, creates a synergistic system that is far more resilient than any single strategy applied in isolation. This integrated approach addresses the chronic, cumulative nature of ADHD challenges.

1. The Synergistic EF Gain

The power of this toolkit lies in how each strategy supports the next, leading to a profound conservation of EF:

- **Milestones** (finitude) enable **Prioritization** (clarity of scope).
- **Prioritization** (focus on Q2 / Goals) enables **IC** (Inhibitory Control) because you know exactly what to resist.

- **IC** (resistance) protects **WM** (Working Memory) from CL drain.
- **WM** conservation and **Decision Simplification** reduce the overall **Mental Fatigue**, ensuring energy is available for the next day's activation.

This continuous positive feedback loop replaces the old cycle of chaos, paralysis, and shame with a new cycle of clarity, momentum, and self-efficacy.

2. The Emotional Fuel for the Next Journey

The Executive Function skills you have conserved and strengthened are the essential **psychological fuel** required for the profound emotional mastery work that lies ahead in Book 4 (Tame Intense Emotions).

- **Attention as a Prerequisite for Mindfulness:** The capacity for sustained, anchored attention, honed through **Pomodoro** and **IC practice**, is the critical prerequisite for effective **Mindfulness** (the cornerstone of DBT / CBT). Without the ability to maintain focus, the crucial mindful "pause" between feeling an intense emotion and acting impulsively is impossible.
- **IC as the Emotional Brake:** The muscle of **Inhibitory Control** (resisting the urge to check a notification) is the very same EF muscle required for **emotional regulation**—resisting the urge to react impulsively or explode during conflict. Your IC practice in this book is, fundamentally, training your emotional "brakes."
- **Reduced Anxiety:** The structural predictability of Time Blocking and the knowledge that high-stakes tasks are automated (Toolkit 3) stabilize the nervous system, reducing the chaotic internal anxiety that often triggers emotional dysregulation.

By completing the work of Book 3, you have moved beyond merely coping with the symptoms of ADHD to strategically commanding your cognitive function. You are now equipped with the robust internal and external resilience needed to embark on the crucial journey of emotional mastery and true self-acceptance.

CONCLUSION:

SUMMARY: YOUR EMPOWERED ATTENTION

You have completed the intensive, strategic work of Book 3, systematically defeating the core internal challenges of the ADHD brain: **Time Blindness, Prioritization Failure**, and **Memory Inconsistency**. This accomplishment represents a profound transformation, shifting your state from chaotic reactivity to one of intentional, sustained command over your mental resources.

The core realization solidified here is that consistent focus and productivity are not born from relentless willpower, but from the disciplined, strategic application of **Executive Function (EF) management** and robust **external scaffolding**. You have learned that your struggle was never laziness; it was a neurobiological reality that required an evidence-based toolkit to compensate for deficits in time perception, task initiation, and filtering capacity.

By systematically reducing the internal noise and structuring your time to work *with* your brain's needs, you have reclaimed precious mental bandwidth. This cognitive stability is the most valuable asset you possess, providing the foundation necessary to manage the complex emotional and physiological challenges that lie ahead. You have not just managed your focus; you have successfully future-proofed your capacity for consistent follow-through, providing the ultimate antidote to the pervasive feeling of being perpetually "frenzied, frazzled, and overwhelmed."

Section 1: The Cognitive Victory:
Annihilating Time Blindness and Overload

The most powerful outcome of mastering the EF strategies in this book is the mitigation of two core, debilitating deficits: the inability to perceive time accurately and the chronic drain of high cognitive load. This transformation of the cognitive landscape is the tangible benefit of replacing inconsistent internal effort with predictable external structure.

1. The Banishment of Time Blindness: Finitude and Planning

Time blindness—the inability to accurately perceive or estimate the flow of time—is the primary driver of chronic lateness, poor prioritization, and the anxiety that triggers task paralysis. The Milestone framework directly counteracted this deficit by making time concrete and measurable.

- **Milestones and Time Blocking as an External Clock:** You replaced the overwhelming abstract nature of deadlines with a series of sequential, manageable **Milestones** (Chapter 1), forcing the abstract future into the urgent present. This technique directly addressed the **estimation deficit** (the tendency to underestimate time) by forcing you to apply the **Reverse Timeline** method and intentionally schedule **Estimation Buffers** (25–50% extra time), ensuring your schedule is temporally realistic. The visible, structured schedule minimized the cognitive guesswork of "What to do next?", conserving EF resources.

- **The Power of Pomodoro Finitude:** The customized application of the **Pomodoro Technique** (Chapter 3) strategically attacks the paralysis triggered by the perception of an infinite, daunting task. By committing to short, fixed sprints, you impose **finitude** on the task, lowering the psychological barrier to initiation. The visible timer provides a constant, external cue, anchoring attention and generating the necessary **momentum** through the immediate reward (dopamine hit) of completing a structured sprint, systematically bypassing the internal motivation deficit.

- **Working Memory Conservation:** The consistent implementation of **fixed planning routines** (Chapter 4) and the use of external checklists actively offloaded multi-step instructions from your unreliable **Working Memory (WM)**. This systematic offloading ensured that your cognitive resources are available for high-leverage thinking, not constant recall, thereby mitigating "brain fog" and forgetfulness.

2. Cognitive Load Annihilation: Prioritization and Simplification

The chronic state of overwhelm is rooted in the high **Cognitive Load (CL)** caused by an overstimulated mind that struggles to filter stimuli and manage multiple "open loops." The mastery of **Decision Simplification** (Chapter 5) and **Prioritization** (Chapter 2) is the most direct defense against this drain.

- **Annihilating Decision Fatigue:** By implementing binary frameworks like the **Eisenhower Matrix** (Chapter 2) and **The Rule of Three**, you eliminated the chaotic friction of endless micro-decisions (e.g., *Which task should I start?*). The systematic annihilation of decision points, achieved through automation and the **One-Touch Rule** (Chapter 5), conserved EF resources that were previously consumed by continuous internal negotiation.

- **Defeating Context Switching:** By enforcing **single-tasking** and **Cognitive Load Annihilation** (Chapter 5), you systematically eliminated the draining cost of **Context Switching**—the rapid shifting of attention between different cognitive demands—which incurs a measurable cognitive penalty that rapidly depletes EF reserves and leads to mental exhaustion. The strict implementation of **Notification Annihilation** protected your **Inhibitory Control (IC)**—your brain's "brakes"—from the constant temptation of novelty.

Section 2: The Emotional and Economic Payoff: Building Resilience

The structured focus achieved in this book yields profound emotional dividends, reinforcing the positive feedback loop necessary for long-term consistency and challenging a lifetime of internalized shame.

1. Defeating Shame and Building Self-Efficacy

The chronic failure to maintain focus and follow through—a frequent result of time blindness and fragmentation—is a significant driver of shame and the pervasive feeling of inadequacy for women with ADHD.

- **The Antidote to the Inner Critic:** The mastery of EF strategies replaces the long, overwhelming to-do list (a document of perceived failure) with a realistic, manageable schedule, thereby setting **achievable expectations** and reducing the likelihood of failure and self-criticism. The consistent success in meeting **Milestones** provides tangible, undeniable evidence of competence and follow-through, systematically chipping away at the internalized shame and building **self-efficacy** (the belief in one's ability to execute a plan).

- **Emotional Conservation:** The structured use of the **Pomodoro Technique**, with its mandated restorative breaks, ensures that mental energy is managed proactively, preventing the total depletion of EF reserves that leads to burnout and emotional volatility.

2. Mitigating the ADHD Tax and Economic Strain

The EF mastery achieved here translates into measurable improvements in the outside world, directly mitigating the financial and time cost of the **ADHD Tax**.

- **Economic Stability:** The use of the Milestones framework and Decision Simplification (automation) directly combats the financial costs associated with unmanaged time blindness (late fees, financial instability) and impulsivity (impulsive buying). By systematically prioritizing and meeting deadlines, you reduce the time and money wasted on compensation and mistakes, actively safeguarding your financial well-being.
- **Relational Predictability:** The predictability established through structured scheduling reduces the friction caused by forgetfulness and lateness. Furthermore, the practice of **Inhibitory Control** (Chapter 4) provides the internal capacity needed to pause before responding impulsively in relationships, which is a foundational skill for constructive communication (Book 5).

Section 3: The Bridge to Future Mastery: Preparing for Emotional Regulation

The structural stability of focus achieved in this book is the essential **prerequisite** for engaging with the complex internal work of emotional mastery (Book 4). A brain that is constantly battling chaos and cognitive fatigue lacks the resources necessary to manage intense feelings.

1. EF as the Foundation for Emotional Control

Emotional dysregulation—the most impairing symptom for many women with ADHD—is profoundly linked to the EF skills you have practiced.

- **Activating the "Brakes":** The muscle of **Inhibitory Control (IC)**, honed through resistance practice (Chapter 4), is the very same EF required for **emotional regulation**—resisting the urge to react impulsively during an intense emotional surge. Your IC practice in this book is, fundamentally, training your emotional "brakes" (the PFC) to successfully engage before the emotional accelerator (the amygdala) takes over.
- **Mindfulness and the "Pause":** The capacity for sustained, anchored attention, honed through the **Pomodoro Technique** and **Single-Tasking**, is the critical prerequisite for effective **Mindfulness** (a cornerstone of DBT / CBT). This EF skill creates the critical **"pause"** between feeling an intense emotion and reacting to it, allowing the cognitive strategies (challenging thoughts, etc.) to engage before the emotional storm takes over.

2. The Laws of Sustained Executive Function

You have transformed from a reactive participant in your life to a strategic commander of your time and attention. Your new system is governed by the following laws of sustained EF, which you must commit to maintaining:

- **Law of Finitude:** You conquer paralysis by breaking all large projects into small, finite, manageable **Milestones** and **Pomodoro sprints**.
- **Law of Conservation:** You conserve energy by ruthlessly eliminating distractions (**CL Annihilation**) and automating decisions, preserving WM and IC for high-leverage tasks.
- **Law of Proactive Structure:** You replaced vague intentions with predictable, scheduled action (**Time Blocking**), ensuring that your motivation is anchored to the external calendar, not inconsistent internal dopamine.

The stability achieved here is your most valuable asset. The mental energy that was once consumed by fighting your own brain is now a conserved resource—a stable platform upon which you can build emotional resilience (Book 4) and navigate the complex dynamics of your relationships (Book 5). This powerful new sense of competence and control is the definitive antidote to the shame and overwhelm that has characterized your struggle, equipping you for the profound work of self-mastery that lies ahead.

BOOK FOUR
SYNC HORMONES AND OPTIMIZE TREATMENT
FOR THE ADHD WOMAN

INTRODUCTION

The journey toward defeating chronic overwhelm for a woman with Attention-Deficit / Hyperactivity Disorder (ADHD) requires profound mastery over the structural demands of organization and the cognitive challenges of attention (as addressed in the foundational work of the previous books). However, for women, these struggles are not static; they are dynamically and intensely influenced by a factor often overlooked in mainstream ADHD literature: the powerful and intricate ebb and flow of **hormonal cycles** throughout her entire lifespan.

For many women, living with ADHD is akin to trying to stabilize a ship in a perpetually shifting tide. They report, anecdotally, yet consistently, that their core symptoms of inattention, poor time management, anxiety, and emotional dysregulation can intensify without warning during certain times of the month or at specific life stages, such as puberty, the menstrual cycle, or perimenopause. This crucial link has historically been minimized or dismissed by medical practitioners, leading to a profound sense of not being "believed" when a woman reports that her medication efficacy fluctuates or her focus completely collapses in the days leading up to her period.

This book is a direct intervention into this critical knowledge gap. It provides an evidence-based roadmap that validates the woman's lived experience with rigorous scientific research, empowering her to understand, track, and strategically manage the dynamic role of her hormones. The goal is to move beyond the traditional, male-normed view of ADHD treatment, which often assumes a static neurochemistry, and transition to a holistic, personalized approach that accounts for the powerful hormonal reality unique to the female brain. By syncing your management strategies with your natural hormonal rhythm, you move from reacting to chaos to creating predictable, sustainable stability.

Section 1: The Gender Health Gap and the Unseen Burden

The struggle to have the hormonal connection validated is a stark symptom of the wider **gender health gap** in ADHD research. Historically, research and diagnostic criteria were developed almost exclusively using male populations, leading to a limited understanding of the nuances of female symptom presentation and the profound influence of the female endocrine system.

- **Delayed Diagnosis and Shame:** The female presentation of ADHD, often characterized by internalized struggles, pervasive inattention, disorganization, and emotional volatility, is frequently overlooked or misdiagnosed entirely as anxiety or a mood disorder. This diagnostic disparity is severe: studies confirm that women tend to be diagnosed much later than men, with some finding the mean age of diagnosis for females to be up to 28.6 years, compared to 22.7 years for males. This delayed diagnosis leaves women without a framework to understand their struggles, fueling intense internalization, shame, and a belief that their functional difficulties are personal or moral failings.

- **The Neurochemical Reality of Worsening Symptoms:** When a woman reports that her symptoms worsen cyclically, it is not subjective fluctuation; it is a measurable consequence of her neurobiology being under additional, predictable hormonal pressure. The constant pressure to meet societal expectations for organization and emotional maturity further exacerbates this struggle, compelling many women to engage in **masking**, the exhausting effort to hide their internal chaos. This book provides the language and objective data needed to overcome this invalidation and command a tailored, individualized treatment plan.

Section 2: The Core Neurochemical Link: Estrogen, Dopamine, and Attention

To understand the profound impact of hormones on ADHD, one must first grasp the intricate link between key sex hormones and the brain's neurochemical systems, particularly **dopamine**. This neurochemical connection provides the powerful, scientific explanation for why ADHD is not a static condition in women.

1. Dopamine: The Fuel for Focus and Motivation

At the core of the ADHD experience is a distinct neurochemical reality centered on the dysregulation of **dopamine**. Often called the brain's "motivation" or "reward" chemical, dopamine is crucial for regulating attention, initiation, and sustained focus. For individuals with ADHD, this dysregulation, often manifesting as lower effective dopamine signaling in the synapses, makes it exceptionally difficult to sustain engagement on tasks that are not inherently stimulating or rewarding. This is the neurobiological basis for procrastination, inattention, and the search for novelty.

2. Estrogen: The Supportive Ally

Estrogen, a primary female sex hormone, acts as a crucial supportive ally to this system. Research has consistently shown that estrogen plays a pivotal role in regulating dopamine synthesis and activity. Higher levels of estrogen are linked to increased dopamine levels and receptor sensitivity, which provides a **protective and enhancing effect** on the brain's attentional and emotional systems. This natural boost can make executive functions feel more robust and mood more stable.

Conversely, when estrogen levels drop or fluctuate erratically, this supportive effect diminishes. Lower estrogen levels are linked to lower dopamine levels, which can dramatically exacerbate core ADHD challenges like poor motivation, inattention, and executive dysfunction. This sudden change can feel like a complete collapse of organizational capability or focus, often leading to deep frustration and renewed self-blame.

3. Progesterone: The Complicating Regulator

Progesterone, the other major female sex hormone, further complicates this dynamic. Often referred to as the "calming hormone" due to its role in boosting the inhibitory neurotransmitter GABA, progesterone regulates mood, sleep, and emotional stability. However, its influence is complex: while it promotes calm, its rise, particularly in the context of declining estrogen during the late luteal phase, can increase the sensitivity of the brain's emotional center (the amygdala). This hormonal combination can lead to increased anxiety, irritability, poor emotional regulation, and heightened sensitivity to stress, contributing to the distinct symptoms of the premenstrual phase.

Section 3: The Dynamic Lifespan:
Vulnerable Phases of Hormonal Fluctuation

ADHD symptoms are known to correlate with hormonal shifts, creating distinct periods of vulnerability across a woman's entire reproductive lifespan. This dynamic nature is why a static treatment plan often fails to provide stable support.

1. Puberty: The Initial "Double Whammy"

The onset of puberty is a pivotal time when many girls, previously managing their subtle symptoms, begin to struggle. As estrogen and progesterone levels surge and fluctuate, the balance of the brain's neurochemistry is disrupted. Experts refer to this phase as a **"double whammy,"** where the combination of transient hormonal effects and long-lasting organizational changes sets the stage for increased impairment in adulthood. This hormonal shift can exacerbate ADHD symptoms, including increased irritability and impulsivity, making the girl's presentation harder to manage and often leading to misdiagnosis as a mood or anxiety disorder, further widening the diagnostic gap.

2. The Menstrual Cycle: A Monthly Challenge

The natural, rhythmic fluctuations of the menstrual cycle create a constant, predictable source of internal volatility. Research and clinical monitoring strongly suggest that attention and executive function are significantly impaired during the low-estrogen phases of the cycle.

- **The High-Risk Luteal Phase:** Symptoms demonstrably worsen during the **luteal phase**, the period immediately following ovulation and preceding menstruation, which is characterized by declining estrogen and rising progesterone. This low-estrogen environment exacerbates the existing dopaminergic dysregulation, leading to more pronounced challenges in:
  - **Inattention and Focus:** Difficulty sustaining concentration and increased distractibility.
  - **Emotional Volatility:** Heightened anxiety, irritability, and stress.
  - **Executive Function:** Worsening of organization, planning, and task initiation deficits.

233

- **The PMDD Intersection:** This period of vulnerability is further intensified for the significant percentage of women with ADHD who also experience **Premenstrual Dysphoric Disorder (PMDD)**, a severe form of PMS characterized by debilitating emotional and physical symptoms. The combination of ADHD and PMDD creates a neurobiological perfect storm that makes emotional regulation nearly impossible during the premenstrual days.

3. Perimenopause and Menopause: The "ADHD Squared" Effect

The hormonal influence culminates in midlife, during the transition into **perimenopause and menopause**. As estrogen and progesterone levels undergo a significant, sustained decline, underlying ADHD symptoms that a woman may have compensated for throughout her life often become unmanageable.

- **Cognitive Collapse:** Experts refer to this as the "**ADHD squared**" effect, the compounding of already low dopamine with the sustained decline of estrogen. The symptoms of menopause, such as **"brain fog," memory lapses, poor organization, and difficulty with concentration**, often mirror and drastically intensify the symptoms of ADHD, leading to a confusing and frustrating experience that can feel like early-onset dementia.

- **Emotional Vulnerability:** The decline in progesterone during this phase further exacerbates anxiety, irritability, and emotional dysregulation by reducing its supportive, calming effect on the nervous system (GABA). This loss of neurochemical buffer makes the woman more susceptible to stress and emotional overwhelm, highlighting the intense need for individualized, integrated treatment.

Section 4: Implications for Optimized Treatment and Self-Advocacy

The knowledge of this hormonal connection is the key to moving from reactive coping to proactive, personalized treatment. You are now equipped to advocate for a plan that is dynamic, not static, addressing a long-standing **gender health gap** in medical care.

1. Cycle Dosing: Tailoring Medication Efficacy

One of the most critical implications of this research is the finding that the effectiveness of stimulant medication used to treat ADHD may be **menstrual cycle-dependent**. Because estrogen influences the dopamine system that these medications target, the natural decline in estrogen during the low-estrogen phases can lead to a diminished response to the stimulant, causing a temporary, frustrating return of symptoms.

- **The Guidance for Personalization:** Clinical observations and preliminary studies strongly suggest the potential benefit of **"cycle dosing"**, tailoring medication dosages to a woman's hormonal status, often involving a slight increase in dose during the premenstrual week when symptoms and medication challenges are most pronounced. This must be implemented only under the supervision of a specialized physician, but the evidence empowers the woman to initiate the conversation for a safe, optimal, and individualized treatment approach.

- **HRT Integration:** For women in perimenopause and menopause, combining **Hormone Replacement Therapy (HRT)** to increase estrogen with existing ADHD medication often yields the most effective improvement in memory, reasoning, and overall symptom control, demonstrating the critical interplay between neurochemistry and endocrinology.

2. The Power of Tracking: Moving from Anecdote to Data

The most powerful tool a woman possesses in this journey is objective data collection. For years, women were dismissed because their reports were subjective. Now, you can transform that anecdotal experience into undeniable evidence.

- **The Symptom Log:** By diligently tracking your menstrual cycle alongside your ADHD symptoms (inattention score, anxiety level, medication efficacy) for two to three months, you create a clear, measurable pattern. This data provides the concrete proof necessary to validate your experience and present an informed, strategic request to your healthcare provider for a dosage adjustment or personalized therapy plan.

- **The Bridge to Self-Compassion:** Tracking shifts the narrative from "I am failing to focus" to **"My body is currently experiencing a neurochemical shift due to lower estrogen levels, and this is a predictable, manageable challenge."** This perspective fosters **self-compassion**, recognizing that the struggle is a neurobiological reality, not a moral failure, and actively counters the shame that has long accompanied the female ADHD experience.

Section 5: The Holistic Path: Building Resilience Against Fluctuations

The structural stability achieved through organization and focus (Books 1 and 3) is the vital buffer that prevents hormonal fluctuations from leading to emotional or cognitive collapse. Sustaining hormonal harmony requires a proactive, holistic commitment to physiological self-care.

- **Proactive Scheduling:** Use the Time Blocking skills (Book 3) to strategically schedule high-leverage, cognitively demanding tasks (e.g., report writing, complex planning) during the high-estrogen phases and save routine, low-energy tasks (e.g., administrative work, organizing simple areas) for the challenging low-estrogen phases. This works with, rather than against, your fluctuating energy.

- **Physiological Buffering:** Prioritize factors that stabilize neurochemistry. Consistent, high-quality **sleep hygiene** is crucial, as sleep deprivation exacerbates both ADHD and hormonal symptoms. Regular **physical exercise** is a potent, natural tool for regulating dopamine levels, reducing restlessness, and improving mood, acting as a direct buffer against the emotional volatility of the luteal phase.

- **Stress Management:** High stress levels further disrupt hormonal balance and cognitive function. Maintaining a low baseline of stress through the elimination of chaos (Book 1) and the use of **mindfulness and grounding techniques** is crucial for protecting the Executive Functions that hormonal dips make vulnerable.

Conclusion: A Holistic Approach to Hormonal Harmony

The journey through this book provides a groundbreaking validation of the female ADHD experience. You have learned that your symptoms are not static; they are dynamic, measurable, and profoundly influenced by the ebb and flow of your hormonal cycles.

By understanding the neurochemical link between estrogen and dopamine, navigating the vulnerabilities of the menstrual cycle and menopause, and embracing the necessity of personalized treatment and proactive self-care, you move from feeling powerless against your symptoms to a place of informed, strategic action. This knowledge empowers you to command a truly holistic treatment plan, ensuring that your journey toward balance is not a rigid prescription but a dynamic, lifelong process that accounts for the complete reality of your unique neurobiology.

The harmony you cultivate here is the essential foundation for the intense internal work that follows: managing the unique emotional volatility and building the robust, stable connections that define integrated success.

CHAPTER 1

MAP YOUR CYCLE: TRACK SYMPTOMS TO PINPOINT HORMONAL HIGH-RISK DAYS

The journey to achieve sustainable calm and focus requires the integration of all facets of your neurobiology. As established in previous books, structural stability (Book 1) and cognitive command (Book 3) are essential, but for the female brain, these efforts are continuously modulated by the predictable, powerful rhythm of your **hormonal cycle**. For women with Attention-Deficit / Hyperactivity Disorder (ADHD), core symptoms, inattention, anxiety, and emotional volatility, are not static; they intensify dynamically with the ebb and flow of **Estrogen** and **Progesterone**.

This chapter provides the critical first step in taking command of this dynamic system: the transformation of subjective experience into objective, actionable data. By systematically tracking your menstrual cycle alongside your Executive Function (EF) deficits and emotional shifts, you move from feeling like a victim of unpredictable chaos to becoming a strategic commander of your own physiology. This data is the single most powerful tool for **self-advocacy**, enabling you to identify your personalized **Vulnerability Window**—the high-risk days when low estrogen levels demand a strategic adjustment to your work, self-care, and treatment protocols.

The goal is not to eliminate hormonal shifts, but to **anticipate** them. By recognizing the pattern, you neutralize the shame that accompanies the sudden, overwhelming dips in performance, allowing you to replace self-criticism with strategic self-compassion and proactive buffering.

Section 1: The Neurobiological Blueprint of the Monthly Shift

The need for cycle tracking is rooted in the measurable neurochemical reality of how ovarian hormones interact with the brain's attention system, which is already dysregulated in ADHD. This interaction provides the scientific basis for the worsening of symptoms.

1. The Low-Estrogen Trigger: Dopamine Diminishment

The effectiveness of the brain's attention and motivation system is highly dependent on **dopamine**. Since ADHD is fundamentally characterized by dopamine dysregulation, the supporting role of **Estrogen**, which increases dopamine synthesis and receptor sensitivity, is critical.

- **The Follicular Advantage:** During the late follicular phase (pre-ovulation), when estrogen levels are high and steadily rising, women often report experiencing a period of relative cognitive clarity and focus, and may find it easier to stay organized. This high-estrogen environment provides a **neurochemical buffer**, offering temporary support to the dopamine system, which can enhance motivation and Executive Functions.

- **The Luteal Collapse (The Vulnerability Window):** The challenge emerges during the **luteal phase** (post-ovulation and pre-menstruation), which is characterized by a significant drop in estrogen and a sharp rise in **Progesterone**. As estrogen diminishes, its supportive effect on the dopamine system collapses, exacerbating the underlying dopaminergic deficit of ADHD. This predictable neurochemical dip leads to a pronounced worsening of core ADHD symptoms, including:

  o **Exacerbated Inattention:** Difficulty sustaining focus and planning, and increased distractibility.

  o **Emotional Volatility:** Heightened irritability, anxiety, and stress, often linked to the drop in the supportive, calming effects of progesterone on GABA.

This phenomenon is not anecdotal; studies suggest that within-person declines in estrogen are associated with **meaningful increases in ADHD symptoms** (specifically hyperactivity-impulsivity post-ovulation and inattention perimenstrually). Recognizing this pattern transforms a confusing, painful experience into a predictable neurobiological event that can be planned for.

2. The Link to Emotional Dysregulation and PMDD

The cyclic hormonal shifts intensify the most impairing aspects of female ADHD, particularly emotional dysregulation. For women with ADHD, this struggle is often compounded by a high incidence of **Premenstrual Dysphoric Disorder (PMDD)**, a severe form of PMS.

- **Emotional Amplification:** The low-estrogen, high-progesterone environment of the late luteal phase makes the brain's emotional center (the amygdala) more reactive while simultaneously reducing the inhibitory control of the prefrontal cortex. This combination leads to rapid, unpredictable mood shifts, where minor triggers can escalate into a disproportionate emotional storm, the "green-to-red" phenomenon often reported by those with emotional dysregulation.

- **Heightened Sensitivity:** This period of heightened emotional vulnerability also exacerbates sensitivity to perceived criticism or rejection, magnifying the debilitating pain of **Rejection Sensitive Dysphoria (RSD)**. During the vulnerability window, a woman may be more prone to catastrophizing and internalizing negative feedback, reinforcing the cycle of shame and self-blame.

Section 2: The Tracking Toolkit: From Anecdote to Objective Data

The most powerful form of self-advocacy and strategic management is moving from subjective reports of feeling "bad" to objective data that clearly identifies the correlation between your cycle day and symptom severity. Tracking is the process of building an **objective, measurable pattern** that your Executive Function can use to plan and that your doctor must respect.

1. Designing Your Symptom Log (The Four-Point Data Set)

Your log must track four key data points simultaneously to reveal the pattern:

Data Point	What to Track	Why It Matters
1. Cycle Day	Track Day 1 as the first day of your period (menses). This is the anchor for all subsequent hormonal phases.	Pinpoints the predictable decline in estrogen that triggers the dip.
2. Core ADHD Symptoms (Cognitive)	Rate Inattention, Task Initiation, and Working Memory (Forgetfulness) using a consistent scale (e.g., 1 to 5, where 5 is Severe).	Quantifies the functional impact on productivity and focus.
3. Emotional / Physical Symptoms	Rate Irritability / Anxiety, Fatigue / Brain Fog, and Sleep Quality (1 to 5).	Identifies the compounding effect of low Progesterone / low Estrogen on mood and energy.
4. Medication Efficacy	Rate how effective your stimulant medication feels each day (1 to 5, where 1 is Highly Effective, 5 is Ineffective).	Provides the necessary data for discussing **cycle dosing** options with your physician.

Consistency is the Goal: The tracking does not need to be complex; a simple journal or a dedicated app is sufficient. The key is to rate your symptoms **at the same time each day** (e.g., end of the workday) for a minimum of two to three full cycles. This consistency ensures the data is reliable and not influenced by transient events.

2. Pinpointing Your Vulnerability Window

After two cycles, review your data log to identify the predictable **Vulnerability Window**, the high-risk phase where scores for Inattention and Irritability consistently spike (e.g., Days 22–28, or the final week before menses).

- **Predictability is Power:** By pinpointing this window, you gain the ability to **anticipate** the dip. This pre-knowledge is an immense act of self-compassion, as it transforms the sudden onset of chaos into a predictable event. Instead of internalizing the sudden inability to focus as "I am falling apart," the thought becomes, "This is Cycle Day 24; my estrogen is low, and my system needs to buffer."

- **Strategic Planning Anchor:** This window now becomes the central anchor for your **Optimize Your Flow** plan (Chapter 2). During these days, you know you must enforce your external EF scaffolding (Time Blocking, micro-steps) more rigorously and reduce external demands to protect your finite energy reserves.

Section 3: Data as Self-Advocacy: Overcoming the Gender Health Gap

The intentional collection of objective data is the most crucial tool in navigating the often-skeptical medical environment and addressing the historical lack of research into female-specific ADHD symptoms, the **gender health gap**.

1. Challenging the Narrative of Dismissal

For years, women were dismissed because their reports were subjective. Clinicians often lack training in the dynamic relationship between hormones and neurochemistry, relying instead on a static model of ADHD.

- **From Anecdote to Evidence:** Your Symptom Log provides the concrete evidence needed to shift the conversation from general mood reporting to a specific correlation between hormonal status and functional impairment. You are presenting **measurable data** that demands a tailored response, effectively bypassing the historical tendency toward dismissal.

- **Targeted Request:** Instead of saying, "My medication doesn't work right before my period," the advocacy statement becomes: "My data shows that during Cycle Days 22–28, my average Inattention score increases by 4 points, and my stimulant efficacy drops by 50%. I would like to discuss evidence-based options for managing this predictable impairment, starting with cycle dosing."

2. The Intersection of ADHD and PMDD

For a significant number of women, the symptoms of the Vulnerability Window are so severe they align with **Premenstrual Dysphoric Disorder (PMDD)**. Tracking is essential here because PMDD, like ADHD, is a condition rooted in neurochemical sensitivity, and its high co-occurrence with ADHD creates a perfect storm of emotional and cognitive distress.

- **Dual Diagnosis:** Tracking allows you to isolate the predictable, cyclical nature of severe mood swings, hopelessness, and intense irritability. This data is critical for seeking a PMDD diagnosis alongside your ADHD, which can open up specialized treatment options (often involving SSRIs or hormonal contraceptives) tailored to stabilize the emotional volatility of the luteal phase, thereby reducing the stress that exacerbates your core ADHD symptoms.

Section 4: The Emotional Payoff: Self-Compassion and Predictability

The most profound outcome of cycle tracking is the liberation from shame and the cultivation of radical self-compassion.

1. Neutralizing Shame with Knowledge

For the woman with ADHD, the sudden, unpredictable collapse of focus and control leads to immediate **shame** and internal judgment ("I'm a failure," "I'm lazy").

- **Anticipation is Self-Kindness:** By anticipating the symptom spike, you neutralize the shame. You replace the harsh self-judgment with **radical acceptance**, acknowledging the reality of the emotional / cognitive state without judgment. The thought is transformed from: *"Why can't I just focus today? I'm useless."* to *"Ah, my energy is low because my body is following a predictable hormonal rhythm. I need to pivot to a lower-effort task and engage my self-care buffer."*

- **Conserving Emotional Energy:** This compassionate response stops the cascade of self-criticism and stress, which would otherwise consume the limited emotional bandwidth required for resilience. You conserve vital emotional energy by refusing to fight against a temporary, neurobiological reality.

2. The Bridge to Long-Term Resilience

The data collected in this chapter is the essential link that connects all the pillars of this guide. It allows you to transform the external stability of time and focus management (Book 3) into a flexible, dynamic system that is resilient to internal volatility. You are using the language of science to honor the unique complexity of your brain and body, creating a foundation for true, integrated hormonal harmony.

Chapter 1 Workbook: Map Your Cycle: Track Symptoms to Pinpoint Hormonal High-Risk Days

Objective: To systematically collect objective data on how hormonal fluctuations impact ADHD symptoms and cognitive function, transforming subjective experience into actionable evidence.

Scientific Anchor: Tracking links perceived symptoms (e.g., anxiety, inattention) to measurable hormonal phases, providing the evidence needed to predict symptom spikes (especially in the low-estrogen luteal phase) and advocate for tailored support.

Activity 1.1: The Monthly Symptom / Cycle Tracker (Initial Audit)

Instructions: Commit to tracking for 30 consecutive days (Cycle Day 1 is the first day of your period). Use a scale of 1 (Minimal Impact) to 5 (Severe / Debilitating Impact) for consistency.

1. **Identify High-Risk Symptoms:** List the three ADHD symptoms that cause you the most distress during your known challenging times.

   Symptom 1 (Cognitive / Focus): _____

   _____

   _____

   Symptom 2 (Emotional / Mood): _____

   _____

   _____

   Symptom 3 (Functional / Task Initiation): _____

   _____

   _____

2. **Daily Tracking Log (Sample):** Record your data daily. After 30 days, identify your **Vulnerability Window** (the 3 to 7 days where the scores are consistently highest).

Cycle Day	Symptom 1 (Focus Score 1-5)	Symptom 2 (Irritability Score 1-5)	Medication Efficacy (1-5)	Notes (e.g., High Stress Day, Poor Sleep)
Day 1 (Period Start)				
Day 14 (Approx. Ovulation)				
Day 24 (Late Luteal)				
Day 28 (Premenstrual)				

Activity 1.2: Identifying Your Vulnerability Window

Instructions: Based on your completed 30-day log, review the data to pinpoint the predictable window where your EF and emotional resilience consistently dip.

1. **Peak Impairment Window:** Identify the range of days where your symptoms (scores of 4 or 5) consistently spike.

   My Vulnerability Window (Cycle Days):

   From Day _____

   To Day_____

2. **The Neurobiological Cause:** During this window, what functional change do you feel is the most detrimental (e.g., Working Memory collapses, or Task Activation is impossible)?

Functional Collapse: _____

_____

_____

_____

_____

Reflection 1.3: Data as Self-Advocacy

Instructions: Reflect on how this objective data shifts your emotional narrative and empowers your treatment plan, transforming anecdote into evidence.

1. **Shift from Shame:** Before tracking, when your symptoms worsened, what was your automatic internal thought (e.g., "I'm falling apart," "I can't handle this")?

Old Thought: _____

_____

_____

_____

2. **New Narrative:** How does having the **objective data** from your log allow you to replace that thought with a compassionate, non-judgmental, neurobiological explanation (e.g., "My estrogen is low; this dip is predictable")?

New, Empowered Narrative: _____

_____

_____

_____

3. **Advocacy Preparation:** Create one specific, data-informed sentence you can now use to start a conversation with your healthcare provider about your symptoms during the Luteal Phase.

Advocacy Sentence (e.g., "My tracking data shows a 40% drop in focus during Days X-Y, which aligns with low estrogen. What are our options for addressing this?"):

CHAPTER 2

OPTIMIZE YOUR FLOW: STRATEGICALLY SCHEDULE TASKS AROUND ENERGY PEAKS

In Chapter 1, you achieved the critical first step in managing hormonal chaos: systematic tracking of your cycle and the objective identification of your **Vulnerability Window**, the high-risk days characterized by low estrogen and a corresponding dip in neurochemical support. This data transforms your struggle from a confusing, subjective experience into a predictable, measurable pattern that demands strategic action.

This chapter moves from data collection to **strategic application**. The goal is to leverage the robust scheduling skills you mastered in Book 3 (**Time Blocking**, **Task Breakdown**) to intentionally **Optimize Your Flow** by aligning your cognitive demands with your hormonal energy peaks and troughs. This practice, often referred to as **Cycle Syncing**, is the definitive method for transforming unpredictable internal volatility into a manageable, structured rhythm. It is a necessary intervention for the ADHD brain, whose executive functions (EFs) are already inconsistent and become exacerbated by hormonal shifts.

For the woman with Attention-Deficit / Hyperactivity Disorder (ADHD), the key to defeating chronic overwhelm is to stop fighting her fluctuating neurochemical energy and start working *with* her unique neurobiology. By proactively scheduling high-leverage, complex tasks during periods of natural cognitive enhancement (high-estrogen phases) and reserving low-stakes, routine tasks for periods of inevitable cognitive drain (low-estrogen phases), you systematically buffer the impact of hormonal shifts, conserve precious mental energy, and achieve a sustainable state of control.

Section 1: The Neurochemistry of Cognitive Peaks and Troughs

The foundation of flow optimization lies in recognizing the distinct cognitive profiles associated with the two main phases of the menstrual cycle, the **Follicular Phase** and the **Luteal Phase**. These differences are a direct result of the varying levels of **Estrogen** and **Progesterone** and their powerful influence on the brain's neurotransmitter systems.

1. Estrogen: The Fuel for Focus and Organization

Estrogen, the primary hormone of the first half of the cycle, is a powerful ally to the ADHD brain. Research consistently confirms that estrogen plays a pivotal role in regulating the synthesis and activity of **dopamine**, the key neurotransmitter for attention, motivation, and Executive Function. Given that ADHD is fundamentally characterized by dopamine dysregulation, the level of estrogen directly dictates the brain's baseline capacity for focus and organization.

- **High Estrogen (Follicular / Ovulatory Phase):** When estrogen levels are high and rising (during the late follicular phase, leading up to ovulation), women often report finding it **easier to focus, sustain attention, stay organized, and engage in high-level cognitive tasks**. This is the period of peak cognitive function, your natural productivity advantage, making it ideal for deep work, planning, and problem-solving.

- **Low Estrogen (Luteal / Perimenstrual Phase):** The symptoms spike during the **luteal phase** (post-ovulation and preceding menstruation), which is characterized by a significant drop in estrogen. As estrogen diminishes, its supportive effect on the dopamine system collapses, exacerbating the underlying dopaminergic deficit of ADHD. This predictable neurochemical dip leads to a pronounced worsening of core ADHD symptoms, including **inattention, organization deficits, and executive dysfunction**.

2. Progesterone: The Complicating Factor in Emotional Regulation

Progesterone, which rises significantly during the **Luteal Phase**, further complicates the cognitive and emotional landscape. While often termed the "calming hormone" due to its role in boosting the inhibitory neurotransmitter GABA, its sustained presence in the context of declining estrogen leads to distinct challenges for the emotionally vulnerable ADHD brain:

- **Emotional Volatility:** The low-estrogen environment, coupled with the influence of progesterone, can increase the sensitivity of the brain's emotional center (the amygdala), leading to heightened irritability, anxiety, and low frustration tolerance.
- **Mental Sluggishness ("Brain Fog"):** The decline in both estrogen and progesterone in the late luteal / perimenstrual phase directly contributes to the feeling of **"brain fog,"** increased forgetfulness, mental fatigue, and sleep disturbances, which further impair focus and memory, core EF skills already challenged by ADHD.

The intentional goal of flow optimization is to use the structural integrity of your schedule (Time Blocking) to buffer these neurochemical dips, preventing the **Vulnerability Window** from triggering functional collapse and emotional overwhelm.

Section 2: The Cycle Syncing Framework: Aligning Task Demand

Cycle Syncing is the strategic process of aligning the **demand** of your scheduled tasks with the **supply** of your neurochemical energy. This framework utilizes the predictable energy shifts to schedule work that is easiest for your brain to manage in that specific phase, conserving your limited EF when support is low.

1. Phase 1: The Follicular / Ovulatory Phase (Peak Cognitive Function)

When: Typically from the end of the period until ovulation (approximately Days 6–14). Estrogen levels are rising or high.

Cognitive Profile: This is your **peak cognitive window**. Attention is generally more stable, motivation is higher (dopamine supported), and executive functions are most robust. You possess the greatest capacity for deep, sustained work and resistance to frustration.

Strategic Task Scheduling (High-Leverage Work):

- **Deep Work and Focused Sprints:** Schedule your most complex, cognitively demanding tasks, such as report writing, coding, complex planning, studying, and learning new skills. Utilize your longest **Pomodoro sprints** (e.g., 45–50 minutes) during this time, maximizing the mental acuity provided by high estrogen.

- **Goal Setting and Planning:** Dedicate time for strategic planning, setting major goals, tackling ambiguous projects (which require high EF), and initiating new creative work.

- **Communication and Socializing:** Schedule high-stakes meetings, difficult conversations, or challenging social engagements, as your emotional regulation, confidence, and verbal fluency are at their best.

2. Phase 2: The Luteal / Perimenstrual Phase (Strategic Conservation)

When: Typically from post-ovulation until the start of the period (approximately Days 15–28). Estrogen is dropping, and symptoms are worsening. This is your **Vulnerability Window** identified in Chapter 1.

Cognitive Profile: This is your low-energy phase. Focus, working memory, and emotional regulation dip. Irritability, anxiety, and task initiation deficits (paralysis) increase. The brain is conserving energy due to low estrogen support.

Strategic Task Scheduling (Low-Friction / Routine Work):

- **Routine and Maintenance:** Prioritize low-stakes, routine, and highly structured maintenance tasks that require minimal EF input. Examples include filing, performing the **Daily 15-Minute Reset** (Book 1), simple administrative chores, running established errands, or answering low-priority emails.

- **Review and Editing:** Schedule tasks that require detailed, but non-creative, focus—such as proofreading, editing a report drafted in the Follicular Phase, or organizing established systems (e.g., sorting the Junk Drawer).

- **Self-Care and Recovery:** Schedule mandatory blocks for rest, relaxation, and proactive stress management. This is the time to aggressively enforce boundaries and decline commitments that will overextend your limited EF reserves.

Section 3: Tactical Adaptation of Executive Function Tools

The Time Blocking system you built in Book 3 must be flexible enough to adapt its parameters during the low-energy Luteal Phase. Successfully optimizing your flow requires modifying your approach to planning and focus based on your current neurochemical reality.

1. Adjusting Time Blocks and Buffers (Chapter 1, Book 3)

During the Luteal Phase, the **Estimation Deficit**, the tendency to underestimate task duration, is likely to be exacerbated by mental fatigue and compromised Working Memory. Your scheduled blocks must adjust proactively.

- **Increase the Estimation Buffer:** Double your usual time buffer. If you typically schedule 25% extra time for a task, increase it to **50% extra time** during the Vulnerability Window. Acknowledge that the process of loading information into your working memory will be slower, and transitions will be harder. This proactive adjustment reduces the stress of rushing, which would otherwise compound EF deficits.

- **Shorter, More Frequent Transition Blocks:** The high cognitive cost of **context switching** is intensified when focus is low. Schedule a **mandatory 10-minute break** between all major time blocks, rather than the standard 5-minute break. Use this time for physical movement (a brief walk) or sensory grounding to clear the mental slate before the next activity, conserving EF.

- **Color-Code for Energy:** When creating your time-blocked calendar, use a specific color (e.g., red or gray) to designate the high-risk Luteal Phase days, serving as a constant **external cue** to manage expectations for performance and prioritize self-compassion.

2. Modifying the Pomodoro Technique (Chapter 3, Book 3)

The customized Pomodoro cycle must contract during the low-energy phase to maintain its effectiveness and prevent burnout. The goal is to maximize the short bursts of attention available.

- **Contract the Work Sprint:** If your optimal work sprint is usually 45 minutes, contract it to **20 or 25 minutes** during the low-energy window. The commitment must feel short and finite to overcome the **task activation deficit** (paralysis) that flares up when motivation is low.

- **Lengthen the Break (Intentional Recovery):** Increase the break duration to 7 or 10 minutes. Use this mandated time for active recovery, movement, stretching, or engaging in a simple, non-productive reward. This intentional recovery period counteracts the high levels of **mental fatigue** that accompany the drop in estrogen, providing the novelty needed for the ADHD brain to re-engage.

- **Anchor with External Accountability:** During the low-motivation Luteal Phase, the need for **external scaffolding** is highest. Proactively schedule Body Doubling sessions (Book 1) for the tasks that you know will be difficult to initiate, as the presence of a non-judgmental peer provides the external executive function necessary to bridge the gap between intention and action.

Section 4: Holistic Buffering: Protecting Vulnerable Energy

Optimizing your flow is not just about moving tasks on a calendar; it is about building holistic resilience against the stress and emotional volatility that impair executive functions. When hormonal support is low, proactive self-care becomes the most critical EF strategy.

1. Prioritizing Sleep Hygiene and Physiological Support

Quality sleep and stable physical health are the non-negotiable foundations for robust EF and mood regulation. Sleep deprivation exacerbates both ADHD and hormonal symptoms.

- **The Circadian Anchor:** Enforce strict, consistent sleep hygiene, particularly during the Vulnerability Window, by maintaining a fixed bedtime and wake time. This regularity helps anchor the brain's circadian rhythm, which is vital for stabilizing the neurochemistry that governs attention and mood.

- **Movement for Neurochemistry:** Regular **physical exercise** is a potent, evidence-based tool for regulating dopamine levels, reducing restlessness, and improving mood, acting as a direct buffer against the emotional volatility of the luteal phase. Schedule a brisk walk or light exercise during this time, ensuring movement is prioritized over static work.

- **Nutritional Stability:** Maintain stable blood sugar levels through consistent consumption of lean protein and complex carbohydrates. Avoiding the sharp energy spikes and crashes from excessive sugar intake is essential, as these crashes exacerbate EF and mood deficits, particularly when estrogen levels are already low.

2. Enforcing Emotional Boundaries and Self-Compassion

Stress consumes immense EF resources. During the high-risk Luteal Phase, you must ruthlessly enforce boundaries to minimize stress and engage compassionate self-talk.

- **Enforce the Boundary Matrix:** Limit exposure to emotionally taxing situations and people (Q3 demands) that are harder to handle when emotional regulation is compromised by hormonal shifts. Use the prioritization frameworks from Book 3 to confidently decline external demands that would overwhelm your schedule.

- **Mindfulness and Stress Reduction:** Schedule brief, non-negotiable **mindfulness practices**, such as deep breathing or the 5-4-3-2-1 grounding exercise, to manage the increased anxiety and internal restlessness. The goal is to prevent the physiological arousal of stress from further depleting your already limited EF reserves.

- **Radical Acceptance:** When a symptom spike occurs during the Vulnerability Window, the response is not criticism, but **self-compassion**, treating yourself with the same kindness and understanding you would offer a friend. This compassionate response stops the cascade of self-criticism and stress, which would otherwise consume the limited emotional bandwidth required for resilience. The narrative shifts from "I am failing" to "My body is following a predictable pattern."

Conclusion: Sustaining Predictability in a Dynamic System

The journey of optimizing your flow is the definitive step toward integrated self-mastery for the ADHD woman. By recognizing the profound, dynamic influence of your hormones on your executive functions, you stop fighting against your own neurobiology and start building a supportive, resilient framework.

You have learned to align the powerful, external structure of **Time Blocking** with the internal reality of your **hormonal cycle**. This strategic approach ensures that the mental energy you conserved through organization and focus mastery is deployed with maximum efficiency. You are moving from a frantic cycle of reactive overwhelm and symptom spikes to a calm, self-directed rhythm that honors your brain's unique need for both structure and self-compassion.

This mastery of cyclical stability is the essential platform for the high-stakes conversations that follow, advocating for medication adjustment (Chapter 3) and navigating the profound cognitive shifts of perimenopause (Chapter 4), and for engaging in the deep emotional work of the rest of the guide.

Chapter 2 Workbook: Optimize Your Flow: Strategically Schedule Tasks Around Energy Peaks

Objective: To practice aligning cognitive demands with the specific energy peaks and troughs of your Follicular (High Energy) and Luteal (Low Energy) phases.

Scientific Anchor: Strategically scheduling high-demand tasks during high-estrogen phases and low-demand tasks during low-estrogen phases conserves EF resources and reduces the shame of underperformance, providing a necessary buffer against hormonal shifts.

Activity 2.1: The Task Alignment Audit

Instructions: Identify the cognitive demands of your common tasks and assign them to the most supportive hormonal phase.

1. **Follicular / Ovulatory Phase (High Energy / Focus):** List three tasks requiring high **Working Memory, planning, or Inhibitory Control**.

   Task 1 (Example: Financial Planning / Budgeting):

   Task 2 (Complex Communication / Deep Work):

   Task 3 (Goal Setting / Strategy):

   ----

2. **Luteal / Vulnerability Phase (Low Energy / Routine):** List three tasks requiring minimal cognitive effort or tasks that are routine and established (low activation energy).

   Task 1 (Routine Maintenance): (Example: Filing receipts, simple chores.)

   Task 2 (Low-Cognitive Output / Review):

   Task 3 (Self-Care / Recovery):

Activity 2.2: Adapting Your Time Block Parameters

Instructions: Select a standard, recurring task (e.g., "Work on project X"). Show how you will change the **Time Block** and **Pomodoro** parameters during your identified **Vulnerability Window** (Luteal Phase) to compensate for low focus.

1. Standard Follicular Phase (High Focus):

Time Block / Interval	Duration	Neuro-Adjustment
Core Work Block	90 minutes	Standard commitment.
Pomodoro Cycle	45 min Work / 5 min Rest	Long, sustained effort.
Time Buffer	15% extra time	Standard Estimation Buffer.

2. Luteal / Vulnerability Phase (Low Focus):

Time Block / Interval	Duration	Neuro-Adjustment (The Buffer)
Core Work Block	90 minutes	Reduce work time to **60 minutes** or break into shorter blocks.
Pomodoro Cycle	Min Work ____ Min Rest _____	Contract work sprint (e.g., 20 / 10) to honor low focus and lengthen break for recovery.
Time Buffer	Extra time ____%	Increase buffer to 50% extra time for slow processing / fatigue.

Reflection 2.3: Shifting from Shame to Acceptance

Instructions: Reflect on how proactive planning impacts the emotional burden of performance.

1. **Defeating the Inner Critic:** When you fail to complete a complex task during the Luteal Phase, the inner critic often says, "You're useless, you should be able to do this." How does the simple act of looking at your calendar and seeing the block color-coded as "Low-Energy / High-Risk" provide a compassionate, factual response to that critic?

    Factual Response: _____
    _____
    _____
    _____

2. **Conserving Energy:** How does scheduling intentional, low-friction tasks (like maintenance) during the Luteal Phase contribute to your overall **Executive Function conservation**?

    EF Conservation: _____
    _____
    _____
    _____

3. **Future-Proofing:** What is one specific, non-work activity (e.g., physical movement, social buffer) that you will now **proactively schedule** during your next Vulnerability Window to act as a buffer against emotional volatility?

    Scheduled Buffer: _____
    _____
    _____
    _____

CHAPTER 3

ADVOCATE FOR ADJUSTMENT: DISCUSS CYCLE DOSING OF STIMULANTS WITH YOUR DOCTOR

You have successfully achieved the essential foundation of hormonal self-management: objective tracking of your cycle and the identification of your **Vulnerability Window**, the high-risk days when low estrogen causes a predictable collapse in focus, organization, and emotional resilience (Chapter 1). This data is not just for internal use; it is your single most powerful tool for **self-advocacy** in the medical setting.

This chapter addresses the critical next step: translating your personal data into an informed discussion with your healthcare provider about **optimizing your pharmacological treatment**. The traditional, male-normed approach to ADHD often assumes a static effective dose of medication, but a woman's neurochemistry is dynamic, fluctuating monthly with her hormones. The goal is to initiate a dialogue about **Cycle Dosing**, tailoring the dose of psychostimulants to align with your hormonal status, a strategy that addresses the documented **gender health gap** and aims to stabilize your cognitive function during your most challenging days.

This is a powerful act of informed self-care, moving you from passively accepting a fluctuating standard of care to proactively commanding a treatment plan that is personalized, dynamic, and neurobiologically accurate.

Section 1: The Neurochemical Reality of Medication Efficacy

The anecdotal experience of many women, that their ADHD medication seems to "stop working" in the days leading up to their period, is validated by the core neurochemistry of ADHD and the hormonal cycle. This phenomenon has a clear, scientific basis rooted in the interaction between estrogen and dopamine.

1. Estrogen's Role in Stimulant Response

Stimulant medications, such as amphetamines, work by increasing the availability and efficacy of **dopamine** and **norepinephrine** in the brain, thereby improving attention and executive function. However, the efficacy of this process is not independent of hormonal context.

- **Dopamine Dependence:** Estrogen acts as a supportive ally to the dopamine system, enhancing dopamine synthesis and receptor sensitivity.

- **Diminished Response:** Research, including clinical monitoring and preliminary studies, suggests that during the **late luteal phase** (the days preceding menstruation), the significant drop in estrogen levels diminishes this supportive effect. This hormonal drop can reduce the overall dopamine baseline, making the prescribed static dose of psychostimulant medication less effective at managing symptoms.

- **The Symptom Spike:** Consequently, during this low-estrogen phase, women often report a return or worsening of core ADHD symptoms, including pronounced **inattention, task paralysis, and emotional volatility**, even while taking their regular medication.

This neurochemical reality provides the foundation for demanding a dynamic, rather than static, approach to dosage.

2. The Unmet Need and the Gender Health Gap

The recognition of this cycle-dependent efficacy highlights a significant **gender health gap** in ADHD treatment. For decades, the fluctuations experienced by women were often dismissed as subjective or attributed to premenstrual moodiness, leaving a major unmet clinical need.

- **Lack of Research:** Only a very limited number of studies have formally investigated the effects of sex hormones on stimulants in women with ADHD, and even fewer have provided specific treatment recommendations tailored to the menstrual cycle.
- **Mismatched Treatment:** The current standard of care, a fixed, unchanging dose, is often mismatched to the dynamic neurobiological reality of the menstruating female brain, potentially leading to unnecessary suffering and self-blame during the high-risk Luteal Phase.

Section 2: The Strategy of Cycle Dosing

Cycle dosing refers to the clinical strategy of tailoring psychostimulant medication dosages to align with a woman's hormonal status. This approach aims to proactively counteract the anticipated neurochemical dip before symptoms intensify.

1. The Rationale for Dose Adjustment

The goal of increasing the dose during the vulnerability window is to compensate for the reduction in estrogen's supportive effect, thereby stabilizing the dopamine system and preventing the symptomatic collapse that typically occurs premenstrually.

- **Targeted Intervention:** Preliminary studies suggest that increasing the dosage of psychostimulant medication premenstrually may help combat the worsening of cognitive and emotional symptoms in vulnerable women with ADHD. This strategy offers a more refined, individualized approach to treatment, addressing a period where treatment outcome is often compromised.
- **Clinical Guidance:** While extensive research is still required, clinical monitoring and small studies provide guidance for the management of women with ADHD, suggesting that dosage adjustments in the late luteal phase may be beneficial for those who experience predictable, clinically significant symptom worsening.

2. The Necessity of Physician Oversight

Crucially, cycle dosing must be individually explored and implemented only under the close supervision of a physician or psychiatrist specialized in adult female ADHD. The process is highly individualized and depends on the specific medication, dosage, and a woman's unique symptom profile.

- **Implementation Strategy:** The typical approach involves identifying the specific **Vulnerability Window** (e.g., the 5–7 days before the period begins) and establishing a structured protocol for a minor, temporary increase in the prescribed stimulant dose during that window, followed by a return to the standard dose for the remainder of the cycle.
- **Focus on Symptoms:** The decision to adjust the dose should be based entirely on the **functional impairment** experienced during the low-estrogen phase (e.g., severe collapse in Working Memory, profound emotional dysregulation, or task paralysis), not merely on the calendar date.

Section 3: Empowering Self-Advocacy with Objective Data

To initiate a successful discussion about dose adjustment, you must provide your physician with objective data that transforms your anecdotal experience into measurable, quantifiable evidence of a cycle-symptom correlation. This is where the tracking completed in Chapter 1 becomes indispensable.

1. The Data Presentation: From Feeling to Factual Evidence

Instead of reporting vague feelings of being "more irritable" or "less focused," you should present your **Symptom Log** (Chapter 1) as factual evidence:

- **Quantify the Dip:** "My data shows that during Cycle Days 23–28 (the late luteal phase), my average score for **Inattention / Focus** increases from 2 to 5, and my self-rated **Medication Efficacy** drops by 40%. This decline consistently impairs my ability to perform scheduled work tasks during this window."
- **Target the Problem:** This shifts the conversation from addressing a mood issue to managing a documented neurochemical fluctuation that impairs executive function, aligning the discussion with the mechanisms of ADHD treatment.
- **Frame the Solution:** Propose the strategy as a proactive measure for stability: "Given this predictable pattern, I would like to explore evidence-based options for compensating for this dip, starting with a monitored, temporary dose increase during the last five days of my luteal phase."

2. Partnering with Specialized Professionals

Navigating hormonal treatment requires a multidisciplinary approach, often involving coordination between several professionals:

- **ADHD Specialist:** Seek a psychiatrist or medical doctor who has explicit experience treating **adult female ADHD** and is knowledgeable about the impact of hormonal fluctuations (the **ADHD health gap**).
- **Hormone Therapy Integration (Midlife):** For women in perimenopause or menopause (Chapter 4), coordinating treatment with a gynecologist or endocrinologist who is open to **Hormone Replacement Therapy (HRT)** is essential. HRT often works synergistically with stimulant medication to stabilize cognitive and emotional symptoms by increasing the baseline level of supportive estrogen.

Section 4: The Holistic Context: Conserving Energy and Defeating Shame

The strategy of cycle dosing is an essential part of a holistic plan, not the entire solution. Its true power is realized when it works in conjunction with the structural strategies you have already mastered.

1. EF Strategies as a Buffer Against Hormonal Chaos

Even with optimized medication, the low-estrogen phase still presents a challenge. The structural stability you created in Book 3 acts as the critical behavioral and cognitive buffer that prevents the internal dip from becoming an external crisis.

- **Time Blocking and Prioritization:** During the Vulnerability Window, you should rigidly enforce your **Time Block schedule** and **Prioritization Frameworks** (Q2 / Goal tasks only). The external structure compensates for the internal loss of Working Memory and Inhibitory Control, ensuring functional stability even when the brain is struggling internally.
- **Reducing Cognitive Load:** Aggressively reduce **Cognitive Load** during this phase (e.g., eliminating all non-essential meetings, enforcing strict **Notification Annihilation**) to conserve the limited EF reserves you have.

2. Defeating Shame through Knowledge and Self-Compassion

Perhaps the greatest payoff of understanding cycle-dependent efficacy is the liberation from shame. For years, the woman blamed her own effort when her focus collapsed.

- **The Factual Response to the Inner Critic:** Knowledge transforms the internal conversation. When symptoms worsen, the self-talk shifts from, *"I'm useless; I can't focus"* to, *"My estrogen support has dipped; this is a predictable neurochemical* *reality. I am being strategic by adjusting my demands and relying on my schedule."*

- **Sustainable Self-Efficacy:** By taking proactive, informed control over her treatment, the woman builds a profound sense of **self-efficacy** and agency. She replaces the cycle of frustration and failure with a system of compassionate, effective management, moving toward genuine self-acceptance.

Conclusion: Committing to Dynamic, Personalized Care

The journey through this chapter marks the shift to personalized, dynamic care that honors your unique neurobiology. You have moved beyond the static, one-size-fits-all model of treatment and armed yourself with the data and knowledge necessary to command an optimized plan.

By combining the rigor of cycle tracking with the external scaffolding of your Time Blocks and the willingness to advocate for appropriate pharmacological support, you stabilize your neurochemistry across the entire month. This stability is the vital bridge to mastering emotional resilience and building lasting, healthy relationships in the final books of this guide.

Chapter 3 Workbook: Advocate for Adjustment: Discuss Cycle Dosing of Stimulants with Your Doctor

Objective: To prepare objective data and strategic communication points to advocate for a personalized medication approach (Cycle Dosing) with a healthcare professional.

Scientific Anchor: Clinical data suggests that psychostimulant efficacy can diminish during the low-estrogen luteal phase. Proactive, temporary dose adjustments may help compensate for the premenstrual worsening of cognitive and emotional symptoms.

Activity 3.1: Data Consolidation for Advocacy

Instructions: Based on your Symptom Log (Chapter 1), consolidate the objective data needed to make your case.

1. **My Vulnerability Window:** Identify the exact days your symptoms peak (Luteal Phase).

   From Cycle Day: _____

   To Day: _____

2. **Quantify Functional Impairment:** Calculate the average change in your focus and medication efficacy during this window.

    Average Inattention / Focus Score (Peak Window): _____ (e.g., 4 or 5)

    Average Medication Efficacy Score (Peak Window) :_____ (e.g., 1=Effective, 5=Ineffective)

3. **Specific Behavioral Impairment:** Name one high-leverage task you consistently struggle to complete or initiate during this window (e.g., financial administrative tasks, deep work, or managing conflict).

    Impaired Task: _____

    _____

    _____

    _____

Activity 3.2: The Advocacy Script Preparation

Instructions: Craft a concise, professional script to initiate the conversation with your doctor, using factual data rather than subjective complaints.

1. **Opening Statement (Factual):** State the correlation between your cycle and your function.

    Script: "Doctor, I've been tracking my ADHD symptoms and medication response over the last months, and my data shows a clear pattern." _____

2. **The Solution Proposal (Informed Request):** Propose the evidence-based strategy you wish to explore.

    Script: "Given this predictable decline, I would like to explore the potential benefit of a monitored, temporary dose increase during Cycle Days _____ to _____to prevent the premenstrual worsening of my symptoms, as supported by current guidance on cycle dosing."

3. **Holistic Context:** Briefly mention the non-pharmacological buffers you already have in place to show commitment to self-management.

    Buffer: "I am proactively managing my schedule by using **Time Blocking** and **Body Doubling** during this phase."

Reflection 3.3: Partnering with Your Care Team

Instructions: Reflect on the emotional significance of this act of advocacy.

1. **Defeating the Gender Gap:** How does bringing objective data to your appointment help you overcome the historical tendency of the medical system to dismiss or misattribute female symptom fluctuations?

   Benefit: _____

   _____

   _____

   _____

   _____

2. **Self-Efficacy Gain:** Regardless of the immediate outcome of the discussion, how does the act of preparing this data and making a clear, informed request increase your sense of control and self-efficacy?

   Control Gained: _____

   _____

   _____

   _____

   _____

3. **Midlife Preparation:** If you are approaching perimenopause or menopause, what is one question you will ask your doctor about **Hormone Replacement Therapy (HRT)** in relation to stabilizing your Executive Function?

   Question: _____

   _____

   _____

   _____

   _____

CHAPTER 4

MANAGE THE TRANSITION: NAVIGATE PERIMENOPAUSE AND MENOPAUSAL BRAIN FOG

The hormonal influence on the female ADHD brain culminates in midlife, presenting what is often the most profound and challenging period of cognitive shift. While the previous chapters focused on the monthly fluctuations of the menstrual cycle, this chapter addresses the sustained, systemic decline of hormones during **perimenopause** and **menopause**. This transition is frequently the tipping point where underlying Attention-Deficit / Hyperactivity Disorder (ADHD) symptoms, which a woman may have successfully masked or compensated for over decades, become significantly and often suddenly unmanageable.

Experts refer to this phenomenon as the **"ADHD Squared"** effect: the compounding of an already dopamine-dysregulated system with the severe, sustained decline of supporting hormones. This chapter provides the strategic roadmap for understanding this crisis, managing the ensuing "brain fog," and advocating for the integrated, dynamic treatment required to stabilize Executive Function (EF) and emotional resilience during this high-risk life stage.

The goal is to provide validation that the cognitive collapse you may be experiencing is a measurable neurobiological reality, not a personal failure or a sign of premature aging, and to empower you to maintain command over your attention and well-being.

Section 1: The Neurobiological Crisis: The "ADHD Squared" Effect

Perimenopause is the transition period leading up to menopause, characterized by unpredictable and often severe fluctuations in estrogen and progesterone. Menopause is defined as twelve months after a woman's final menstrual period. This hormonal shift directly impacts the neurochemistry that supports attention, memory, and emotional control, thereby intensifying pre-existing ADHD deficits.

1. Estrogen Decline and the Collapse of Cognitive Support

The sustained decline of **Estrogen** is the primary driver of the cognitive crisis in midlife ADHD. Estrogen, as established, acts as a crucial supportive ally to the brain's **dopamine system**, enhancing dopamine synthesis and receptor sensitivity.

- **The Compounding Deficit:** Because the ADHD brain is already deficient or dysregulated in dopamine, the removal of estrogen's supportive effect creates a profound neurochemical vulnerability. The resulting sustained drop in dopamine levels exacerbates core ADHD symptoms, a compounding effect that is experienced as a major functional decline.

- **Impact on EF:** This decline, in turn, directly impacts the neurotransmitters required for attention, regulating emotions, organizational skills, and memory. For women without ADHD, this decline may manifest as mild "brain fog"; for women with ADHD, these symptoms become significantly more severe, magnifying organizational difficulties, attention lapses, and the need for specialized treatment.

2. Progesterone Loss and Emotional Volatility

The decline in **Progesterone** further compromises emotional stability and sleep quality, both of which are critical for maintaining functional EF.

- **Loss of Calming Buffer:** Progesterone is often referred to as the "calming hormone" due to its role in boosting **GABA** (gamma-aminobutyric acid), a neurotransmitter that helps reduce feelings of stress and promote relaxation. As progesterone levels decline or fluctuate erratically, this crucial inhibitory (calming) effect is lost.

- **Increased Reactivity:** For women whose emotional regulation is already vulnerable due to ADHD, the loss of this GABA-boosting buffer leads to **increased anxiety, irritability, and heightened sensitivity to stress**. This makes the woman more reactive and prone to emotional outbursts, complicating relationships and increasing the risk of burnout. The sleep disturbances associated with this phase further compound the issue, as chronic fatigue drastically impairs Working Memory and Inhibitory Control.

Section 2: The Manifestation: Navigating Menopausal Brain Fog

The physiological effects of hormonal decline translate into a crisis of Executive Function that often mirrors the worst unmanaged ADHD symptoms, leading to confusion and self-doubt.

1. Profound Working Memory Failure ("Brain Fog")

The term "brain fog" accurately describes the collapse of Working Memory (WM) and processing speed that many women experience. WM is the temporary "mental scratchpad" needed for multi-tasking, complex planning, and holding instructions in mind.

- **Impaired Multi-Tasking and Planning:** The decline in estrogen directly impairs the ability to multitask, reason, plan, and problem-solve, skills that are foundational to EF mastery. A woman who previously compensated for her ADHD by meticulously planning may suddenly find her organizational systems ineffective and her capacity for managing multiple demands severely diminished.

- **Memory Lapses and Forgetfulness:** Memory problems become more pronounced, going beyond misplaced keys to include difficulty retrieving words, forgetting recent conversations, or losing the thread of complex projects. This loss of reliable recall feeds anxiety and undermines the confidence that the woman painstakingly built through her EF strategies.

2. Worsening of Core ADHD Symptoms

The symptoms that might have been manageable in early adulthood, inattention, disorganization, and low motivation, are likely to become the dominant feature of daily life, potentially "unmasking" a previously undiagnosed condition or severely intensifying a diagnosed one.

- **Loss of Inhibitory Control:** Increased anxiety and irritability, stemming from progesterone loss, weaken **Inhibitory Control (IC)**, making it harder to pause before speaking, resist impulsive spending, or manage frustration. This can lead to increased relational friction and renewed feelings of being "out of control."
- **Diminished Medication Efficacy:** The low-dopamine environment created by low estrogen can reduce the effectiveness of stimulant medication, leading to the frustrating feeling that the dose is no longer adequate, even if the woman's body size or activity level has not changed. This requires immediate reevaluation of the treatment plan.

Section 3: The Strategic Imperative: Integrating Dynamic Treatment

Managing ADHD during this transition requires abandoning the static treatment model in favor of an integrated, dynamic approach that utilizes both pharmacological and hormonal support.

1. HRT and Stimulant Integration: Offsetting the Decline

The goal of treatment in this phase is to offset the sustained loss of estrogen and its supportive effect on the dopamine system. This often requires a combined therapeutic approach, which is considered the most helpful strategy.

- **Hormone Replacement Therapy (HRT):** HRT is a primary tool for increasing estrogen levels, which can directly mitigate the cognitive and emotional severity of the menopause transition. HRT works synergistically with stimulant medication by restoring the supportive hormonal environment, making the ADHD medication more effective at stabilizing dopamine. Research suggests that taking HRT can improve menopausal women's memory, reasoning, multi-tasking, planning, and problem-solving, which are all critical EF skills.
- **Stimulant Adjustment:** For women already taking ADHD medication, a physician may offer an increase in dose to directly offset the effects of the changing hormone levels and the corresponding drop in dopamine. The decision to use HRT, adjust stimulants, or combine both is highly individualized and must be done under specialized medical supervision.

2. The Necessity of Coordinated Care and Self-Advocacy

Navigating midlife ADHD requires a woman to become a fierce advocate for personalized care, often coordinating treatment between specialists who understand this intersection.

- **Multidisciplinary Approach:** It is critical to work with professionals who recognize the ADHD-hormone link, typically coordinating care between a psychiatrist (for ADHD medication / dose adjustment) and a gynecologist or internist (for hormone management / HRT).

- **Demand Data-Driven Care:** A woman must continue to track her symptoms (Chapter 1) to provide objective evidence of the correlation between the hormonal transition and the severity of her EF deficits. This data is essential to validate her experience and ensure the treatment plan is tailored to her specific need for cognitive stability.

Section 4: Non-Pharmacological Buffering: Supporting the PFC

When the brain is experiencing persistent decline, the external EF strategies mastered in Book 3 become non-negotiable structural buffers that prevent total functional collapse.

1. Enforcing Structural and Memory Systems

The memory and organizational systems that were once helpful now become essential survival tools against "brain fog."

- **Offload Working Memory:** Rigorously enforce the externalization of all instructions and schedules. Use fixed **Checklists** and **Templates** (Chapter 4, Book 3) for all multi-step processes, ensuring that unreliable WM is not the keeper of essential information.

- **Simplify Decisions:** Combat decision fatigue (Chapter 5, Book 3) by automating choices (e.g., automated bill pay, fixed meal plans) and strictly adhering to the **Constraint Principle** (limiting options). This conserves the highly limited EF reserves for critical thinking.

- **Routines as Anchors:** Maintain rigorous **fixed routines** (e.g., Nightly Offload, Time Blocking) to provide a predictable structure that the vulnerable PFC can rely on, minimizing the stress and cognitive effort associated with uncertainty.

2. Proactive Self-Care for Mood and Focus

The physical and emotional well-being factors that support the PFC must be aggressively prioritized during this phase to mitigate the severity of symptom worsening.

- **Prioritize Rest and Recovery:** Schedule mandatory, non-negotiable **recovery blocks** into the Time Block schedule. Recognizing and honoring the profound **mental fatigue** that accompanies this transition is essential for preventing burnout.

- **Movement and Neurochemistry:** Regular physical exercise remains a potent tool to stimulate dopamine release and improve mood, directly buffering the negative effects of the hormonal decline.

- **Emotional Support:** Given the heightened emotional volatility and anxiety caused by progesterone loss, actively use **mindfulness and grounding techniques** (Chapter 1, Book 4) to manage stress and prevent emotional escalations. Maintaining a low stress baseline is crucial, as stress further impairs EF function.

Conclusion: A New Era of Self-Acceptance

The journey through perimenopause and menopause can feel like a profound test of self-control and identity, especially for the woman with ADHD. However, armed with scientific knowledge, this transition becomes a predictable phase that can be strategically managed.

The mastery gained here allows you to move beyond the shame of cognitive decline, replacing self-criticism with **radical acceptance** and a focused, data-driven approach. You are commanding an integrated system, combining pharmacological and hormonal support with the rigorous structural management of your EF toolkit, to maintain your cognitive stability and emotional resilience during this complex, powerful era of change. This ability to navigate the shifting sands of your neurobiology with informed grace is the ultimate expression of self-mastery.

Chapter 4 Workbook: Manage the Transition: Navigate Perimenopause and Menopausal Brain Fog

Objective: To create a personalized, proactive plan for managing the sustained cognitive and emotional dips associated with the perimenopausal / menopausal transition, using data to inform self-advocacy.

Scientific Anchor: ADHD symptoms worsen due to the decline of estrogen / progesterone. Strategic management involves integrated treatment (HRT / medication) and rigid EF scaffolding to buffer WM / IC deficits.

Activity 4.1: The Midlife Symptom Audit

Instructions: Identify the three cognitive and emotional symptoms that have become most problematic *since* starting perimenopause (or in the last two years), as these represent the "ADHD Squared" effect.

1. **Symptom 1 (Cognitive / WM Collapse):** (e.g., Forgetting words, losing items, difficulty multitasking / planning)

   Symptom: _____

2. **Symptom 2 (Emotional / Anxiety):** (e.g., Increased anxiety, low patience, irritability / snapping)

   Symptom: _____

3. **Symptom 3 (Functional / Initiation):** (e.g., Severe task paralysis, constant fatigue / brain fog)

   Symptom: _____

Activity 4.2: Integrated Treatment Advocacy Plan

Instructions: Prepare a strategic statement for your healthcare provider regarding integrated treatment options, based on evidence.

1. **Data Point:** My most prominent cognitive deficit is ___ (*Symptom 1*).

2. **HRT Question:** To address this decline in Executive Function, I would like to discuss whether **Hormone Replacement Therapy (HRT)** could stabilize the hormonal support for my attention.

   Commitment: I will schedule an appointment with a gynecologist or internist to discuss HRT options.

3. **Medication Adjustment Proposal:** If you are taking stimulants, draft the question you will ask your psychiatrist about offsetting the sustained decline.

   Question: "Given the sustained hormonal decline, is an increase in my **stimulant dosage** a possible strategy to offset the loss of estrogen's neurochemical support, or should we consider an alternative medication to support cognitive function?"

Reflection 4.3: Buffering the Brain Fog

Instructions: Reflect on how the structured EF strategies from Book 3 act as a non-pharmacological buffer against the worsening symptoms of this transition.

1. **WM Offload Strategy:** When you are experiencing severe "brain fog" (Symptom 1), what single **external system** (e.g., a specific checklist, writing everything down immediately, using a visible timer) will you rely on most heavily to ensure you complete tasks?

   External System: _____

   _____

   _____

   _____

   _____

2. **Self-Compassion and Acceptance:** When you find yourself forgetting something critical, the inner critic often attacks. How will the knowledge that your struggles are due to a predictable, documented **sustained hormonal change** help you replace self-criticism with self-compassion?

   Compassionate Reframe: _____

   _____

   _____

   _____

   _____

3. **Stress Buffer:** Given that anxiety and irritability (Symptom 2) worsen due to progesterone loss, what **physiological reset** (e.g., 10 minutes of walking, deep breathing) will you commit to scheduling daily to mitigate stress and conserve your vulnerable EF?

   Scheduled Buffer: _____

   _____

   _____

   _____

   _____

CHAPTER 5

BUILD YOUR BUFFER: PRIORITIZE SLEEP AND NUTRITION TO STABILIZE MOOD

You have achieved the essential structural and advocacy goals of this book: objective tracking of your hormonal cycle (Chapter 1), strategic alignment of your workflow (Chapter 2), and informed advocacy for optimizing medication during hormonal dips (Chapter 3) and midlife transitions (Chapter 4). This foundation of knowledge and external support is vital, but sustainable stability requires integrating this strategy with your basic physiology.

This chapter addresses the final, non-negotiable pillar of hormonal harmony: building a resilient **physiological buffer** against volatility. For the woman with Attention-Deficit / Hyperactivity Disorder (ADHD), who already struggles with neurochemical stability, insufficient **sleep**, poor **nutrition**, and chronic **stress** act as direct hormonal disruptors. These factors not only exacerbate ADHD symptoms but actively impair Executive Functions (EFs) and undermine emotional regulation, especially during the low-estrogen phases.

The goal here is to transform foundational self-care into a strategic, evidence-based tool for stability. By prioritizing consistent sleep hygiene and steady, brain-supporting fuel, you proactively regulate the nervous system, conserve vital EF reserves, and build a buffer of emotional resilience that is resistant to both hormonal shifts and the daily friction of life.

Section 1: Sleep Hygiene:
The Non-Negotiable Foundation of Executive Function

For anyone, quality sleep is crucial, but for the woman with ADHD, sleep consistency is the bedrock of sustained focus, emotional control, and Working Memory (WM). Disruptions to sleep directly impair the prefrontal cortex (PFC), the brain's command center for EF.

1. The Neurobiological Cost of Sleep Deprivation

Research shows that sleep problems are highly prevalent in adults with ADHD, with studies indicating that sleep deprivation in this population can be as functionally impairing as the core ADHD symptoms themselves. Sleep problems are often linked to both the hyperactivity / restlessness symptoms and the difficulties with consistent routine required for good sleep hygiene.

- **EF Impairment:** During sleep, the brain restores the PFC's capacity. Lack of sleep directly depletes **Working Memory** and weakens **Inhibitory Control (IC)**, the ability to resist impulses and regulate emotions. This results in pronounced "brain fog," forgetfulness, and lowered patience, making task completion and emotional regulation significantly harder the following day.

- **Exacerbating Emotional Volatility:** Sleep deprivation increases emotional reactivity. When tired, the amygdala (the brain's emotional accelerator) becomes more reactive, while the PFC (the emotional "brakes") is less effective. This increases the likelihood of a minor trigger escalating into a disproportionate emotional outburst, particularly during the high-risk, low-progesterone phases of the hormonal cycle.

2. Strategic Sleep Hygiene for the ADHD Brain

Since the ADHD brain struggles with consistent routines and shutting down an active mind, sleep hygiene must be treated as a structured, intentional ritual.

- **The Fixed Bedtime Anchor:** Establish a consistent **bedtime and wake-up time**, even on weekends. The human body, and especially the neurodiverse brain, thrives on regularity (circadian rhythm). This consistency helps anchor the brain's neurochemistry and regulates its sleep-wake cycle, minimizing difficulties with falling asleep.

- **The Nightly Offload Ritual:** To combat a racing mind and rumination (internal noise), commit to the **Nightly Offload Ritual** (introduced in Book 3). Before bed, write out your **To-Do List** for the next day, capturing all "open loops" (tasks and worries) that consume WM. This externalizes the cognitive burden, signaling to the brain that the day's tasks are secured on the schedule, allowing the mind to quiet down and transition smoothly toward rest.

- **Avoid the Final Dopamine Hit:** In the hour before sleep, avoid screens (blue light interferes with melatonin), caffeine, sugar, and stimulating work projects that can trigger **hyperfocus**. Use this time for low-stimulation activities that signal relaxation, such as listening to a calming audiobook or music, or taking a warm bath.

Section 2: Nutrition and Hydration: Fueling the Neurochemical System

The PFC's capacity for focus and regulation requires stable, high-quality fuel. Erratic energy supply, through poor nutrition or dehydration, mimics and exacerbates ADHD symptoms, directly undermining the efficacy of optimized treatment.

1. Stabilizing Blood Sugar for Consistent Focus

The ADHD brain is highly susceptible to energy spikes and crashes caused by erratic blood sugar levels. These crashes amplify inattention, irritability, and mental fatigue, directly opposing the effort to build EF resilience.

- **Protein and Complex Carbs:** Focus on balanced meals that combine **lean protein** (for amino acids needed to build neurotransmitters like dopamine) and **complex carbohydrates** (for sustained energy release) at every meal. This prevents the rapid energy peaks from simple sugars that are inevitably followed by a crash, which exacerbates impulsivity and mood instability.

- **The Morning Focus Fuel:** Never skip breakfast. The morning meal should be rich in protein and fiber to anchor stable blood sugar, supporting sustained attention through the challenging first work blocks of the day.

2. Essential Neuro-Nutrients: Omega-3s and Magnesium

Specific nutrients are crucial building blocks for the brain structures and neurochemistry that support EF. Prioritizing these nutrients acts as a direct buffer against neurochemical volatility.

- **Omega-3 Fatty Acids:** Omega-3s (especially EPA and DHA) are essential for brain health, supporting cell membranes and neurotransmitter function. Research has linked low omega-3 levels to ADHD symptoms, including learning difficulties and emotional regulation problems. Supplementation, or dietary focus on fatty fish (salmon, sardines), can improve mood, reduce hyperactivity, and potentially enhance **Working Memory**.

- **Hydration:** Dehydration, even mild, can impair cognitive function, mood, and mental clarity, often mimicking or worsening the "brain fog" associated with ADHD and hormonal decline. Consistent, intentional hydration throughout the day is a simple, high-leverage strategy to maintain optimal brain performance.

Section 3: Stress Management: The Circuit-Breaker for Emotional Storms

High stress levels are a major hormonal disruptor, increasing cortisol production which, over time, depletes dopamine and serotonin and directly impairs EF function. Stress also magnifies emotional dysregulation, creating a vicious cycle of chaos. Managing stress is the final, essential buffer against hormonal and emotional volatility.

1. Proactive Grounding Techniques

When stress or anxiety levels rise, the nervous system enters a state of physiological arousal ("fight or flight"). Grounding techniques are immediate circuit-breakers that shift the body back to the calm, restorative state (parasympathetic nervous system).

- **Deep Breathing Exercises:** Practicing paced, deep breathing (e.g., inhaling for 4 counts, holding for 2, exhaling for 6 counts) immediately calms the nervous system and reduces heart rate, mitigating the physical effects of stress.

- **Sensory Reset (Grounding):** Use the 5-4-3-2-1 grounding technique (focusing on 5 things you see, 4 things you feel, etc.) to pull attention away from overwhelming internal thoughts and anchor it to the immediate, external reality. This simple redirection of focus utilizes your attentional skills (Book 3) to calm the emotional system.

- **Movement as Release:** Physical movement is a direct and healthy way to discharge the pent-up energy of frustration and anxiety. Utilize the mandatory breaks from the Pomodoro Technique (Book 3) for short bursts of intense movement (e.g., brisk walking, stretching) to act as a physiological "reset button," preventing emotional escalation.

2. Mindfulness and Psychological Buffering

Sustaining a calm baseline requires the intentional practice of mindfulness to manage intrusive thoughts and emotional reactivity.

- **Mindful Awareness:** Mindfulness, the practice of paying attention to the present moment without judgment, is crucial for supporting **Emotional Regulation** (the focus of Book 5). It strengthens the ability to observe a racing thought or an intense emotion without immediately reacting, creating the crucial "pause" that allows IC to engage.

- **Stress as Data:** Instead of reacting impulsively to stress, use the EF skills of reflection and analysis: *What caused this spike? Am I hungry? Did I skip my rest block?* Framing stress as valuable data allows you to apply a strategic solution (e.g., eating a protein-rich snack, taking a rest block) rather than engaging in self-blame.

Section 4: The Integration: A Stable Internal Ecosystem

The work of Book 4 is not about fighting hormones; it is about establishing a robust, stable internal ecosystem that supports the neurobiology of the ADHD brain against all forms of volatility, monthly, lifelong, and environmental.

1. The Synergistic Buffer

The EF resilience gained in Book 3 works synergistically with the physiological buffers established here:

- **Sleep / Nutrition** restores the PFC, maximizing **EF capacity** (Working Memory, Inhibitory Control).

- **Stress Management** lowers the baseline anxiety, minimizing **Emotional Reactivity** (Anger, Irritability).

- **EF Strategies** (Time Blocking, Milestones) prevent environmental chaos, minimizing the **Stress Triggers** that disrupt the hormonal and cognitive systems.

This continuous positive feedback loop ensures that when the inevitable low-estrogen dip occurs, your system is not depleted, but ready to rely on the robust reserves you have built.

2. The Bridge to Emotional Mastery

The physiological stability achieved in this chapter is the essential precursor to the emotional work of Book 5. A brain that is well-rested, well-fed, and less stressed is a brain that is capable of deep introspection, self-compassion, and intentional emotional regulation. You have built the stable neurological and physiological platform needed to successfully navigate the intense emotional landscape of ADHD.

Chapter 5 Workbook: Build Your Buffer: Prioritize Sleep and Nutrition to Stabilize Mood

Objective: To implement consistent, strategic physiological routines (Sleep and Nutrition) to build a robust buffer against hormonal volatility and mental fatigue.

Scientific Anchor: Quality sleep and stable blood sugar are essential for restoring the Prefrontal Cortex and maintaining Inhibitory Control, which are highly vulnerable to stress and hormonal decline.

Activity 5.1: The Sleep Hygiene Offload Ritual

Instructions: Create a fixed, low-stimulation ritual for the **60 minutes before bed** to signal rest and offload working memory (WM).

1. **Fixed Bedtime Commitment:** My committed bedtime is:

   _____

   _____

   _____

2. **The 60-Minute Wind-Down Sequence:** Detail the three non-negotiable steps you will take to close out the day, avoiding all screens / caffeine.

Time Slot	Activity	Neuro-Benefit (WM / IC Protection)
(Example: -60 to -45 min)	Read a physical book / Take a bath.	Low stimulation; avoids blue light / dopamine hit.
(Example: -45 to -30 min)	**Nightly Offload Ritual (Write List)**	**Externalizes open loops / worries from WM.**
(Example: -30 to 0 min)	Gentle stretching / Deep breathing.	Activates parasympathetic nervous system (calm).

Activity 5.2: The Neuro-Nutrient Focus Plan

Instructions: Plan two meals tomorrow to maximize focus and stability by ensuring adequate protein / fiber and hydration.

1. **Morning Focus Fuel:** Detail your breakfast, ensuring it contains **protein and fiber** to anchor stable blood sugar for the first work block.

   Breakfast Plan: _____

2. **Hydration Commitment:** Set a reminder to track your water intake during your peak focus block (e.g., 9:00 AM–1:00 PM).

   Hydration Reminder Text: _____

Reflection 5.3: The Stress and Buffer Analysis

Instructions: Reflect on how proactive physiological care impacts your stress and emotional regulation.

1. **Stress as Data:** Identify one specific moment this week where you felt an intense emotional surge (e.g., snapping at someone, feeling sudden anxiety). If you had immediately applied a **Deep Breathing / Grounding Technique**, how might the intensity of that moment have been reduced?

   Intensity Reduction: _____
   _____
   _____
   _____

2. **EF Conservation:** How does the intentional scheduling of a **Morning Focus Fuel** (protein / fiber) breakfast support your **Inhibitory Control** (your ability to resist distractions or impulsive spending) compared to starting the day with high sugar or skipping the meal entirely?

IC / Impulsivity Benefit: _____

_____

_____

_____

3. **Hormonal Buffer:** During your next **Vulnerability Window** (low-estrogen phase), what single self-care activity (e.g., 15-min walk, early bedtime) will you commit to prioritizing to serve as your non-negotiable **Emotional Buffer**?

Committed Buffer: _____

_____

_____

_____

CHAPTER 6

REFLECT AND INTEGRATE:
YOUR HORMONAL HARMONY JOURNEY SO FAR

You have completed the most complex and neurobiologically intricate phase of your journey toward self-mastery. The work of Book 4 has been a focused campaign to bring order and predictability to the dynamic internal forces, your **hormonal cycles**, that profoundly impact Executive Function (EF) and emotional regulation. This is the integration chapter, a dedicated space to reflect upon the profound cognitive, physiological, and emotional gains achieved by challenging the historical notion of static treatment and embracing your unique, dynamic neurobiology.

The core achievement of this book is the replacement of unpredictable, chaotic symptom spikes with a predictable, manageable rhythm. You have learned that your struggles with focus and emotional volatility were never random failures; they were **measurable, neurochemical events** driven by the ebb and flow of estrogen and progesterone. By acquiring this scientific knowledge and the data to back it up, you have transformed from a passive victim of hormonal chaos to a strategic manager of your own physiology. This is the ultimate victory of **self-advocacy** and **self-compassion**.

The stability cultivated here, the reliable synchronization of your internal body clock with your external structural supports (from Book 3), is the essential, stable base required to successfully embark on the challenging work of emotional mastery (Book 5).

Section 1: The Victory of Validation: Defeating the Gender Health Gap

The first, and arguably most important, victory of this book is the emotional and psychological liberation that comes with **scientific validation**. For years, women's reports of fluctuating focus and mood were dismissed as subjective or moodiness, a reality stemming from the **gender health gap** in ADHD research.

1. From Subjective Anecdote to Objective Data

You systematically gathered objective data that provided undeniable evidence of a cycle-symptom correlation (Chapter 1).

- **Quantifying the Dip:** By tracking the decline of estrogen in the **Luteal Phase** against functional symptoms (inattention, poor WM, and emotional volatility), you quantified your unique **Vulnerability Window**. This data moves the conversation with providers from subjective complaints to objective facts: "My data shows a 40% drop in focus during Cycle Days X-Y, correlating with low estrogen, which requires a strategic intervention."

- **Empowering Advocacy:** This data provided the necessary fuel for informed **self-advocacy** regarding **Cycle Dosing** (Chapter 3) and navigating the compounded challenges of **Perimenopause / Menopause** (Chapter 4). You now understand that when medication efficacy dips, it is not the fault of the dose or your effort; it is a neurochemical reality that demands a dynamic, tailored pharmacological solution to offset the loss of estrogen's supportive effect on dopamine.

2. Neutralizing Shame with Self-Compassion

The knowledge that your symptoms worsen during your Vulnerability Window is the ultimate antidote to the shame that accompanies unmanaged ADHD.

- **Radical Acceptance:** You replaced the harsh self-judgment, *"I'm falling apart; I can't handle this routine"*, with the compassionate, factual statement: *"My body is following a predictable hormonal rhythm. My system needs intentional buffering today."* This act of **radical acceptance** stops the cascade of stress and self-criticism, which would otherwise consume the limited emotional bandwidth required for resilience.

- **Managing the "ADHD Squared" Effect:** For those navigating midlife, the knowledge that "brain fog" and cognitive decline are often the predictable **"ADHD Squared"** effect (compounding low estrogen and low dopamine) provides crucial psychological safety, preventing the spiral into fear of premature cognitive decline.

Section 2: The Command Over Flow: Strategic Integration

The true power of this book lies in the integration of hormonal knowledge with the structural EF strategies mastered in Book 3. This synthesis ensures that your management plan is flexible enough to withstand internal volatility.

1. Cycle Syncing as an EF Strategy

You learned to use the **Cycle Syncing Framework** (Chapter 2) to proactively match **task demand** with **neurochemical supply**.

- **Strategic Allocation:** You maximize efficiency by scheduling cognitively complex tasks (planning, analysis, deep work) during the **High-Estrogen Follicular Phase** (Peak Focus) and reserving low-stakes, routine tasks (filing, maintenance, passive learning) for the **Low-Estrogen Luteal Phase** (Strategic Conservation). This prevents the highly taxing effort of trying to force focus when the brain is neurochemically unsupported.

- **EF Buffering:** During the low-energy Luteal Phase, you learned to rigidly adapt your scheduling parameters, including **increasing the Time Buffer** to 50% extra time and **contracting the Pomodoro work sprints** (e.g., 20 / 10 cycle) to prevent burnout and compensate for slower Working Memory and harder transitions. The external structure acts as the resilient scaffolding when the internal cognitive mechanisms are compromised.

2. The Power of the Physiological Buffer

The disciplined prioritization of foundational self-care (Chapter 5) transformed sleep, nutrition, and stress management into strategic tools for neurochemical stability.

- **Restoring the PFC:** Consistent **sleep hygiene** and the **Nightly Offload Ritual** were established as non-negotiable foundations for restoring the Prefrontal Cortex (PFC) and maximizing **EF capacity** (WM, IC) for the following day.

- **Neuro-Nutritional Support:** Stable blood sugar (protein / complex carbs) and essential nutrients (Omega-3s) were integrated to provide consistent fuel, mitigating the energy crashes that exacerbate impulsivity and emotional volatility during low-hormone periods.

- **Stress Management and IC:** You integrated **Grounding Techniques** and **Movement** into your routine as immediate **circuit-breakers** (Chapter 5), effectively engaging the parasympathetic nervous system to reduce stress arousal and protect your already vulnerable **Inhibitory Control** from emotional overload.

Section 3: The Bridge to Emotional Mastery (Book 5)

The stability achieved in this book is the essential prerequisite for navigating the intense emotional landscape of Book 5 (Tame Intense Emotions). A system that is constantly being hijacked by hormonal or physiological stress lacks the bandwidth for deep psychological work.

1. Stabilizing the Emotional Baseline

The primary outcome of Book 4 is the profound reduction in **chaotic input** that triggers emotional flares.

- **Reducing Reactivity:** By managing stress, prioritizing sleep, and buffering the low-estrogen dip, you stabilize the emotional baseline, making the brain less reactive and preventing minor triggers from escalating into a disproportionate emotional storm (the "green-to-red" phenomenon).

- **Conserving Emotional Bandwidth:** The conserved EF resources and reduced physiological stress are now available for **emotional labor**, the challenging work of introspection, cognitive reframing, and intentional response that defines emotional regulation.

2. The Foundation for DBT Skills

The structural stability provided by this book supports the efficacy of the therapeutic tools explored in the next book.

- **IC as Emotional Brake:** The **Inhibitory Control** trained through EF practice is the very same muscle required for **emotional regulation**, the ability to pause between stimulus and response.
- **Mindfulness Prerequisite:** A body that is well-rested and neurochemically stable is better equipped to engage in sustained attention, which is the necessary prerequisite for effective **Mindfulness** (the core skill of DBT / CBT), allowing for greater self-awareness and non-judgmental observation of intense feelings.

Conclusion: Committing to Dynamic, Personalized Care

The journey through Book 4 is the definitive step in achieving dynamic, personalized self-mastery. You have moved beyond feeling powerless against internal chaos to commanding a truly holistic system that honors the unique intersection of your neurobiology and your physiology.

Your ongoing commitment must be to **consistency in self-advocacy** and **self-compassion**. By maintaining your tracking data, adhering to your structural buffers, and refusing to succumb to the shame of neurobiological differences, you ensure that the stability you have fought for is sustained. This resilient foundation now fully equips you to tackle the crucial final phase: achieving emotional mastery and building robust, resilient connections with others.

Chapter 6 Workbook: Reflect and Integrate: Your Hormonal Harmony Journey So Far

Objective: To synthesize the cognitive and emotional gains achieved in Book 4, solidifying the shift from reliance on static treatment to dynamic, data-driven hormonal management.

Scientific Anchor: Reflective practice and self-compassion reduce the impact of stress on Executive Functions. Synthesis of tracking data ensures proactive buffering against neurobiological shifts (low estrogen / dopamine dips).

Activity 6.1: The Hormonal Harmony Scorecard

Instructions: Rate the severity of your challenges **before** Book 4 (Initial) and **now** (Current), focusing on the impact of hormonal stability. (Scale: 1 = Minimal Challenge, 5 = Severe Challenge)

Challenge Area	Before Book 4 (Initial)	After Book 4 (Current)	Reflection: The Tool That Helped Most
Inattention / Focus Dip (Pre-Menses)			(Example: Cycle Syncing / Time Blocking)
Anxiety / Irritability (Hormonal)			(Example: Progesterone Buffer / Deep Breathing)
Brain Fog / Working Memory Collapse			(Example: Sleep Hygiene / Nutritional Support)
Sense of Control Over Symptoms			(Example: Tracking Data / Advocacy)

Reflection 6.2: Shifting from Shame to Strategy

Instructions: Use this space to integrate the core concept that symptoms are neurobiological consequences, not moral failures, and assess your progress in building self-advocacy.

1. **The Crisis to Strategy Shift:** Recall a moment this week when a hormonal or stress dip made you feel overwhelmed. How did the ability to identify your **Vulnerability Window** (Chapter 1) or your **Physiological Buffer** (Chapter 5) prevent you from escalating to a full emotional crisis?

The Intervention: _____

_____

_____

_____

_____

2. **The Antidote to the Inner Critic:** Identify one self-critical thought you had about your performance during a low-energy moment. Rephrase this thought using the compassionate, neurobiological reality you learned (e.g., "My brain is low on estrogen support today; this dip is predictable. I choose to prioritize rest to restore my PFC.")

   New, Empowered Narrative: _____

_____

_____

_____

_____

_____

3. **Self-Advocacy Gain:** In one sentence, summarize the most important piece of data you now possess (quantified symptom dip or medication fluctuation) that empowers you to demand personalized care from a medical professional.

   Data for Advocacy: _____

_____

_____

_____

_____

Activity 6.3: Bridge to Emotional Mastery (Book 5 Prep)

Instructions: The EF and physiological stability achieved here are the foundation for emotional regulation. Prepare your system for the challenging emotional work ahead.

1. **EF Buffer Check:** Emotional dysregulation (Book 5) is often fueled by external chaos. Name one specific, low-friction EF tool (e.g., Time Blocking, Nightly Offload) you will rigorously maintain, even during periods of high stress, to ensure you have maximum **emotional bandwidth**.

EF Tool Commitment: _____

_____

_____

_____

_____

2. **IC and the Emotional Brake:** The first step in emotional regulation is creating a **pause**. What single **Grounding / Sensory Technique** (e.g., deep breathing, 5-4-3-2-1) will you commit to practicing daily, even when you feel calm, to strengthen your ability to deploy your Inhibitory Control when an emotional surge hits?

Daily IC Practice: _____

_____

_____

_____

_____

_____

CHAPTER 7

PRACTICE AND APPLY:
YOUR HORMONAL HARMONY ACTION TOOLKIT

You have completed the essential, intricate work of Book 4, moving from anecdotal struggle to informed command over your internal physiological environment. This journey has been defined by the profound recognition that the consistency of your Executive Function (EF) is inextricably linked to the ebb and flow of your hormones, particularly the supportive presence of **Estrogen** and the regulatory effects of **Progesterone**. The primary achievement is the transformation of unpredictable, chaotic symptom spikes into a predictable, manageable pattern through objective tracking.

This final chapter provides the comprehensive **Action Toolkit**, designed to translate the neurobiological knowledge mastered in Chapters 1 through 5 into a seamless, resilient system of daily self-management. The goal is to integrate your data, scheduling skills (from Book 3), and physiological buffers into a cohesive framework that ensures the stability of your neurochemistry, and thus, your focus and emotional regulation, across the entire month and throughout life transitions.

The power of this toolkit lies in its synergistic effect: consistency in applying these tools minimizes the **Cognitive Load (CL)** and **stress** that deplete EF, ensuring that when the inevitable low-estrogen dip occurs, your system is buffered and ready. This is the final step in moving beyond reactive coping to a life defined by dynamic, personalized, and proactive hormonal harmony.

Section 1: Toolkit 1: The Cycle Syncing Command Protocol

Objective: To leverage your monthly tracking data to proactively schedule and adjust your Executive Function demands, thereby conserving limited neurochemical energy during the Vulnerability Window.

Scientific Anchor: Symptoms worsen due to low estrogen support for dopamine pathways during the Luteal Phase. Strategic scheduling (Cycle Syncing) ensures high-leverage tasks are performed during the high-estrogen Follicular Phase, conserving finite EF resources during the neurochemically unsupported Low-Energy Phase.

Activity 7.1: Creating the Luteal Phase Protection Plan (LPPP)

Instructions: Based on your completed cycle tracker (Chapter 1), design a non-negotiable plan for your 7-day **Vulnerability Window** (e.g., Cycle Days 22–28) that proactively adjusts your cognitive workload using EF tools (Book 3).

1. **Define the Conservation Window:**

   My Vulnerability Window (Days): ____ to ____

2. **Strategic Task De-Allocation (The "Q2 Freeze"):** Identify the high-leverage tasks (Q2 work) that require peak planning, creativity, and Working Memory. These tasks must be **moved out** of the LPPP.

   Complex Task to AVOID: _____

   Routine Task to PRIORITIZE: _____

   (e.g., Simple filing, routine chores, email triage)

3. **EF Buffer Augmentation (Schedule Adjustment):** Detail how your scheduling parameters (Book 3) must be augmented during this week to compensate for fatigue and WM collapse.

EF Strategy	Standard Follicular Phase (Baseline)	Luteal / Vulnerability Phase (Augmented Buffer)
Time Buffer (Chapter 3, Book 3)	25% extra time	**50% extra time** for every task (compensates for slow processing).
Pomodoro Cycle (Chapter 3, Book 3)	45 min Work / 5 min Rest	Contract to **20 min Work / 10 min Rest** (Finitude is shorter; rest is longer to prevent fatigue).
Cognitive Load Annihilation	Enforced 9 AM-11 AM	**All day enforcement** (Strict Notification Annihilation to conserve limited WM).

Commitment: I commit to viewing any work outside this LPPP structure during my Vulnerability Window as an act of **self-sabotage**, not productivity.

Section 2: Toolkit 2: The Treatment Optimization and Advocacy Audit

Objective: To systematically compile objective, measurable evidence for a dynamic treatment plan, empowering self-advocacy for hormonal support and medication adjustment.

Scientific Anchor: The decline in estrogen / progesterone during the luteal phase (menstrual cycle) and menopause exacerbates ADHD symptoms and may diminish stimulant efficacy. Objective data on this correlation is required to discuss "cycle dosing" or integrated HRT support with medical professionals.

Activity 7.2: The Efficacy Data Log Compilation

Instructions: Consolidate your tracking data (Chapter 1) and midlife symptoms (Chapter 4) into a factual summary that provides measurable evidence for your physician.

1. **Quantifying the Monthly Dip (Menstruating Women):** Summarize the functional decline based on your tracking log.
   - *During Cycle Days ____ to ____my Inattention / Focus score increased by ____ % (e.g., from 2 / 5 to 4 / 5).*

- During this same window, my self-rated **Medication Efficacy** consistently dropped, aligning with guidance that low estrogen can impair dopamine response.

2. **The Midlife Symptom Inventory (Perimenopausal / Menopausal Women):** Identify the key cognitive deficits resulting from the "ADHD Squared" effect (sustained low estrogen / progesterone).

Symptom 1 (Working Memory): _____

_____

(e.g., Word retrieval failure, losing train of thought)

Symptom 2 (Emotional Volatility): _____

_____

(e.g., Sudden irritability, increased anxiety)

3. **Developing the Informed Advocacy Script:** Draft a concise, factual script to initiate the conversation, using data to frame the problem as a neurobiological imbalance, not a personal failing.

- *Script (Cycle Dosing):* "Doctor, my data shows a quantifiable EF decline during my Luteal Phase. I am seeking to explore the clinical approach of **cycle dosing**, a small, monitored dose increase during my high-risk days, to stabilize my dopamine baseline, as research suggests stimulant efficacy is diminished by low estrogen."

- *Script (Midlife / HRT):* "Since my Executive Function (WM, planning) has significantly worsened during perimenopause, I would like to discuss the integration of **Hormone Replacement Therapy (HRT)** with my current ADHD treatment, as combining them has been shown to support cognitive function in this transition."

Section 3: Toolkit 3: The Physiological Resilience Builder

Objective: To automate essential self-care practices (Sleep, Nutrition, Stress Management) that act as a physiological buffer, conserving EF reserves and minimizing the impact of stress hormones (cortisol) on the PFC.

Scientific Anchor: Stress, poor sleep, and blood sugar instability directly impair EF skills (WM / IC). Prioritizing these foundational needs minimizes their negative impact, maximizing cognitive resilience against hormonal dips.

Activity 7.3: The Nightly Hormone Reset Checklist

Instructions: Create a non-negotiable 60-minute wind-down ritual that targets WM offload and physiological calming, ensuring restorative sleep for PFC recovery.

1. **Time Commitment:** My fixed bedtime is _____.

   I start this ritual 60 minutes prior.

2. **The Nightly Offload Sequence (The Final 60 Minutes):**

Time Slot	Action	Neuro-Benefit (WM / IC Protection)
-60 to -45 min	**Physical Disconnect / Offload:** (Example: Write out tomorrow's **Rule of Three** tasks, turn off all screens.)	Closes "open loops" to conserve WM; prevents blue light interference with sleep.
-45 to -30 min	**Routine Body Care / Low-Stimulation:** (Example: Take warm bath / shower, read physical book.)	Signals safety and promotes the physiological shift to rest mode.
-30 to 0 min	**Sensory Calming:** (Example: 5 minutes of paced, deep breathing or gentle stretching.)	Engages the parasympathetic nervous system, strengthening Inhibitory Control against ruminating thoughts.

Activity 7.4: The Stress-to-Calm IC Protocol

Instructions: Practice deploying immediate **Inhibitory Control (IC)** and **Grounding** as a circuit-breaker when stress or intense emotion hits, preventing escalation.

1. **The Trigger Identification:** My most common emotional trigger during the Luteal Phase is _____

   (e.g., unexpected loud noise, partner criticism, task failure).

2. **The IC Circuit-Breaker:** When the trigger hits, commit to deploying the following **STOP** sequence before speaking or reacting impulsively. This is IC in action.

- ○ **S:** Stop (Freeze all physical action).
- ○ **T:** Take a breath (3 deep, paced breaths).
- ○ **O:** Observe (Acknowledge the emotion without judgment: "I observe that I feel intense frustration.").
- ○ **P:** Proceed with Opposite Action / Plan (E.g., Walk away for 10 minutes, or use a specific coping skill).

3. **Nutritional Anchor:** What single action will I take tomorrow (e.g., eat a protein-rich snack, drink a glass of water) when I feel the first sign of **Mental Fatigue** to stabilize my blood sugar and prevent an EF crash?

Fatigue Action: _____

_____

_____

_____

Section 4: Integration and Long-Term Resilience (Reflective Summary)

The culmination of Book 4 is the creation of a dynamic, interconnected system that ensures the structural gains of your EF mastery (Book 3) are not derailed by internal physiological volatility.

1. The Synergistic Buffer

The power of this toolkit lies in how the components support each other: **Tracking** informs **Scheduling**, and **Physiological Buffers** protect **EF Capacity.** You are moving beyond the frantic, low-energy cycle of coping to a sustainable rhythm where your body and schedule work in harmony. This sustained effort conserves the necessary **emotional bandwidth** required to manage the inevitable conflicts and intense feelings that define the emotional mastery journey of Book 5.

2. The Final Step to Emotional Mastery

The physiological and cognitive stability achieved here is the essential precursor to the emotional work of Book 5: Tame Intense Emotions. A brain that is well-rested, regulated by stable blood sugar, and buffered against hormonal chaos is a brain fully capable of engaging in the challenging work of **cognitive reframing** and **assertive communication** (DBT skills) that leads to profound self-acceptance and resilient relationships. You are ready to transform internal turmoil into intentional action.

CONCLUSION

SUMMARY: A HOLISTIC APPROACH TO HORMONAL HARMONY

You have completed the intensive, intricate work of Book 4, moving from anecdotal struggle to informed command over your internal physiological environment. This journey has been a focused campaign to bring order and predictability to the dynamic internal forces, your **hormonal cycles**, that profoundly impact Executive Function (EF) and emotional regulation.

The core achievement of this book is the replacement of unpredictable, chaotic symptom spikes with a predictable, manageable rhythm. You have learned that your struggles with focus, organization, and emotional volatility were never random failures; they were **measurable, neurochemical events** driven by the predictable ebb and flow of estrogen and progesterone. By acquiring this scientific knowledge and the data to back it up, you have transformed from a passive victim of hormonal chaos to a strategic manager of your own physiology. This is the ultimate victory of **self-advocacy** and **self-compassion**.

The stability cultivated here—the reliable synchronization of your internal body clock with your external structural supports (from Book 3)—is the essential, stable base required to successfully embark on the challenging work of emotional mastery (Book 5).

Section 1: The Victory of Validation and Data-Driven Care

The first and most crucial victory of this book is the emotional and psychological liberation that comes with **scientific validation**. By challenging the historical **gender health gap** (Chapter 1), you have equipped yourself with the tools to demand personalized, dynamic care.

1. Quantifying the Neurochemical Dip

You systematically gathered objective data (Chapter 1) that provided undeniable evidence of a cycle-symptom correlation.

- **Luteal Collapse:** You quantified your unique **Vulnerability Window**, the high-risk days characterized by low estrogen and a corresponding dip in dopamine support that exacerbates inattention and disorganization. This knowledge neutralizes the shame and anxiety that accompanies the sudden, overwhelming dips in performance, allowing for **radical acceptance**.

- **Targeted Advocacy:** This data provided the necessary fuel for informed **self-advocacy** regarding **Cycle Dosing** (Chapter 3), a dynamic strategy to offset the loss of estrogen's supportive effect on dopamine by monitoring a temporary dose adjustment of stimulants during the low-estrogen phase.

2. Mastering the Lifespan Transitions

You prepared for the most complex hormonal shifts, recognizing that the symptoms of midlife are often the result of the **"ADHD Squared"** effect (Chapter 4).

- **Perimenopausal Buffer:** The knowledge that cognitive decline, "brain fog," and severe anxiety during perimenopause are predictable consequences of sustained low estrogen empowers you to advocate for integrated pharmacological support, such as the strategic use of **Hormone Replacement Therapy (HRT)** combined with stimulants, to stabilize Working Memory and emotional regulation.

Section 2: Strategic Integration: Building the Physiological Buffer

The true power of this book lies in the strategic integration of hormonal knowledge with the structural strategies you have already mastered. This ensures that your management plan is flexible enough to withstand internal volatility.

1. Cycle Syncing as an EF Strategy

You learned to use the **Cycle Syncing Framework** (Chapter 2) to proactively match **task demand** with **neurochemical supply**, conserving limited cognitive energy.

- **Strategic Allocation:** You maximize efficiency by scheduling cognitively complex tasks (planning, analysis, deep work) during the **High-Estrogen Follicular Phase** (Peak Focus) and reserving low-stakes, routine tasks (filing, maintenance) for the **Low-Estrogen Luteal Phase** (Strategic Conservation).

- **Augmented Buffering:** During the **Vulnerability Window**, you learned to rigidly adapt your scheduling parameters by **increasing Time Buffers** and **contracting Pomodoro work sprints** (e.g., 20 / 10 cycle) to compensate for slower Working Memory and mitigate the high cognitive cost of context switching.

2. The Non-Negotiable Physiological Buffer

You established essential physiological practices (Chapter 5) that act as a crucial buffer against volatility, conserving EF reserves and regulating the nervous system.

- **Sleep and EF Restoration:** Consistent **sleep hygiene** and the **Nightly Offload Ritual** were established as non-negotiable foundations for restoring the **Prefrontal Cortex (PFC)** and maximizing **EF capacity** (WM, IC) for the following day.

- **Stress and Mood Stabilization:** You committed to using **Neuro-Nutritional Support** (protein, complex carbs) to stabilize blood sugar and prevent energy crashes. Furthermore, you learned to deploy immediate stress management techniques (Grounding, Deep Breathing) to act as a **Circuit-Breaker**, preventing stress arousal from further impairing your vulnerable **Inhibitory Control (IC)**.

Section 3: The Bridge to Emotional Mastery

The physiological and emotional stability achieved in this book is the essential precursor to the emotional mastery work of Book 5. A brain that is well-rested, regulated, and buffered against hormonal chaos has the emotional bandwidth necessary for deep psychological growth.

- **EF for Emotional Control:** The structural stability of your external systems reduces the chronic input that triggers emotional flares. The disciplined practice of **IC** (Chapter 5) is the very muscle required for **emotional regulation**, the ability to pause between stimulus and response, preparing you for the application of advanced behavioral therapies (DBT / CBT) in the next book.

- **Sustaining the Buffer:** Your ongoing commitment must be to **consistency in self-advocacy** and **self-compassion**. By maintaining your tracking data, adhering to your structural buffers, and refusing to succumb to the shame of neurobiological differences, you ensure that the stability you have fought for is sustained, equipping you for the profound work of Taming Intense Emotions (Book 5).

BOOK FIVE

TAME EMOTIONS AND STRENGTHEN RELATIONSHIPS IN WOMEN WITH ADHD

INTRODUCTION

You have successfully established the three foundational pillars of stability: external organization (Book 1), cognitive command (Book 3), and physiological resilience against hormonal volatility (Book 4). This comprehensive structural work has conserved the mental energy necessary for consistent follow-through and reduced the systemic chaos that fuels overwhelm. Now, the final volume addresses the challenges that define integrated success in adulthood: **Taming Emotions** and navigating the high-stakes friction points of **Relationships** and **Financial Management**.

For the woman with Attention-Deficit / Hyperactivity Disorder (ADHD), these two domains, money and love, are not merely areas of life; they are mirrors reflecting her deepest struggles with Executive Function (EF), emotional regulation, and self-worth. Both require consistent planning, impulse control, and active communication, all skills that are profoundly compromised by core ADHD symptoms. The result is often a persistent feeling of inadequacy and a chronic struggle to manage finances and nurture relationships in a way that feels effortless to a neurotypical individual.

This book provides the final, essential bridge, empowering you to translate structural stability into authentic connection and tangible financial health. We will confront the debilitating pain of **Rejection**

Sensitive Dysphoria (RSD) and the heavy emotional burden of **shame**, while building proactive systems for assertive communication and financial control. The ultimate goal is to move beyond merely coping with adult responsibilities to achieving genuine integration, building a life defined by financial security, profound emotional resilience, and deep, lasting connection.

Section 1: The Emotional Core: RSD and the Cost of Internalization

For many women with ADHD, the journey of self-mastery is defined by the unique challenge of **Emotional Dysregulation**, the difficulty in managing and appropriately expressing emotions. This is not a character flaw, but a core symptom rooted in a neurological disconnect between the brain's emotional accelerator (the amygdala) and its inhibitory "brakes" (the frontal cortex, or PFC). This volatility leads to disproportionate emotional responses and intense frustration.

1. The Debilitating Pain of Rejection Sensitive Dysphoria (RSD)

A particularly painful and pervasive manifestation of this dysregulation, highly common in women with ADHD, is **Rejection Sensitive Dysphoria (RSD)**, an extreme emotional responsiveness and intense pain in anticipation of, or response to, **perceived** criticism or rejection.

- **Neurobiological Amplification:** The pain of RSD is more than hurt feelings; it is an immediate, overwhelming emotional pain that can feel physically agonizing, often described as being punched in the gut. This profound hypersensitivity is fueled by a lifetime of internalizing struggles and the fear that their "perceived failures" will be discovered.
- **The Shame Cycle:** For women, RSD fuels a deep sense of shame and inadequacy, driving compensatory behaviors like **perfectionism** and **people-pleasing** in an attempt to avoid any potential criticism. This painful feedback loop, where emotional dysregulation leads to RSD, and RSD feeds shame, creates a devastating barrier to authentic connection and self-acceptance, often leading to co-occurring anxiety and depression.

2. Healing Through Skills-Based Intervention

The solution lies not in suppressing emotions, but in building a robust, evidence-based toolkit that provides a crucial **pause** between stimulus and impulsive response. This book draws heavily on the therapeutic principles of **Dialectical Behavior Therapy (DBT)** and **Cognitive Behavioral Therapy (CBT)**, which are highly effective for managing the anxiety, emotional intensity, and interpersonal friction associated with ADHD.

The toolkit focuses on:

- **Mindfulness and Distress Tolerance:** Creating immediate behavioral interventions (e.g., grounding, deep breathing) to calm the activated nervous system when a storm hits, allowing the PFC time to re-engage.
- **Cognitive Reframing:** Identifying and challenging the irrational thought patterns (e.g., catastrophizing, mind reading) that amplify emotional pain, replacing self-criticism with strategic, compassionate alternatives.

Section 2: The Relational Toll: Communication and Shared Responsibility

The emotional intensity and EF challenges inherent in ADHD often create significant friction in close relationships, which require consistent communication, follow-through, and empathy.

1. Communication Challenges: Attention and Interruptions

One of the most common sources of conflict is difficulty with **active listening** and **impulsivity**. A woman's mind may wander or "zone out" during a conversation (inattention), leading her partner to feel unheard. Conversely, she may impulsively interrupt or blurt out her thoughts (impulsivity) because she fears her thought will be lost due to compromised Working Memory.

The solution is structural: utilizing tools of **Interpersonal Effectiveness** (a core skill of DBT) to build trust. This includes using techniques like:

- **Mirroring and Validation:** Restating what the partner said ("Mirroring") to confirm understanding and acknowledging their feelings ("Validation") to boost their sense of being heard. This is a direct strategy to counteract the appearance of inattention.
- **"I" Statements:** Employing assertive communication that focuses on one's own feelings ("I feel overwhelmed...") rather than the other person's actions ("You never help...") to de-escalate conflict and prevent defensiveness.

2. Navigating the Parent-Child Dynamic

Unmanaged EF deficits often lead to a dysfunctional **"parent-child"** **dynamic** in neurodiverse couples. The neurotypical partner may unintentionally take on the role of a **taskmaster** or reminder for household chores or finances, leaving the ADHD partner feeling like a scolded child, which triggers shame and avoidance.

The solution is collaboration and externalization:

- **External Systems:** Offload shared responsibilities from the neurotypical partner's memory onto neutral, external systems (e.g., shared digital calendars, whiteboard chore charts). This shifts accountability from the person to the system.

- **Collaborative Planning:** Schedule brief, dedicated **weekly check-ins** to discuss logistics and tasks in a calm environment, building a routine of open dialogue and shared problem-solving rather than reactive arguments.

Section 3: The Financial Drain: Conquering the ADHD Tax

The financial challenges faced by women with ADHD are a direct, measurable consequence of core EF deficits—impulsivity, time blindness, and poor organization, that lead to the **"Financial ADHD Tax."**

- **The Cost:** Studies show that adults with a history of ADHD exhibit substantially worse financial outcomes, earning significantly less and having 66% less money in savings by age 30 compared to their peers. This disparity is due to chronic issues like:

  - **Impulsive Buying:** Driven by the search for immediate dopamine reward, leading to spontaneous purchases and debt.

  - **Time Blindness Penalties:** Chronic forgetfulness regarding deadlines leads to late fees, fines, and interest accrual.

- **The Solution: Automation and Boundaries:** Financial stability is achieved by bypassing compromised EF with strict external structures. This includes automating all bill payments and savings transfers to eliminate the need for memory and manual initiation (Chapter 5, Book 3), and creating clear **financial boundaries** (e.g., using specific accounts, implementing a mandatory "pause" before spending) to protect savings from impulse decisions.

Conclusion: Your Integrated Success

This book culminates the entire journey of self-mastery. You have moved beyond structural and cognitive stability to address the highest-stakes areas of life: your inner emotional world and your connections with others. By integrating the resilience gained from EF mastery and hormonal stability, you are now equipped to navigate conflict with intention, manage profound emotional pain with self-compassion, and build a financially secure, authentically connected life.

The final act of self-mastery is the commitment to this integrated system, moving from the shadow of shame into the light of self-acceptance and a truly fulfilling existence.

CHAPTER 1

GROUND YOURSELF: APPLY SENSORY TECHNIQUES TO INTERRUPT ACUTE DISTRESS

You have successfully built the robust external and cognitive structures necessary for stability (Books 1–4), conserving the mental energy required for sustained follow-through. Now, this book addresses the final, most vulnerable area of the ADHD experience: **Emotional Dysregulation**, the pervasive difficulty in managing and appropriately expressing intense feelings. For the woman with Attention-Deficit / Hyperactivity Disorder (ADHD), the onset of a profound emotional surge, whether anger, anxiety, or the overwhelming pain of Rejection Sensitive Dysphoria (RSD), often feels like a traffic light that skips yellow, flipping instantly from calm ("green") to crisis ("red").

This surge, rooted in a neurobiological disconnect between the emotional accelerator (amygdala) and the cognitive "brakes" (prefrontal cortex), compromises the ability to think rationally or employ learned strategies. This chapter provides the immediate, evidence-based toolkit to address these moments of acute distress using **Sensory Grounding**

Techniques. These techniques serve as a crucial **physiological circuit-breaker**, actively calming the activated nervous system and creating the essential "pause" that allows your Executive Function (EF) skills, honed in Book 3, to re-engage and prevent a spiral into meltdown or impulsive action.

The goal is to shift your focus from overwhelming internal chaos to anchoring in the immediate, external reality, transforming emotional volatility into a manageable process.

Section 1: The Neurobiology of the Emotional Surge

To effectively interrupt acute distress, you must understand that the "emotional storm" is a real, physiological event driven by the brain's threat system.

1. The Amygdala-PFC Disconnect

Emotional dysregulation in ADHD is not a character flaw; it is a neurological vulnerability. When a strong trigger occurs (internal stress, external conflict, or perceived rejection):

- **The Accelerator (Amygdala) Overreacts:** The brain's threat system is highly sensitive, leading to an immediate, intense, and disproportionate emotional response. Emotions feel "all or nothing."

- **The Brakes (PFC) Fail:** The prefrontal cortex (PFC), responsible for **Inhibitory Control (IC)**, thinking before acting, is often less active in the ADHD brain. This diminished IC makes it difficult to suppress the automatic, intense reaction.

The result is a rapid, often unpredictable escalation of feelings that compromises the ability to judge, think, and make decisions, leading directly to mental or emotional paralysis.

2. Distress Tolerance vs. Emotional Change

This chapter introduces **Distress Tolerance** (a core skill of Dialectical Behavior Therapy, or DBT), which is the strategic skill of managing a crisis without making it worse.

- **Crisis Management:** When an emotion is at peak intensity ("red light"), it is physically impossible to use complex cognitive strategies (like challenging a thought). Distress Tolerance skills are immediate, physiological interventions designed to endure the intense, painful emotion long enough for the intensity to naturally subside—without resorting to impulsive, unhelpful behaviors (e.g., self-harm, yelling, avoidance).

- **Creating the Pause:** The goal of grounding is to activate the **Parasympathetic Nervous System** ("rest and digest") and force the attention to the external environment. This provides the necessary **physiological pause** that allows the PFC time to return online and deploy the cognitive and interpersonal skills mastered later in this book.

Section 2: Immediate Physiological Circuit-Breakers (TIPP)

The most effective distress tolerance skills are those that provide a rapid, intense sensory shock to the system, overriding the emotional alarm in the amygdala. The DBT toolkit utilizes the **TIPP** skills for this purpose.

1. Temperature (The Cold Shock Reset)

Using cold temperature is a rapid way to activate the body's **mammalian dive reflex**, which immediately slows the heart rate and calms the nervous system, forcing the body to transition from fight-or-flight to rest-and-digest.

- **Action:** Splash cold water on your face, or hold a frozen compress or a bag of ice on the back of your neck or wrists for 30–60 seconds.
- **Neuro-Benefit:** This intense, sudden sensory input provides a powerful distraction and rapidly shifts the body's physiological state, overriding the stress response and reducing the intensity of the emotional surge.

2. Intense Exercise (The Energy Discharge)

Intense physical movement provides a direct, healthy outlet for discharging the pent-up emotional energy that fuels anger, anxiety, or internal restlessness.

- **Action:** Engage in brief, intense physical activity, such as sprinting in place, rapid walking up and down a set of stairs, or performing 20 jumping jacks. The movement must be sufficient to trigger a change in heart rate and breathing.
- **Neuro-Benefit:** This burst of activity uses the physical energy of the stress response, preventing it from spiraling into a mental or emotional meltdown.

3. Paced Breathing (The Nervous System Anchor)

Slow, intentional breathing directly impacts the nervous system, shifting it from a high-arousal stress state to a calmer, more controlled state.

- **Action:** Practice paced, deep breathing, such as inhaling slowly for **four counts**, holding briefly, and exhaling slowly for **six counts**. This focuses attention on the rhythm and sensation of the breath.
- **Neuro-Benefit:** The extended exhale signals to the brain that the danger has passed, activating the restorative parasympathetic nervous system and reducing heart rate and blood pressure, which physically counteracts the panic response.

Section 3: The 5-4-3-2-1 Sensory Grounding Technique

When a woman is experiencing a rapid emotional surge or feels trapped in a cycle of rumination and intrusive thoughts, her mind is fixated on the overwhelming **internal chaos**. Sensory Grounding shifts attention immediately to the safe, neutral reality of the **external environment**.

1. Anchoring Attention to External Reality

The 5-4-3-2-1 method forces the mind, which struggles with internal filtering, to perform a sequential, structured task focused entirely on sensory input. This process utilizes the cultivated attentional skills (Book 3) to create a distraction that is constructive and calming.

- **5 Things You Can See:** Look around and name five distinct things, focusing on color, texture, or shape. *This forces visual attention.*
- **4 Things You Can Feel:** Notice four distinct physical sensations (e.g., the pressure of your feet on the floor, the texture of your shirt, the air temperature, the warmth of your hands). *This anchors physical reality.*
- **3 Things You Can Hear:** Listen for three distinct sounds (e.g., distant traffic, your own breathing, the hum of a computer). *This shifts auditory focus from internal noise to external sound.*
- **2 Things You Can Smell:** Notice two distinct scents (even if faint).
- **1 Thing You Can Taste:** Notice one taste in your mouth (e.g., mint, coffee residue, water).

2. Integrating Grounding with Self-Compassion

Once the acute emotional peak has subsided (after using TIPP or 5-4-3-2-1), the crisis is over, but the residual distress remains. This is the moment to engage the skills of **self-compassion** (Chapter 5) to prevent the distress from spiraling into shame and self-criticism.

- **Affirmation Anchor:** Pair the grounding technique with a compassionate, non-judgmental phrase. After the 5-4-3-2-1 sequence is complete, take a deep breath and repeat: *"This is a moment of suffering, and it is okay. I am here for myself. I am safe."* This reinforces self-kindness, which research shows helps deactivate the brain's threat-defense system.
- **Journaling as Offload:** If the emotional surge was triggered by overwhelming thoughts (e.g., a massive to-do list, a fear of failure), immediately write down those weighty thoughts in a journal (the **Brain Dump**). This externalizes the internal chaos, helping to contain the distress and prevent further rumination, which consumes valuable WM and emotional energy.

Section 4: The Emotional Payoff: Creating Space for Intentional Response

Mastering immediate distress tolerance is the single most important action a woman with ADHD can take to improve her emotional well-being and relationships.

1. Protecting Executive Function and Relationships

By preventing the emotional surge from spiraling into a meltdown, you protect your vital EF reserves and your relational bonds.

- **IC Conservation:** When a sensory shock (TIPP) or distraction (Grounding) creates a crucial pause, it allows the Inhibitory Control (IC) to return online and prevent the impulsive verbal reaction (e.g., snapping at a partner, sending an angry email) that leads to profound regret and relational damage (Book 5).
- **Reducing Shame:** Successfully navigating a crisis without making it worse, without resorting to impulsive, destructive behaviors, provides powerful **evidence of competence** and follow-through, actively dismantling the shame and feeling of inadequacy that accompany unmanaged emotional outbursts.

2. The Bridge to Emotional Mastery (DBT / CBT)

Grounding is merely the first step. The stability gained here is the bridge to the complex cognitive and behavioral work that follows in this book.

- **Readying the Mind:** Once the intensity of the emotion has dropped from "red" to "yellow," the mind is calm enough to engage in rational thought. You are now prepared for the work of **Challenging Thoughts** (Chapter 2) and applying **Opposite**

Action (Chapter 3), the crucial, high-leverage steps that actually change long-term emotional response patterns.

Chapter 1 Workbook: Ground Yourself: Apply Sensory Techniques to Interrupt Acute Distress

Objective: To practice immediate, sensory-based techniques to interrupt acute emotional distress (anxiety, anger, RSD pain) and activate the calming Parasympathetic Nervous System.

Scientific Anchor: Grounding and sensory shock (TIPP) provide rapid physiological interventions that override the emotional alarm system (amygdala), creating the necessary pause for Inhibitory Control to re-engage.

Activity 1.1: The TIPP Circuit-Breaker Plan

Instructions: Create a clear, pre-planned sequence of physiological action for when an intense emotional surge hits.

1. **The Trigger:** Identify a frequent trigger that leads to rapid emotional escalation (e.g., Partner criticism, unexpected task failure, social rejection).

   My Trigger: _____

   _____

   _____

2. **The TIPP Sequence (The "Immediate Action" Plan):** Commit to these three low-friction, rapid interventions.

DBT Skill	Action (Must be pre-planned)	Time / Duration	Neuro-Benefit
T: Temperature	(Example: Splash cold water on face / hold ice pack on wrists.)	30 seconds	Activates the dive reflex / calms heart rate.
I: Intense Exercise	(Example: 20 jumping jacks / brisk walk to mailbox.)	1 minute	Discharges physical energy of stress response.
P: Paced Breathing	(Example: 4-count inhale, 6-count exhale.)	3 cycles	Engages parasympathetic nervous system.

Activity 1.2: The 5-4-3-2-1 Grounding Practice

Instructions: Practice the 5-4-3-2-1 technique now, deliberately slowing down and forcing your focus onto external cues. This trains your attention muscle for crisis situations.

1. **5:** List five things you see in your immediate environment:

    _____
    _____
    _____
    _____
    _____

2. **4:** List four things you can feel (e.g., temperature, texture of clothing, chair pressure):

    _____
    _____
    _____
    _____

3. **3:** List three things you can hear (external sounds):

    _____
    _____
    _____

4. **2:** List two things you can smell:

    _____
    _____

5. **1:** List one thing you can taste:

    _____

Reflective Commitment: If my mind is racing with shame or anger, I commit to performing this full sequence to achieve the **pause**.

Reflection 1.3: Analyzing the Gain in Control

Instructions: Reflect on the functional benefit of distress tolerance skills.

1. **The Crisis Pause:** If a small trigger (e.g., a partner's tone of voice) leads to a rapid emotional surge, how does the deliberate act of performing **Intense Exercise** (Action 1.1) provide the necessary physical and cognitive **interruption** to prevent you from immediately spiraling or shouting?

Interruption Mechanism: _____
_____
_____
_____
_____

2. **IC Protection:** By successfully calming the intensity of the emotion using **Grounding**, you protect your **Inhibitory Control**. How does this conserved IC benefit your relationship in that moment (e.g., prevents you from sending an angry text, prevents an impulsive apology)?

    IC / Relational Benefit: _____
    _____
    _____
    _____
    _____

3. **The Bridge to Cognition:** Once the emotion drops from an intensity of 8 / 10 to 4 / 10, what is the first, small **cognitive task** you are now able to perform (e.g., pick up your journal, apply a rational thought) that was impossible before grounding?

    Cognitive Regain: _____
    _____
    _____
    _____
    _____

CHAPTER 2

CHALLENGE THE CRITIC: IDENTIFY AND REFRAME UNHELPFUL, SHAME-BASED THOUGHTS

In Chapter 1, you learned the crucial first response to acute emotional distress: grounding your body and mind using sensory techniques to create a **physiological circuit-breaker**. That essential pause successfully dropped your emotion from a crisis "red light" to a manageable "yellow light." Now, this chapter introduces the second, transformative step in achieving emotional mastery: engaging the cognitive brain to challenge the destructive, shame-based narratives that fuel emotional volatility.

For the woman with Attention-Deficit / Hyperactivity Disorder (ADHD), emotional dysregulation is rarely just about the feeling; it is amplified by the automatic, pervasive presence of a harsh **Inner Critic**. This voice, fed by a lifetime of internalizing struggles and feeling inadequate, converts minor setbacks into massive personal failures, often through the mechanism of **cognitive distortions** (unhelpful thinking traps).

This chapter equips you with the toolkit of **Cognitive Behavioral Therapy (CBT)**, an evidence-based approach proven highly effective for managing the anxiety, emotional intensity, and chronic shame associated with ADHD. You will learn to become a detective of your own mind, systematically identifying, challenging, and reframing the irrational thought patterns that compromise your Executive Function (EF) and sabotage your self-worth. The goal is to dismantle the source of internalized blame and replace the inner critic with a powerful, compassionate inner ally.

Section 1: The Neurobiological Bridge: Thoughts, Feelings, and Actions

To conquer the inner critic, we must first understand the powerful, instantaneous link between thoughts, feelings, and actions, particularly as it functions in a neurobiologically vulnerable system.

1. The Disconnect: Amygdala Amplification and PFC Failure

The intense, unpredictable nature of ADHD emotions stems from a fundamental disconnect: the **Amygdala** (the brain's emotional accelerator) is often highly sensitive, leading to a quick trigger for strong emotions, while the **Prefrontal Cortex (PFC)** (the cognitive "brakes") is less effective at inhibiting or modulating that intense reaction.

- **Thoughts as Triggers:** In this sensitive neurobiological context, a fleeting negative thought, unexamined and unchallenged, can immediately be amplified by the overactive amygdala, leading to a full-blown emotional storm, a phenomenon far more likely in the context of emotional dysregulation.

- **The Shame Loop:** Because the woman with ADHD is prone to interpreting her symptoms (forgetfulness, disorganization) as moral failings, her automatic thoughts often center on deep inadequacy (e.g., "I'm useless," "I'll never succeed"). This self-blaming thought acts as a **stress trigger**, increasing cortisol and anxiety, which further impairs the function of the PFC, making it even harder to think clearly and regulate the emotion, a destructive shame loop.

2. CBT's Core Principle: Thoughts are Interpretations, Not Facts

The fundamental premise of CBT is that events do not cause feelings; your **interpretation** of events causes your feelings and subsequent actions. By identifying and challenging the automatic thought, you interrupt the emotional chain reaction.

- **Intervention Point:** CBT focuses on creating a cognitive intervention point in the "yellow light" phase of the emotional surge (after grounding has calmed the initial physical alarm). This pause allows the woman to use her cognitive skills to challenge the thought before it fully dictates her emotional and behavioral response.
- **Building the Cognitive Buffer:** Through consistent practice, the CBT approach empowers the individual to develop a systematic framework for mental processing, effectively training the PFC to engage and override the automatic, unhelpful thoughts that often lead to emotional dysregulation and impulsivity.

Section 2: Unmasking Common Cognitive Distortions

Cognitive distortions are irrational or exaggerated thought patterns that reinforce negative thinking, undermine self-esteem, and exacerbate emotional distress. Recognizing these "thinking traps" is the crucial first step toward challenging them.

1. Distortions Amplified by Emotional Intensity

These distortions are common, but they become particularly damaging for the ADHD brain due to the intensity of its emotional regulation and its history of masking and shame.

- **Catastrophizing:** This involves exaggerating the negative consequences of an event, jumping to the worst possible conclusion, even when it's highly unlikely.
  - *ADHD Example:* "I missed that deadline by one hour. Now my boss will think I'm incompetent, I'll be fired, and I'll never find another job." This distortion turns a small mistake into an apocalyptic scenario, fueling intense anxiety and shame.
- **All-or-Nothing Thinking (Black-and-White Thinking):** Seeing things only in extremes, with no middle ground. Everything is either a complete success or an utter failure.
  - *ADHD Example:* "I didn't finish everything on my to-do list today, so the day was a total waste, and I'm a complete failure." This distortion ignores partial progress and effort, reinforcing the shame of imperfection.
- **Mind Reading:** Assuming you know what others are thinking or feeling, usually negatively, without any actual evidence. This is especially painful for those with Rejection Sensitive Dysphoria (RSD).

- ○ *ADHD Example:* "My partner gave me a curt reply. He must be disappointed in me and thinks I'm a mess." This jumps to rejection-based conclusions, triggering intense emotional pain without factual basis.
- **"Should" Statements:** Holding rigid, often unrealistic, expectations for yourself that often ignore the neurobiological reality of ADHD.
  - ○ *ADHD Example:* "I should be able to focus for three hours without checking my phone, just like my colleagues." When this unrealistic expectation is not met, it leads to intense guilt, shame, and self-punishment.

2. Shame-Based Distortions (Internalization)

The distortions of **Personalization** and **Emotional Reasoning** are directly linked to the shame felt by women who internalize their struggles.

- **Personalization:** Blaming yourself for external events or taking things personally that are not your fault.
  - ○ *ADHD Example:* "Our team project failed because I didn't push hard enough on my part," even when multiple factors were involved. This ties into the deep-seated belief that one's inadequacy is the root of all problems.
- **Emotional Reasoning:** Believing something is true solely because you feel it strongly, treating intense feelings as definitive evidence of reality.
  - ○ *ADHD Example:* "I feel like a lazy, unproductive person today, so I must be lazy and incapable." The intensity of ADHD emotions makes this distortion particularly compelling and difficult to challenge.

Section 3: The Practice: Becoming a Thought Detective

The key to breaking free from the grip of distorted thoughts is to become a detective of your own mind. This is an active, structured process of observation, questioning, and re-framing, a strategic application of your cognitive skills.

Step 1: Catch the Thought (The "Pause and Observe")

When you feel a sudden surge of a strong negative emotion (anger, shame, intense anxiety), use the **Grounding Techniques** (Chapter 1) to create a physiological pause. Once the intensity has dropped, engage your cognitive self.

- **Identify the Trigger:** Ask: "What just happened?" (The external event).
- **Catch the Narrative:** Ask: "What thought just went through my mind right before I felt this intense emotion?" Write the exact thought down immediately. The act of externalizing the thought helps you gain crucial distance from it, allowing you to view it as an object of analysis rather than an undeniable truth.

Step 2: Challenge the Thought (The "Courtroom Test")

Once you have externalized the thought, put it on trial. Imagine you are a neutral judge or lawyer, rigorously examining the evidence for and against the thought.

- **Test the Evidence:** What is the **concrete, factual evidence** that this thought is 100% true? (Focus only on facts, not feelings or past assumptions). What are the **facts against** the thought (e.g., "I finished 80% of the project," "My partner used a neutral tone of voice")?
- **Name the Distortion:** Am I falling into a specific thinking trap? Naming the distortion (e.g., "This is Catastrophizing") helps you depersonalize the thought and strip it of its power.
- **Practice Perspective-Taking:** What would I tell a friend in this exact situation? Use the self-compassion skills you have trained to apply rationality to the situation.

Step 3: Reframe and Replace (The "Constructive Alternative")

Based on your rigorous questioning, formulate a more balanced, realistic, and ultimately more helpful thought. This is not about forced positive affirmations; it is about finding a more accurate, nuanced, and empowering perspective that reflects reality more fully.

Original Distorted Thought (Shameful)	Reframed, Balanced Thought (Strategic / Compassionate)
"I'm a total failure for messing up that small task; I can't do anything right."	**Reframe:** "I made a mistake, which is human. I finished three Milestones today, and that's solid progress. The mistake is fixable; it does not define my worth."

Original Distorted Thought (Shameful)	Reframed, Balanced Thought (Strategic / Compassionate)
"My boss ignored me. I'm sure she thinks I'm incompetent (Mind Reading / RSD)."	**Reframe:** "I observed a neutral behavior (she was busy). I'm feeling fear of rejection, which is RSD. I will gather factual evidence later by checking in about the report."
"Since I procrastinated, the whole project is ruined, and there's no point in starting (All-or-Nothing / Paralysis)."	**Reframe:** "The project is not ruined. I can allocate 25 minutes now to the first micro-step, and that momentum is better than paralysis."

Section 4: The Emotional Payoff: Healing Shame and Building Resilience

The consistent practice of identifying and challenging distorted thoughts yields profound emotional and psychological liberation, reinforcing self-worth and increasing resilience.

1. Healing from Shame and RSD

The single greatest payoff is the active dismantling of the Inner Critic, which is the relentless source of shame for the woman with ADHD.

- **Dismantling the Narrative:** By rigorously testing and replacing shame-based thoughts, you systematically dismantle a lifetime of internalized narratives about inadequacy and failure. This builds a robust, internal foundation of self-worth that is resistant to external criticism and the debilitating pain of RSD.

- **Building Self-Acceptance:** The commitment to approaching your own suffering with kindness and rational inquiry is a powerful act of **self-compassion** (Chapter 5), creating a psychological buffer that allows you to learn from mistakes without being crippled by them.

2. Protecting Executive Function and Relationships

Challenging thoughts directly protects the EF skills you have mastered and improves relational outcomes.

- **Conserving IC:** By interrupting the cascade of anxiety and anger that a distorted thought triggers, you conserve vital **Inhibitory Control (IC)** resources. This preserved IC is necessary to engage the behavioral skills (like Opposite Action) that prevent impulsive shouting or emotional outbursts.

- **Reducing Relational Friction:** Since strong emotional reactions often spiral from distorted, fear-based thoughts (e.g., Mind Reading / Catastrophizing), challenging these thoughts reduces the intensity of the feeling, allowing you to approach difficult conversations with clarity and calm. This promotes constructive communication and prevents the friction that damages relationships (Book 5).

Conclusion: Your Cognitive Command

You have achieved cognitive command over the inner critic. By consistently applying the CBT framework, you transform your mind from a source of perpetual self-criticism and shame into a reliable engine for self-compassion and intentional action. This mastery of your thought patterns is the essential cognitive anchor that supports the intense behavioral and interpersonal work that follows in this book, allowing you to use your emotions as information, not as masters.

Chapter 2 Workbook: Challenge the Critic: Identify and Reframe Unhelpful, Shame-Based Thoughts

Objective: To practice identifying common cognitive distortions that fuel shame and emotional dysregulation, and to systematically challenge and reframe them using the CBT method.

Scientific Anchor: Identifying and challenging cognitive distortions is a cornerstone of CBT, helping to interrupt the thought-emotion-action cycle that compromises emotional regulation and drives self-criticism.

Activity 2.1: The Thought Detective Audit (Catch & Name)

Instructions: Identify a recent moment when you felt a sudden, strong negative emotion (e.g., shame, anger, overwhelming anxiety). Use the framework to catch and name the distortion.

1. **The Trigger Event:** Briefly describe the objective event (e.g., "I forgot to send an important work email this morning").

   Event: _____

   _____

2. **The Automatic Thought (The Inner Critic's Voice):** Write the exact thought that immediately followed the event.

Thought: _____

_____

3. **Name the Distortion:** Which thinking trap best describes that thought? (Catastrophizing, All-or-Nothing, Mind Reading, Emotional Reasoning, "Should" Statements, Personalization).

Distortion: _____

_____

Activity 2.2: The Courtroom Test (Challenge & Evidence)

Instructions: Put your automatic thought from Activity 2.1 on trial. You are the lawyer testing the evidence.

1. **Evidence FOR the Thought:** What is the factual evidence supporting the thought? (Focus on facts, not feelings).

Factual Evidence: _____

_____

_____

2. **Evidence AGAINST the Thought:** What facts contradict the thought? (e.g., "I met three Milestones this week," "The email is only one hour late," "My boss sent a neutral email earlier").

Contradictory Evidence: _____

_____

_____

3. **The Verdict:** Based on the evidence, is the original thought 100% true? ____

Reflection 2.3: Reframe and Empower

Instructions: Formulate a compassionate, strategic reframe for your thought, using the evidence you collected.

1. **The Balanced Reframe:** Write a new, realistic, and compassionate statement that acknowledges the mistake but rejects the shame.

Reframed Thought: _____

_____

_____

2. **RSD Healing:** If the thought was related to fear of rejection or shame (RSD), how does having a **factual list of evidence against** the thought help reduce the intense, physical pain associated with RSD?

   RSD Benefit: _____

   _____

   _____

3. **IC Conservation:** How does the act of stopping to **Challenge** the thought (Step 2) conserve the **Inhibitory Control (IC)** you need to manage your emotions, rather than letting the anger / shame immediately fuel an impulsive reaction?

   IC Conservation: _____

   _____

   _____

CHAPTER 3

CHANGE THE SCRIPT: USE "OPPOSITE ACTION" TO INTERRUPT EMOTIONAL IMPULSES

In the journey toward emotional mastery, you have secured the crucial foundations: grounding the body during crisis (Chapter 1) and challenging the destructive narratives of the inner critic (Chapter 2). However, cognitive insight alone is often insufficient when faced with the raw, intense force of an emotional surge. For the woman with Attention-Deficit / Hyperactivity Disorder (ADHD), the urge to act on an intense emotion, to yell, to withdraw, or to lash out, is powerful and immediate, driven by deficits in Inhibitory Control (IC).

This chapter introduces the essential behavioral skill for managing these moments: **Opposite Action**. This core principle of **Dialectical Behavior Therapy (DBT)** provides a structured, actionable framework for interrupting the destructive emotional cycle. Opposite Action mandates that when an intense emotion leads to an unhelpful or destructive urge, you must intentionally execute the **opposite** behavioral response.

This is a powerful, strategic intervention that bypasses compromised IC by using intentional behavior to change the emotional trajectory itself. You move from passively enduring an emotion to actively changing the internal script, transforming automatic, regrettable reactions into thoughtful, intentional responses that build long-term emotional resilience and strengthen relationships.

Section 1: The Neurobiology of the Impulsive Urge

To effectively deploy Opposite Action, you must understand that the destructive urge is a neurological event rooted in the ADHD brain's structural deficits, not a failure of character.

1. The Amygdala-PFC Disconnect and IC Failure

Emotional dysregulation in ADHD is defined by a disconnect between the emotional accelerator (the amygdala) and the cognitive brakes (the prefrontal cortex, or PFC).

- **Disproportionate Urges:** When a trigger occurs, the amygdala fires, creating an immediate, intense urge (e.g., anger, despair). Because the PFC's Inhibitory Control (IC) is inconsistent, the urge translates quickly into an impulsive action (yelling, snapping, avoiding) before the logical brain can assess the situation.

- **Emotions vs. Action:** The intense emotion is real, but the action it urges is often disproportionate or unhelpful to the situation. For instance, sadness over a minor setback is real, but the urge to isolate for three days (the action) is unhelpful because it only increases despair and shame.

- **The Behavioral Solution:** Opposite Action recognizes that if you change the destructive behavior, the emotion that fueled it will eventually change too. This behavioral intervention is often faster and more effective in the moment of crisis than trying to force a cognitive change (e.g., trying to convince yourself to *not* be angry).

2. The Unhelpful Nature of Emotional Responses

Opposite Action is deployed only when the emotion or its associated urge is **unjustified** by the facts of the situation, or when the emotion is **justified but the resulting action is unhelpful** (i.e., makes the situation worse).

Emotion	Urge (Action)	When Opposite Action is Needed
Anger / Irritation	Attack, yell, criticize, lash out.	When the situation is minor (e.g., spilled coffee) or the action will lead to negative relational consequences (Book 5).
Shame / Guilt	Hide, isolate, avoid communication, apologize excessively.	When the urge to isolate perpetuates sadness, or when avoidance guarantees task failure (Task Paralysis).
Fear / Anxiety	Avoid the situation, procrastinate, run away, seek constant reassurance.	When the avoidance is disproportionate to the actual threat (e.g., avoiding a necessary phone call), increasing anxiety in the long term.

Section 2: The Opposite Action Framework in Practice

Applying Opposite Action requires a swift, methodical three-step sequence, utilizing the **Pause** created by grounding (Chapter 1) to deploy intentional action.

Step 1: Identify the Emotion and the Urge

Use the tools of mindfulness (Chapter 3) to label the feeling and the subsequent urge. You must separate the emotion (the feeling) from the impulse (the behavior).

- *Example*: **Emotion:** Intense Anger. **Urge:** To interrupt my partner and shout that I am overwhelmed.
- *Example*: **Emotion:** Shame / RSD pain. **Urge:** To immediately send a long text message apologizing for a minor mistake and withdraw from social interaction.

Step 2: Determine Justification and Impact

Rigorously test the emotion (using CBT skills from Chapter 2). Is the emotion justified by the facts, or is the resulting urge helpful?

- *Anger Scenario*: Is my partner's neutral comment truly a massive attack (justification)? No. Is yelling at them helpful (impact)? No, it will only increase conflict and shame. *Conclusion: Opposite Action is required.*

- *Shame Scenario:* Is my minor mistake (unpaid bill) a complete and total catastrophe that warrants three days of self-isolation (impact)? No. *Conclusion: Opposite Action is required.*

Step 3: Execute the Opposite Behavior

Immediately engage in a behavior that is completely contrary to the destructive urge. The action must be immediate, visible, and sustained for a period long enough to allow the emotional intensity to subside.

Unhelpful Urge (ADHD Impulse)	Opposite Action (DBT Strategy)	Neurobiological Effect
Urge to Attack / Yell (Anger / Irritability)	**Use a Gentle Voice / Avoid Aggression.** Avoid eye contact, relax facial muscles, use "I" statements, or implement a pre-planned **Time Out** (walk away for 10 min).	Deactivates the physiological fight-or-flight response, allowing the PFC to re-engage Inhibitory Control.
Urge to Avoid / Isolate (Shame / RSD / Paralysis)	**Engage Socially / Approach Task.** Force yourself to initiate a micro-step of the avoided task (Paralysis), or call a supportive friend (Isolation).	Displaces the unhelpful emotional energy with productive, non-shaming action, building momentum.
Urge to Ruminate / Worry (Anxiety)	**Focus on External Reality.** Use **5-4-3-2-1 Grounding** (Chapter 1), engage in intense physical exercise (Intense Exercise TIPP skill), or switch focus to a neutral, absorbing task.	Diverts Working Memory from the anxious thought loop to an external anchor, disrupting the spiral.
Urge to Withdraw / Give Up (Despair / Sadness)	**Increase Activity.** Force yourself to engage in gentle, positive activity (e.g., listen to music, go outside, walk briskly), even if you don't feel like it.	Increases positive affect, which is the opposite of the despairing urge.

Section 3: Applying Opposite Action to Relationship and Task Friction

Opposite Action is a powerful tool for women with ADHD because it targets the precise behavioral consequences that most damage self-worth and relationships.

1. Managing Anger and Relational Conflict

Anger and irritability are highly prevalent ADHD symptoms that profoundly damage close relationships, often leading to arguments over seemingly trivial issues.

- **The Gentle Communication Script:** When Anger flares, the urge is to attack or criticize (e.g., "You never listen!"). The opposite action is to immediately shift the physical posture (relaxed hands, slow speech) and use **"I" statements** (Chapter 5, Book 5) to express the need without attacking the partner's character. For example, replace "You never listen!" with, "I feel unheard when you look at your phone while I'm talking."

- **The Time Out Protocol:** If the emotional surge is too high (high "red light"), the opposite action is to take a pre-agreed **Time Out** (e.g., "I need 10 minutes to cool down, I will return at 7:30 PM"). This is crucial IC in action, physically removing the threat of an impulsive outburst that would cause lasting damage.

2. Defeating Shame, RSD, and Task Paralysis

Shame and RSD often manifest as the paralyzing urge to hide or avoid tasks that carry the risk of failure (Task Paralysis).

- **Opposite Action for Avoidance:** If the urge is to stay paralyzed and avoid starting a daunting project (e.g., filing taxes), the opposite action is **immediate, non-judgmental initiation of a micro-step** (Chapter 1, Book 3). For example, if the urge is to zone out on the couch, the opposite action is to force yourself to walk to the desk and simply open the file folder. This breaks the shame / paralysis cycle with momentum.

- **Opposite Action for Shame / RSD:** When RSD strikes (urge to apologize profusely or withdraw after a perceived snub), the opposite action is to **engage socially** or **assert self-respect**. Instead of withdrawing, force yourself to make brief social contact. Instead of collapsing into excessive apologies, make a short, factual apology and then engage in self-compassionate thought-reframing (Chapter 2).

Section 4: The Behavioral Chain Analysis (BCA): Proactive Intervention

Opposite Action is best used proactively. The **Behavioral Chain Analysis (BCA)** is a DBT skill that helps you analyze a past regretted action to pinpoint the precise environmental and internal triggers that occurred *before* the impulsive urge, allowing for strategic future intervention.

1. Analyzing the Sequence of Events

BCA recognizes that impulsive behavior is the end of a long chain of smaller, often unnoticed, events. Analyzing this chain reveals where your EF and emotional regulation broke down.

- **The Regretted Action:** Start with the impulsive behavior (e.g., snapping at your child, making a massive impulsive purchase).
- **The Chain:** Work backward, identifying the precise sequence:
  1. **Vulnerability:** What made me vulnerable? (e.g., Low sleep, skipped meal, low-estrogen Luteal Phase).
  2. **Trigger:** What was the final external event? (e.g., Child asked for help while I was hyperfocused).
  3. **Thought / Feeling:** What was the immediate thought / emotion? (e.g., "I can't take this interruption, I'm going to fail!" -> Intense Anger / Frustration).
  4. **Action / Urge:** What was the resulting urge? (e.g., Urge to yell).

2. Strategic Intervention Points

BCA allows you to identify *where* to apply the Opposite Action skill before the urge hits.

- **Proactive Buffer:** The optimal point for intervention is at the vulnerability and trigger stage (Step 1 / 2). (e.g., Schedule a **Meal / Rest Block** in the Time Block to reduce hunger vulnerability).
- **Immediate Action:** The immediate application of Opposite Action occurs between Step 3 (Thought / Feeling) and Step 4 (Action / Urge). This pause and subsequent opposite action prevents the chain from culminating in the regretted behavior.

Conclusion: Your Internal Command

Mastering **Opposite Action** is the definitive behavioral step in achieving emotional regulation. You have moved from merely reacting to intense feelings to actively changing the emotional script through intentional behavior.

By integrating this skill with your EF mastery (IC / Attention) and your cognitive skills (Challenging Thoughts), you transform emotional turmoil from a source of chaos into a signal for strategic action. This disciplined approach builds profound self-efficacy and is the foundational pillar for building resilient, empathetic, and fulfilling relationships (Chapter 4 and 5). You are now in command of your inner world.

Chapter 3 Workbook: Change the Script: Use "Opposite Action" to Interrupt Emotional Impulses

Objective: To practice identifying unhelpful emotional urges (impulsive behavior) and defining a strategic, contrary action to interrupt the emotional spiral.

Scientific Anchor: Opposite Action is a core DBT skill used to interrupt and eventually change the destructive link between intense, disproportionate emotions and unhelpful behavioral urges, strengthening Inhibitory Control (IC).

Activity 3.1: The Unhelpful Urge Audit

Instructions: Recall a recent instance of intense, regrettable emotional behavior. Identify the emotion, the unhelpful urge it produced, and the strategic opposite action required.

1. **Emotion (e.g., Anger, Shame, Despair):**
2. **The Unhelpful Urge (The Impulse):** What did you want to do impulsively? (e.g., Yell, apologize excessively, isolate, procrastinate).

   Urge: _____

   _____

3. **The Opposite Action (The Strategy):** What is the exact behavioral opposite you should have done? (e.g., Speak softly, engage socially, initiate a micro-step of the task).

   Strategic Opposite Action: _____

   _____

Activity 3.2: The Anti-Anger Protocol (Relational)

Instructions: Create a **relational circuit-breaker** for when anger or irritability flares up with a partner or loved one, using communication and physical boundaries.

1. **Anger Trigger:** (Example: Partner interrupts your hyperfocus block).

   Trigger: _____

2. **The Urge to Attack:** (Example: Shout, use sarcasm, criticize).

   Urge: _____

3. **Opposite Action Commitment:** Commit to two immediate, non-aggressive actions:

   Action A (Physical): (Example: Take a pre-agreed 5-minute time out / walk away).

   Action B (Verbal): (Example: Use a soft voice to state, "I am feeling overwhelmed right now and need 10 minutes to reset").

Reflection 3.3: Analyzing the Gain in Emotional Command

Instructions: Reflect on how deliberately applying the opposite behavior conserves EF and builds self-efficacy.

1. **IC Conservation:** When you successfully execute **Action A (Time Out)** in Activity 3.2, how does that physical removal of yourself from the argument conserve the **Inhibitory Control** (IC) you need to manage your emotions, compared to staying in the fight?

   IC Benefit: _____

   _____

2. **Defeating Paralysis:** If the urge is to avoid and procrastinate on a massive project (shame / fear), how does the Opposite Action of completing a **single micro-step** (Chapter 1, Book 3) transform the emotional state from despair to momentum?

   Momentum Gain: _____

   _____

3. **Self-Efficacy:** When you choose the **Opposite Action** (e.g., engage socially instead of hiding), you are consciously overriding a powerful impulse. How does this successful choice provide **tangible evidence of self-command** that directly counters the inner critic's narrative that you are "out of control?"

   Evidence of Command: _____

   _____

CHAPTER 4

CONNECT THROUGH LISTENING: EMPLOY MIRRORING AND VALIDATION FOR DEEPER COMMUNICATION

You have mastered the foundational work of emotional mastery: creating the crucial pause during crisis (Chapter 1) and challenging the Inner Critic (Chapter 2) through cognitive reframing. This work provides internal stability. Now, the journey shifts to the external sphere: applying this control to the most fragile and high-friction aspect of neurodiverse relationships, **communication**.

For the woman with Attention-Deficit / Hyperactivity Disorder (ADHD), communication is often compromised by core symptoms: **inattention** (mind-wandering during conversation) and **impulsivity** (interrupting due to fear of forgetting a thought). These behaviors, while rooted in compromised Executive Function (EF), frequently lead a partner to feel unheard, ignored, or unprioritized, leading to resentment and emotional isolation, a major cause of relationship stress.

This chapter provides the strategic toolkit of **Interpersonal Effectiveness** (a core skill of Dialectical Behavior Therapy, or DBT) to bridge this communication gap. By mastering the techniques of **Mirroring, Validation, and Empathy**, you actively counteract the perception of inattention, foster genuine understanding, and build the foundation of trust necessary to transform daily friction into collaborative partnership. The goal is to move from defensiveness and misunderstanding to deep, empathetic connection.

Section 1: The Neurobiological Barrier to Active Listening

Effective communication relies on sustained, mindful listening, which directly engages EF skills that are often inconsistent in the ADHD brain.

1. Inattention and the Fragmentation of Listening

The ADHD brain's difficulty with sustained attention and its impaired filtering mechanism make deep listening challenging.

- **Mind-Wandering:** During a partner's conversation, the woman's attention may fragment, pulled away by an external distraction (visual / auditory noise) or internal stimuli (racing thoughts, new ideas). This mind-wandering leads to missed details, difficulty retaining instructions, and the appearance of disinterest, even when the woman is genuinely trying to engage.
- **The Working Memory Sieve:** Active listening requires holding the speaker's points in **Working Memory (WM)** while processing their meaning and formulating a response. Because WM is easily overloaded, the woman may lose the thread of the conversation, making it difficult to accurately summarize or respond coherently, leading the partner to feel unheard.

2. Impulsivity and the Interruptive Urge

Impulsivity, a deficit in **Inhibitory Control (IC)**, creates the painful urge to interrupt or blurt out thoughts, further compromising communication.

- **Fear of Loss:** The urge to interrupt is often driven by the fear that a fleeting thought or insight will be lost forever due to compromised WM if the woman waits for her turn. This impulsive behavior, while rooted in a memory deficit, is often perceived by the non-ADHD partner as rudeness, self-centeredness, or lack of respect.

The DBT communication strategies provided here recognize that the brain must be given a **structured task** to anchor its focus, simultaneously reinforcing IC and WM during vulnerable relational moments.

Section 2: The Interpersonal Effectiveness Toolkit (Mirror, Validate, Empathize)

The core strategy for repairing communication deficits is the active, intentional use of three techniques that provide immediate, tangible proof to the partner that they have been heard and understood, bypassing the negative interpretations caused by past inattention.

1. Mirroring: Anchoring Attention and Ensuring Accuracy

Mirroring (or paraphrasing) is the act of restating or summarizing what your partner said *before* offering your own thoughts or response. This technique anchors your attention and serves as a check for accuracy.

- **Action:** When your partner finishes speaking, pause, take a breath (IC in action), and begin your response with a mirroring phrase: "So, let me make sure I understood: you feel frustrated that the chores haven't been divided fairly, and you specifically need the laundry offloaded from your plate."

- **Neuro-Benefit:** This forces the ADHD brain to engage in **Working Memory retrieval** and sustained attention, ensuring that the critical information is captured and processed. For the partner, it provides immediate, irrefutable evidence that their message was received, directly counteracting the perception of inattention or mind-wandering.

2. Validation: Acknowledging the Emotional Reality

Validation is the act of acknowledging your partner's feelings as real, understandable, and legitimate, even if you do not agree with their perspective or interpretation of the facts.

- **Action:** Connect with your partner's emotional state using a validating phrase: *"That makes complete sense. Given how much you're handling at work, I understand why you feel overwhelmed by the additional mental load of the chores."*

- **Neuro-Benefit:** Validation de-escalates emotional intensity, which is critical for the ADHD partner, who often struggles with heightened emotional reactivity themselves. By showing you are engaged and present, you boost the partner's self-confidence and foster a sense of mutual respect, which is essential for conflict resolution.

3. Empathy: Demonstrating Understanding and Care

Empathy moves beyond simply acknowledging feelings to expressing genuine understanding for your partner's experience.

- **Action:** Use statements that reflect true understanding and remove barriers of distrust: *"I see how you feel. I understand that the pattern of me forgetting things makes you feel unsafe about relying on me."*
- **Neuro-Benefit:** This powerful act of connection reduces the partner's feeling of isolation and resentment, fostering empathy that helps **repair disconnections** caused by previous ADHD-related failures (e.g., missed appointments, impulsive reactions).

Section 3: Structural Communication: Creating Predictability

Communication cannot rely on spontaneous emotional energy alone. For neurodiverse couples, intentional structure and predictability are necessary to prevent issues from escalating into intense emotional conflict.

1. Scheduling the "Relationship Roundtable"

Emotional conversations are difficult for the ADHD brain to navigate on impulse. The solution is to schedule important discussions when both partners are rested and prepared.

- **Fixed Appointments:** Schedule brief, dedicated **weekly check-ins** to discuss logistics, shared responsibilities, and emotional temperature. This creates a routine of open dialogue, preventing issues from compounding and exploding later in a reactive moment.
- **The "Pause Rule":** For spontaneous, emotionally charged conversations, establish a pre-agreed "Pause Rule." Either partner can call a **Time Out** (Chapter 3, Book 5), agreeing to disengage and return to the topic after 20 minutes when both have calmed down. This enforces Inhibitory Control and prevents the conversation from being hijacked by the impulsive emotional surge.

2. Assertiveness through "I" Statements

When communication turns to complaints or requests for change, the most effective tool for preventing defensiveness and promoting clear action is the **"I" Statement.**

- **Focus on Self, Not Blame:** An "I" statement focuses on your own feelings and needs, rather than attacking the partner's character or actions (e.g., replacing "You never listen!" with "I feel frustrated when I am talking and you are looking at your phone"). This de-escalates conflict by removing the immediate trigger for defensiveness, opening the door for collaborative problem-solving.
- **Problem-Solving Focus:** As research suggests, couples are more likely to stay constructively engaged if they look for **common ground** and focus on solutions. Redirecting the argument toward a shared goal ("We both agree that it's important for the kids to get enough sleep, so what might help us achieve the 9 PM bedtime?") reframes the discussion into a collaborative effort.

Section 4: The Emotional and Relational Payoff

Mastering active listening and validation is essential for moving past the shame and friction that define neurodiverse relationship struggles.

1. Reducing Relational Friction and the Parent-Child Dynamic

Poor communication, coupled with organizational deficits, is a major factor in the destructive **"parent-child" dynamic**, where the non-ADHD partner becomes the taskmaster.

- **Shifting Accountability:** By using **Mirroring** and **Validation** when the partner expresses frustration, you demonstrate that you are engaged, you understand the emotional impact of your symptoms, and you are taking responsibility for the problem. This rebuilds trust and reduces the partner's need to constantly remind or police, shifting the dynamic back toward a balanced, respectful partnership.

2. Healing Shame and RSD

The consistent practice of effective communication is a powerful antidote to the shame and chronic anxiety fueled by **Rejection Sensitive Dysphoria (RSD)**.

- **Evidence of Worthiness:** RSD is rooted in the fear of being perceived as unworthy or inadequate. When a woman consistently engages in open, validating communication, especially during conflict, she creates **tangible evidence of her competence and commitment** to the relationship. This steady stream of positive feedback counters the inner critic's negative narrative, strengthening self-worth.

- **Repair Attempts:** After a conflict or impulsive reaction, the ability to offer a sincere apology and validate the partner's experience (e.g., *"I was wrong to snap at you; I understand you feel hurt, and I am committed to using my Pause Rule next time."*) provides an **"olive branch"** that actively repairs disconnections, preventing small arguments from causing lasting emotional damage.

Conclusion: The Bedrock of Connection

Mastering active listening and validation is the essential bedrock of resilient relationships. You have learned to bypass the neurobiological barriers of inattention and impulsivity by using structured communication techniques that build trust and empathy.

By moving from passive coping to intentional engagement, you transform your relationships from a source of high friction and shame into a vital source of support and self-acceptance. This relational competence is the final skill set needed to complete the journey of self-mastery, preparing you to integrate your focus, emotions, and connections into a fully empowered life.

Chapter 4 Workbook: Connect Through Listening: Employ Mirroring and Validation for Deeper Communication

Objective: To practice structured communication techniques (Mirroring and Validation) that actively anchor attention, counteract the perception of inattention, and build relational trust.

Scientific Anchor: Mirroring forces active listening (engaging WM), and validation de-escalates emotional intensity, both crucial for managing high-friction conversations common in neurodiverse couples.

Activity 4.1: The Mirroring and Validation Practice

Instructions: Practice using mirroring and validation on a low-stakes conversation with your partner or a friend this week (e.g., discussing their day, a movie, or a minor logistical issue).

1. **The Scenario:** (Describe the topic of the conversation).
2. **Mirroring Commitment:** After your partner finishes a point, commit to restating the essence of what they said before responding.

   Partner's Statement (Simplified): _____

Your Mirroring Response: "So, what I hear you saying is that you feel because of _____. Did I get that right?"

3. **Validation Commitment:** Find a way to validate their feeling, even if you don't agree with the cause.

   Your Validation Response: "I understand why that would make you feel _____ That frustration makes sense."

Activity 4.2: The Impulsivity Circuit-Breaker

Instructions: Plan for a high-risk communication moment when you typically struggle with impulsive interruption. This is IC in action.

1. **The High-Risk Scenario:** (e.g., A weekly planning session, discussing finances, or a time when you are tired).

2. **The Interruptive Urge:** What thought triggers your urge to interrupt? (e.g., "If I don't say this now, I'll forget it!").

   Urge Thought: _____

   _____

   _____

   _____

   _____

3. **The IC Intervention:** When the urge hits, commit to two steps:

   Step 1 (Grounding): Deploy 3 seconds of paced breathing (Chapter 1) to create the pause.

   Step 2 (Offload): Immediately write down the thought on a notepad to offload it from WM. This reduces the fear of forgetting and allows you to return to listening.

Reflection 4.3: Analyzing Relational Gain

Instructions: Reflect on how intentional communication impacts relational trust and emotional stability.

1. **Counteracting Inattention:** How did using the **Mirroring** technique (Activity 4.1) help to anchor your attention, preventing your mind from wandering and ensuring you captured the important details of the conversation?

   Attention Anchor: _____

   _____

   _____

2. **Building Trust:** When you used **Validation** (acknowledging your partner's feelings), how did they react? How does validating their emotional reality help **rebuild trust** that may have been damaged by past impulsive or inattentive episodes?

   Trust Rebuilding: _____

   _____

3. **RSD Mitigation:** RSD is often triggered by perceived rejection during conflict. How does the practice of **Empathy** (Chapter 4, Section 2) reduce the likelihood that a neutral tone of voice from your partner will be misinterpreted through the "lens of rejection?"

   RSD Buffer: _____

   _____

CHAPTER 5

FIGHT FAIR: USE 'I' STATEMENTS AND REPAIR ATTEMPTS TO RESOLVE CONFLICT

You have established internal control by creating a crucial emotional pause (Chapter 1) and replacing self-criticism with cognitive reframing (Chapter 2). You have also mastered tools for active, validating communication (Chapter 4). This foundation of internal and interpersonal skills is vital, but relationships are dynamic and inevitably involve conflict. For the neurodiverse couple, unmanaged conflict, fueled by emotional intensity and deficits in Inhibitory Control (IC), is a major cause of relationship strain and breakdown.

This chapter addresses the highest-stakes scenario in relationships: **constructive conflict resolution**. You will learn how to apply your hard-won Executive Function (EF) skills (IC, Working Memory) and emotional strategies (Distress Tolerance) to engage in conflict without causing lasting damage. By mastering the use of **"I" Statements** to assert needs and practicing timely **Repair Attempts**, you transform arguments from destructive emotional explosions into opportunities for collaborative problem-solving, ensuring your relationship remains resilient and trust-based.

The goal is to move beyond the dysfunctional "parent-child" dynamic and the pain of impulsive reactions, learning to "fight fair" as equal, empathetic partners committed to a shared future.

Section 1: The Neurobiological Crisis of Conflict

Conflict is often disproportionately difficult for the neurodiverse couple because the core symptoms of ADHD, impulsivity, intense emotionality, and low frustration tolerance, are amplified under stress.

1. Impulsive Escalation and Inhibitory Control (IC)

Arguments are highly triggering because they activate the brain's threat system, demanding that the Prefrontal Cortex (PFC) maintain control while emotions run high.

- **IC Failure under Stress:** The core problem is that stress and high emotions compromise **Inhibitory Control** (the emotional "brakes"), making the woman with ADHD more likely to lash out, interrupt, or say regrettable things during a disagreement. These impulsive verbal actions are often perceived by the partner as unfair attacks or a failure to respect boundaries, which quickly escalates the argument.

- **The Vicious Cycle:** Arguments frequently revolve around ADHD-related deficits: the non-ADHD partner criticizes a lack of follow-through ("You never finished the laundry"), which triggers the ADHD partner's **Shame / RSD** (Chapter 2), leading to an intense, defensive, and disproportionate emotional outburst (e.g., yelling, storming off). This emotional reaction validates the partner's feeling of being in a "parent-child" dynamic, escalating the resentment.

2. Conflict as an Amorphous Problem

For the ADHD brain, which struggles with ambiguity (Chapter 2, Book 3), conflict can feel like an amorphous, unsolvable problem.

- **Focus on the Past vs. Future:** Arguments often get stuck ruminating on past failures ("You missed the deadline last month, too!"), rather than focusing the Executive Function on the present task: *solving the problem and establishing a future plan.*

- **Need for Structure:** Just as you broke down deadlines into manageable Milestones (Chapter 1, Book 3), conflict requires external structure to remain contained and solution-focused. Without boundaries, the argument feels infinite and leads to emotional exhaustion.

Section 2: Assertive Communication: The Power of "I" Statements

The most foundational strategy for productive conflict is shifting the language of the argument from blame to personal need. This is achieved through the disciplined use of **"I" Statements**.

1. Shifting from Blame to Need

"You" statements (e.g., "You never listen," "You always interrupt") are aggressive, accusatory, and immediately trigger defensiveness, making rational problem-solving impossible.

- **The "I" Statement Structure:** The "I" Statement refocuses the conversation on your own feelings, needs, and the factual impact of the behavior, allowing the other person to receive the information without feeling attacked.
  - Example: Replace "You always leave the dishes in the sink, you don't care about the shared space!"
  - With: **"I feel overwhelmed and unsupported when I see the dishes piled up, because it makes me worry that the Daily Reset routine is going to collapse."**
- **Neuro-Benefit:** This approach reduces the stress hormones associated with defensiveness, allowing both partners to stay "constructively engaged" by focusing on the shared concern (the integrity of the routine / the feeling of overwhelm), rather than character assassination.

2. Asserting Needs with DEAR MAN

For high-stakes conflicts, the DBT skill of **DEAR MAN** provides a structured framework for assertive communication, ensuring you express your needs clearly while maintaining self-respect and the relationship.

- **Describe:** Describe the situation objectively (facts only). *"The past two weeks, the bill-pay checklist wasn't completed by Tuesday night."*
- **Express:** Express your feelings using "I" statements. *"I feel anxious and worried about accruing late fees."*
- **Assert:** Clearly and respectfully assert your need. *"I need you to commit to completing the Bill-Pay block on Tuesday night."*
- **Reinforce:** Explain the positive outcome. *"If we can do this, it will save us late fees and reduce my anxiety significantly."*

- **Mindful:** Stay mindful of your goal (getting the bill paid, not blaming the partner).
- **Appear Confident:** Maintain respectful body language and a calm tone (IC in action).
- **Negotiate:** Be willing to negotiate a compromise (e.g., changing the chore to a different day / time block).

Section 3: The Circuit-Breaker: Time-Outs and De-escalation

For the conflict to remain constructive, both partners must have clear, pre-agreed methods for de-escalation when one or both become emotionally "flooded" (overwhelmed by strong physiological arousal).

1. Implementing the Time Out Protocol

The ability to call a **Time Out** is an essential act of **Distress Tolerance** (Chapter 1) and **Inhibitory Control** (Chapter 3). It physically removes the threat of an impulsive emotional outburst.

- **Pre-Agreed Signal:** Establish a clear, non-confrontational signal (e.g., a hand gesture, or a simple phrase like, "I need a 10-minute reset"). This signal must be honored immediately by the receiving partner without argument.
- **The Cool-Down Commitment:** The person calling the time out commits to:
    1. **Immediate Disengagement:** Physically leaving the room and engaging in a **Grounding Technique** (Chapter 1) or a physiological reset (TIPP) to calm the nervous system.
    2. **Fixed Return Time:** Committing to a fixed return time (e.g., "I will return at 7:45 PM") to ensure the pause is for regulation, not avoidance.
- **Neuro-Benefit:** This pause allows the amygdala's alarm to subside and the logical PFC to return online, preserving IC and preventing the conversation from spiraling out of control due to impulsive words or actions.

2. Finding Common Ground and Shared Goals

Conflict resolution is most successful when the focus shifts from **winning** to **problem-solving** the system, using EF skills to find a mutual solution.

- **Redirect to the Goal:** When an argument gets stuck on blame, redirect the focus to the shared goal. *"We might disagree on the details of how to schedule the chores, but at least we're finally in agreement that the gutters need fixing this year!"* or *"We both agree that it's important to get to bed by 10, so what might help us do that?"* This frames both partners as collaborators on the same team, rather than adversaries.
- **Objective Analysis:** Use the skills of **Working Memory** and **Planning** (Book 3) to analyze the problem objectively. Treat the argument not as a character flaw, but as a system failure. (E.g., "The system for keys failed because the bowl isn't intuitive enough; let's find a hook").

Section 4: Repair Attempts: Rebuilding Trust and Connection

Conflict causes damage. The final, critical step in conflict resolution is the intentional act of **repair**, which rebuilds trust and intimacy damaged by emotional outbursts or conflict fatigue.

1. Making the Sincere Apology

A sincere apology is not just saying "sorry"; it must validate the partner's experience and include a commitment to future action.

- **Validate the Impact:** Acknowledge the emotional impact of your action, without qualifying it with an excuse. (e.g., *"I am sorry I snapped at you; my frustration overwhelmed me, and I understand that my tone made you feel attacked."*)
- **Commit to the System:** Commit to using your EF and emotional toolkit next time. (e.g., *"Next time I feel overwhelmed, I will use my Time Out signal immediately."*) This provides tangible assurance that you are actively working on the problem, rebuilding the trust that you are a reliable partner.

2. The Power of Olive Branches and Appreciation

Repair attempts can be small, non-verbal gestures that signal reconciliation and connection.

- **Olive Branches:** During or immediately after a conflict, offer an "olive branch", a small, non-verbal signal of care (e.g., a kind touch, a drink of water, or simply acknowledging their pain). These acts mitigate the relational damage caused by the preceding emotional storm.

- **Show Appreciation:** Demonstrate appreciation for your partner's efforts, especially in areas where they provide scaffolding for your ADHD symptoms. *"I love that you have followed through on starting to exercise,"* or *"I appreciate that you checked the shared calendar this morning."* This reinforces positive behavior and shifts the focus away from chronic deficiencies, nourishing the relationship's core strength.

Conclusion: Conflict as a Catalyst for Growth

By mastering the strategies of **"I" Statements**, **Time Out Protocols**, and **Repair Attempts**, you transform conflict from a destructive, shame-inducing event into a valuable catalyst for relationship growth. You are actively using the emotional regulation and Inhibitory Control skills gained in this book to protect your relationship's integrity.

This relational competence is the definitive step toward building a fulfilling life. You have moved beyond surviving arguments to collaboratively problem-solving, ensuring that your most important connections are resilient, empathetic, and stable, thereby completing the emotional mastery pillar of your self-management journey.

Chapter 5 Workbook: Fight Fair: Use 'I' Statements and Repair Attempts to Resolve Conflict

Objective: To practice assertive communication and de-escalation techniques that replace impulsive reactions with thoughtful, solution-oriented responses.

Scientific Anchor: "I" Statements reduce defensiveness, and Time Out protocols utilize Inhibitory Control to prevent the emotional flooding that leads to destructive impulsive actions in conflict.

Activity 5.1: The "I" Statement Conversion

Instructions: Take three common relationship complaints (which typically start with "You never...") and convert them into constructive "I" **Statements** that focus on your feelings and needs.

1. **Complaint (Blame):** You never help me plan social events; I always have to do it alone.

   "I" Statement (Need): "I feel overwhelmed and alone in planning social events. I need you to commit to taking the lead on one specific step this week."

2. **Complaint (Blame):** You always interrupt me; you don't care about what I'm saying.

   "I" Statement (Need): _____

   _____

   _____

   _____

3. **Complaint (Blame):** You are so micromanaging about the finances!

   "I" Statement (Need): _____

   _____

   _____

   _____

Activity 5.2: The Time Out Protocol and IC Practice

Instructions: Plan for a high-risk conflict moment (e.g., when tired or hungry) by establishing a non-negotiable **Time Out** protocol.

1. **The Trigger:** (Example: Partner asks about the utility bill that was due).

   Trigger: _____

   _____

   _____

   _____

2. **The Time Out Signal:** What is the non-confrontational signal you will use to stop the argument immediately?

   Signal (Verbal / Non-Verbal): _____

   _____

   _____

   _____

   _____

3. **The IC Commitment:** When you call the Time Out, you commit to two actions:

   Action A (Grounding): I will immediately engage in _____ (e.g., a TIPP skill from Chapter 1).

   Action B (Time Frame): I will return to the conversation at (Fixed time).

Reflection 5.3: Analyzing the Gain in Trust

Instructions: Reflect on how strategic conflict management heals relational damage and builds trust.

1. **Relational Damage:** How does a moment where you impulsively yell at your partner compromise the relationship's sense of **safety** and **trust**?

   Compromise: _____

   _____

   _____

   _____

   _____

2. **Repair and Trust:** If you successfully apply the **Time Out** (Activity 5.2) and return with a sincere apology that includes a commitment to use the system next time (a **Repair Attempt**), how does this action actively **rebuild** the trust that your impulsive action damaged?

   Trust Rebuilt: _____

   _____

   _____

   _____

3. **Shame Reduction:** Conflict often triggers shame. By successfully mastering a difficult conversation using **"I" Statements**, how does this successful use of EF skills provide tangible evidence that counters the inner critic's belief that you are "out of control" in relationships?

   Evidence of Control: _____

   _____

   _____

   _____

CHAPTER 6

REFLECT AND INTEGRATE:
YOUR EMOTIONAL MASTERY JOURNEY SO FAR

You have completed the intensive emotional mastery work of Book 5, successfully navigating the turbulent landscape of emotional dysregulation, chronic shame, and relational friction. This journey has been a campaign to stabilize your inner world, transforming intense, automatic reactions into thoughtful, intentional responses that honor both your feelings and your commitment to others.

This chapter is a dedicated moment of pause, a time to **reflect and integrate** the profound psychological and behavioral gains achieved through the disciplined practice of the therapeutic strategies you have mastered: **Sensory Grounding, Cognitive Reframing (CBT),** and **Opposite Action (DBT)**. The aim is to solidify the crucial shift from a life dictated by **emotional overwhelm** to a state of **calm, effective self-command**.

The core achievement of this emotional work is the consistent creation of the **"Pause"**, the critical time lag between an intense emotional stimulus (like perceived rejection or criticism) and your subsequent impulsive reaction. This pause allows your conserved Executive Function (EF) skills, honed in Book 3, to engage, making it possible to choose strategic action over automatic, regrettable behavior. You have moved beyond mere coping to building a robust, resilient foundation for genuine self-acceptance and lasting connection.

Section 1: The Victory Over Internal Chaos: Cognitive and Behavioral Synthesis

The most significant outcome of mastering the emotional strategies in this book is the mitigation of the destructive cycle where intense emotion fuels shame and shame compromises focus.

1. Grounding the Surge: The Physiological Circuit-Breaker

You learned to use immediate, sensory interventions to manage acute emotional distress, thereby preventing the emotional surge from escalating into a full meltdown.

- **TIPP and Sensory Anchors:** By practicing **Sensory Grounding Techniques** (TIPP: Temperature, Intense Exercise, Paced Breathing), you acquired the physical tools to actively calm the activated nervous system. This physiological intervention serves as the essential **circuit-breaker** that immediately drops the emotional intensity from a crisis "red light" to a manageable "yellow light."

- **IC Conservation:** This initial grounding phase is crucial because it provides the necessary time for **Inhibitory Control (IC)** to return online, preventing the impulsive verbal or physical reactions (yelling, isolating, self-harm) that cause profound regret and relational damage.

2. Dismantling the Inner Critic: Cognitive Reframing

Once the emotion is manageable, you moved to dismantle the harsh, automatic self-criticism that is the internal source of shame for women with ADHD.

- **Challenging Distortions:** You mastered the toolkit of **Cognitive Behavioral Therapy (CBT)**, systematically identifying and challenging destructive **cognitive distortions** (e.g., Catastrophizing, All-or-Nothing Thinking) that convert minor setbacks into massive failures.

- **The Reframe:** By rigorously testing the evidence for and against these thoughts, you learned to replace the harsh narrative with a **balanced, compassionate reframe**. This cognitive work strengthens the PFC's ability to engage rational thought, actively dismantling the internalized shame that is a primary driver of anxiety and depression in the female ADHD experience.

3. Interrupting Impulses: Behavioral Change

You learned to apply the ultimate behavioral defense against destructive urges: **Opposite Action**.

- **Opposite Action as Strategy:** This core **DBT** skill mandates that when an emotion leads to an unhelpful urge (e.g., Sadness -> urge to isolate), you must intentionally execute the **opposite behavior** (e.g., engage socially). This action directly changes the emotional trajectory, transforming automatic, regrettable reactions into thoughtful, intentional responses.

- **Analyzing the Chain:** You used the **Behavioral Chain Analysis (BCA)** framework to identify the precise internal and external triggers that lead to impulsive action, allowing you to proactively apply your coping skills before the crisis hits.

Section 2: The Relational Dividend: Building Trust and Safety

The internal mastery achieved in this book yields tangible, profound benefits in close relationships, moving the dynamic from chronic friction to collaborative partnership.

1. Constructive Conflict and Trust Repair

You mastered essential **Interpersonal Effectiveness** skills to navigate conflict without triggering defensiveness or causing lasting damage.

- **Active Listening:** By consistently practicing **Mirroring and Validation** (Chapter 4), you actively anchored your attention during conversations, counteracting the perception of inattention and providing irrefutable evidence to your partner that their message and feelings were received and understood.

- **Fighting Fair:** You learned to use **"I" Statements** (Chapter 5) to express your feelings and needs without blaming your partner's character ("I feel overwhelmed when..." vs. "You never...") and implemented the **Time Out Protocol** to ensure that arguments are paused and regulated before IC collapses.

- **Repair Attempts:** Crucially, you understood that after conflict, sincere **Repair Attempts** (validating the partner's impact, apologizing, and committing to use the system next time) are essential "olive branches" that actively rebuild the trust compromised by past impulsive reactions.

2. Healing Shame and RSD

The consistent use of these skills is the most powerful antidote to the debilitating pain of **Rejection Sensitive Dysphoria (RSD)**.

- **Evidence of Worthiness:** RSD is fueled by the fear of being seen as unworthy. When a woman consistently engages in open, validating communication, especially during conflict, she creates **tangible evidence of her competence and commitment** to the relationship. This steady stream of positive feedback counters the inner critic's negative narrative, strengthening self-worth.

- **Creating Safety:** By demonstrating that you have a proactive plan for managing your impulsivity (e.g., the Time Out signal), you create a sense of **safety and predictability** for your partner, reducing their need to act as a **taskmaster** and thereby dissolving the dysfunctional "parent-child" dynamic that fuels friction.

Section 3: The Integration: Emotional Fuel for Future Success

The mastery of emotions is the final, essential pillar that integrates all previous books, ensuring sustainable success across your life's domains.

1. EF Mastery and Emotional Bandwidth

The EF skills you conserved in Book 3 are the very resources you now deploy for emotional mastery.

- **Conserved CL:** The reduction in **Cognitive Load (CL)** from organizational and scheduling systems ensures that your brain has the necessary bandwidth to engage in the emotionally demanding work of IC and cognitive reframing. A less cluttered mind is a less reactive mind.

- **IC as a Universal Skill:** The **Inhibitory Control** trained through emotional regulation is a universal skill that supports all high-leverage EF demands: resisting the urge to check a notification (Book 3), resisting the urge to impulsively spend (Book 5), and resisting the urge to lash out (Book 5).

2. The Final Step to Integrated Success

You have successfully moved beyond the reactive struggle to a state of internal and relational command. The stability and emotional bandwidth achieved in this book are the essential prerequisites for tackling the final phase of integrating complex adult responsibilities, Relationships and Financial Management, into a harmonious system (Book 5).

The powerful new narrative forged here is one of self-acceptance: recognizing that your emotional intensity is a neurobiological reality that, with strategy and self-compassion, can be managed and harnessed for profound connection and resilience.

Chapter 6 Workbook: Reflect and Integrate: Your Emotional Mastery Journey So Far

Objective: To synthesize the cognitive and behavioral gains achieved in Book 5, assessing the shift from emotional reactivity to self-command and self-acceptance.

Scientific Anchor: Consistent practice of DBT skills strengthens the PFC's Inhibitory Control, creating resilience against emotional flooding and reducing the physiological impact of shame and stress.

Activity 6.1: The Emotional Command Scorecard

Instructions: Rate the severity of your emotional challenges **before** this book and **now**, focusing on the gain in your ability to pause and regulate. (Scale: 1 = Minimal Challenge, 5 = Severe Challenge)

Challenge Area	Before Book 5 (Initial)	After Book 5 (Current)	Reflection: The Tool That Helped Most
Impulse Control (Snapping / Yelling)			(Example: Opposite Action / Time Out)
Intensity of Shame / Self-Criticism			(Example: Cognitive Reframing / Self-Compassion)
Relational Friction / Misunderstanding			(Example: Mirroring / Validation)
Severity of Emotional Meltdowns			(Example: Sensory Grounding / TIPP)

Reflection 6.2: Analyzing the Power of the "Pause"

Instructions: The single greatest gain is the ability to choose a response rather than react impulsively.

1. **The Trigger and the Intervention:** Recall a moment this week when you felt an intense emotional surge. What **Distress Tolerance Skill** (e.g., TIPP, Grounding) did you use to interrupt the feeling, and how long did that intervention last?

   Intervention: _____

   _____

   _____

   Duration of Pause: _____

   _____

   _____

   _____

   _____

2. **IC Success:** How did that pause (even if short) prevent your **Inhibitory Control (IC)** from collapsing, allowing you to avoid the destructive action you were tempted to take?

   IC Protection: _____

   _____

   _____

   _____

   _____

   _____

3. **The Inner Ally:** The Inner Critic often reinforces the pain of RSD. How has the practice of **Self-Compassion** (treating yourself like a friend) helped to neutralize the sting of a perceived rejection this week?

   RSD Mitigation: _____

   _____

   _____

   _____

   _____

Activity 6.3: Bridge to Relationships and Financial Health (Book 5 Prep)

Instructions: Prepare to integrate your emotional skills into the final, practical domains of life, relationships and financial health, by identifying vulnerable areas.

1. **Conflict Strategy:** Name one specific conflict that frequently recurs with a partner or family member. Which tool ("**I**" **Statement** or **Time Out**) will you commit to using first the next time this conflict arises?

   Conflict & Tool: _____

   _____

   _____

   _____

   _____

2. **Impulsivity Protection:** Financial chaos is often fueled by emotional impulses. Name one specific, high-stakes impulse (e.g., buying a non-essential item, starting a new project) that you will now manage using the **Opposite Action** strategy.

   Impulse & Opposite Action: _____

   _____

   _____

   _____

   _____

   _____

CHAPTER 7

PRACTICE AND APPLY:
YOUR EMOTIONAL MASTERY ACTION TOOLKIT

You have completed the entire emotional mastery curriculum, moving from crisis management to cognitive reframing and strategic relationship building. This final chapter provides the comprehensive **Action Toolkit**, designed to translate the therapeutic knowledge of this book into a seamless, resilient system of daily emotional command.

The power of this toolkit lies in its synergistic effect: the **grounding and cognitive skills** (DBT / CBT) create the essential **"Pause,"** which allows your conserved Executive Function (EF) resources to choose intentional action over automatic, regrettable reaction. Consistency in applying these tools is the key to minimizing the intensity of emotional dysregulation, healing shame, and building lasting relational trust.

Section 1: Toolkit 1: Crisis and Distress Tolerance Protocol

Objective: To implement immediate, sensory-based techniques to interrupt acute emotional distress (Red Light), thereby activating the calming Parasympathetic Nervous System and creating the crucial "Pause" for IC to re-engage (Chapter 1).

Scientific Anchor: Sensory shock (TIPP) and focused grounding provide rapid physiological intervention to override the emotional alarm system (amygdala), creating the necessary time lag for Inhibitory Control (IC) to deploy.

Activity 7.1: The Immediate Circuit-Breaker Plan

Instructions: Create a clear, pre-planned sequence of physiological action for when an intense emotional surge (e.g., intense RSD pain, anger, anxiety) hits.

1. **Identify the High-Risk Trigger:** What is the most common trigger that leads to rapid emotional escalation?

   My Trigger: _____

   _____

   _____

   _____

   _____

2. **The TIPP Sequence (The "Immediate Action" Plan):** Commit to this low-friction, rapid intervention when the trigger occurs.

DBT Skill	Action (Must be pre-planned)	Duration	Neuro-Benefit
T: Temperature	(Example: Hold ice cube on wrist, splash cold water on face.)	30 seconds	Activates the dive reflex / calms heart rate.
I: Intense Exercise	(Example: 20 jumping jacks or wall push-ups.)	1 minute	Discharges physical energy of stress response.
P: Paced Breathing	(Example: 4-count inhale, 6-count exhale.)	3 cycles	Engages parasympathetic nervous system.

3. **The Grounding Anchor:** Immediately follow the TIPP sequence with the 5-4-3-2-1 Sensory Grounding Technique to pull attention away from internal chaos and anchor it to external reality.

   Commitment: I will find 5 things I see, 4 things I feel, 3 things I hear, 2 things I smell, and 1 thing I taste.

Section 2: Toolkit 2: Cognitive and Behavioral Interruption

Objective: To use thought-challenging frameworks (CBT) and intentional behavior (Opposite Action) to change the emotional trajectory and reduce shame (Chapters 2 & 3).

Scientific Anchor: Challenging cognitive distortions interrupts the thought-emotion-action cycle. Opposite Action changes the emotion by changing the unhelpful behavior, strengthening IC.

Activity 7.2: The Thought-Action Reframe Protocol

Instructions: Practice applying the Cognitive Behavioral and Opposite Action protocols to a common emotional struggle (e.g., shame, anger, avoidance).

1. **The Automatic Reaction (Anger / Relational Conflict):** Recall a moment when intense anger led to the urge to **yell / attack**.

   The Urge: _____

   Opposite Action (Commitment): _____

   _____

   _____

   _____

   (e.g., Use a gentle voice and an "I" statement, or call a Time Out).

2. **The Shame-Based Distortion (RSD / Avoidance):** Recall a moment when fear of failure led to the urge to **isolate / procrastinate**.

   The Distorted Thought: _____

   _____

   (e.g., "I'm a complete failure for missing that.")

   Cognitive Challenge (Reframe): _____

   _____

   _____

   _____

   (e.g., "This is just Catastrophizing. I made a mistake, which is human. I will start one micro-step now.")

3. **Behavioral Chain Analysis (BCA) Intervention:** Identify a common point of **Vulnerability** that precedes an emotional failure (e.g., low sleep, hunger, high Luteal Phase stress).

Vulnerability: _____

_____

_____

Proactive Intervention (Action): I will proactively schedule a _____ minute rest block / snack break today to prevent this vulnerability from leading to a crisis.

Toolkit 3: Relational Trust and Repair Protocol

Objective: To apply communication skills (Mirroring / Validation) and conflict strategies (Repair Attempts) to reduce relational friction and rebuild trust damaged by impulsive actions (Chapters 4 & 5).

Scientific Anchor: Mirroring anchors attention (reducing perception of inattention). Validation de-escalates conflict. Repair attempts rebuild trust and safety in the relationship, essential for resilience.

Activity 7.3: The Trust-Building Communication Sequence

Instructions: Practice using active listening and repair attempts in your next necessary conversation with a close partner or family member.

1. **Active Listening Commitment:** During the conversation, commit to using **Mirroring** once to confirm you correctly understood the core message.

   Mirroring Script: "So, what I hear you saying is that you feel _____ because of _____."

2. **Validation Commitment:** Commit to using **Validation** once to acknowledge the legitimacy of your partner's emotion.

   Validation Script: "That makes complete sense. I understand why you would feel _____ ."

3. **The Assertiveness Script (Fighting Fair):** When expressing a need for change, commit to using an "I" Statement to avoid blame.

   "I" Statement Script:_____

   _____

   (Focus on *your* feeling, e.g., "I feel frustrated when _____

   _____ ")

4. **Repair Commitment:** Following any conflict (even a small, regulated one), commit to offering a **Repair Attempt**—a small action to rebuild safety and connection.

Repair Action: (Example: A sincere apology and commitment to use a Time Out next time, or a physical gesture of connection / appreciation).

_____

_____

_____

Section 4: Integration and Long-Term Resilience

The EF skills conserved in Book 3 are the resources you now deploy for emotional mastery. This integrated approach ensures sustainable, resilient self-command.

1. The Universal Skill of Inhibitory Control

The **Inhibitory Control (IC)** you trained to stop checking notifications and resist the urge to procrastinate is the universal EF muscle required for emotional mastery. Every time you choose **Opposite Action** (e.g., speaking softly instead of yelling), you are successfully deploying IC under stress. This consistency builds the psychological capital necessary to navigate conflict without lasting damage.

2. The Final Step to Self-Acceptance

By consistently applying these tools, you transform the emotional struggle from a source of shame into a source of **self-efficacy**. You prove to yourself, through repeated, intentional actions, that you are capable of managing intensity, navigating complexity, and building trust. This evidence of competence is the foundation for genuine self-acceptance, moving you beyond the lifetime of internalized inadequacy. You are now fully equipped for the final pillar of integrated success.

CONCLUSION
SUMMARY: YOUR EMOTIONAL STRENGTH

You have completed the intensive, transformative work of Book 5, successfully navigating the turbulent landscape of emotional dysregulation, chronic shame, and relational friction. This final book represents the culmination of your journey toward internal stability, leveraging the structural and cognitive foundations built in the previous volumes (organization, focus, and hormonal synchronization) to master your emotional world and strengthen your most vital connections.

The core achievement of this book is the replacement of automatic, intense reactions with thoughtful, intentional responses. You have learned that your emotional struggles, from sudden anger to the debilitating pain of **Rejection Sensitive Dysphoria (RSD)**, are not signs of a character flaw, but neurobiological realities that can be strategically managed.

This stability, achieved through dedicated practice of therapeutic skills, is the final, essential pillar for realizing integrated success, enabling you to move from a life defined by emotional chaos to one rooted in calm, resilient self-command.

Section 1: The Victory Over Emotional Chaos: The Power of the Pause

The most significant outcome of mastering the strategies in this book is the ability to consistently create the **"Pause"**, the critical time lag between an intense emotional stimulus and a regrettable, impulsive reaction.

1. The Physiological Circuit-Breaker

You gained immediate command over acute distress by learning **Distress Tolerance** techniques (Chapter 1).

- **Grounding and TIPP Skills:** By deploying **Sensory Grounding** and physiological interventions (TIPP: Temperature, Intense Exercise, Paced Breathing), you acquired the capacity to actively calm the activated nervous system and reduce emotional intensity from a crisis "red light" to a manageable "yellow light."

- **IC Conservation:** This physiological pause is crucial because it allows your conserved **Inhibitory Control (IC)**, your brain's emotional "brakes", to re-engage, preventing the impulsive verbal or physical reactions (yelling, withdrawal) that cause profound regret and relational damage.

2. Dismantling Shame and the Inner Critic

Once grounded, you engaged the cognitive brain to dismantle the internal source of shame (Chapter 2).

- **Cognitive Reframing (CBT):** You learned to become a detective of your own mind, systematically identifying and challenging destructive **cognitive distortions** (e.g., Catastrophizing, All-or-Nothing Thinking) that fuel RSD and anxiety.

- **Opposite Action:** You implemented the definitive behavioral intervention, **Opposite Action** (Chapter 3), intentionally choosing to execute the behavior contrary to an unhelpful urge (e.g., engaging socially instead of isolating; speaking softly instead of yelling). This practice systematically changes the emotional script, transforming automatic reactions into thoughtful responses and building resilience against emotional volatility.

The internal mastery achieved is the foundation for navigating the high-stakes friction points of close relationships, moving the dynamic from chronic struggle to collaborative partnership.

1. Mastering Communication and Trust Repair

You mastered essential **Interpersonal Effectiveness** skills (DBT) to bridge communication gaps caused by attention deficits and impulsivity (Chapter 4).

- **Active Listening:** By consistently practicing **Mirroring and Validation**, you actively anchored your attention, counteracting the perception of inattention and providing irrefutable evidence that your partner's message and feelings were understood.

- **Constructive Conflict:** You learned to "fight fair" (Chapter 5) by using **"I" Statements** to express needs without blame, and you implemented the **Time Out Protocol** to ensure arguments are paused and regulated before IC collapses, reducing relational damage.

- **Repair Attempts:** Crucially, you committed to using sincere **Repair Attempts** (validating impact, apologizing, and committing to use the system next time) to actively rebuild the trust damaged by past impulsive reactions, ensuring that conflicts lead to growth, not erosion.

2. The Universal Antidote to Shame

The consistent use of these relational skills is the most powerful antidote to **RSD** and the chronic feeling of inadequacy that defines the female ADHD experience.

- **Evidence of Worthiness:** By successfully managing conflict with intentionality, you create a steady stream of **tangible evidence of your competence and commitment** to the relationship. This positive feedback systematically counters the inner critic's negative narrative, strengthening self-worth and self-acceptance.

- **Dissolving the Dynamic:** You gained the tools to dissolve the dysfunctional **"parent-child" dynamic**, ensuring that accountability for tasks and responsibilities shifts from the personal (blame) to the neutral (the system), fostering equality and respect within your partnership.

The journey through the five books culminates in the realization that integrated success requires all pillars to operate in harmony.

- **System Synergy:** The **IC and Working Memory** strengthened in Book 3 are the universal cognitive resources that enable the emotional **Pause** (Book 5) and the necessary **Impulse Control** for sustained financial health (Book 5). The structural predictability of Book 1 reduces the systemic stress that would otherwise compromise this entire emotional ecosystem.

- **The Empowered Narrative:** You have successfully moved beyond the lifetime of shame and self-blame, recognizing your emotional intensity and cognitive complexity as a neurobiological reality to be managed with strategy and self-compassion. The reward is a life defined by self-acceptance and competence.

You are no longer merely coping with ADHD; you are actively crafting a resilient, fulfilling life, commanding your focus, taming your emotions, and building the enduring connections that define genuine integrated success.

OVERALL CONCLUSION

THE EMPOWERED WOMAN WITH ADHD

The journey through this five-book series has been an intensive, strategic campaign against the systemic chaos and internalized shame that define unmanaged Attention-Deficit / Hyperactivity Disorder (ADHD) in women. This process has not been about finding a cure for ADHD; it has been about recognizing the profound truth that your brain is not broken, but is instead a unique operating system that demands a customized, intentional approach to thrive.

You have successfully moved beyond the reactive struggle, where your energy was a victim of distraction, procrastination, and hormonal chaos, to a state of **integrated self-mastery**.

Section 1: Synthesis of the Five Pillars: The Integrated System

The stability you have achieved is the result of strategically connecting five distinct, yet interdependent, pillars of self-management. The true power of this journey lies in recognizing how the structural, cognitive, and emotional components work synergistically to create resilient neurobiological support.

1. The Foundational Command (Book 1 & Book 3)

The journey began by establishing external and internal structural command, addressing the core deficits in Executive Function (EF) that fuel chaos.

- **External Order (Book 1):** You dismantled **Task Paralysis** and eliminated the anxiety-inducing friction of disorganization by implementing **functional organization** (designated homes, micro-steps). This work successfully reduced **Cognitive Load (CL)**, clearing the runway for cognitive work.

- **Cognitive Command (Book 3):** You conquered **Time Blindness** by making time concrete and visible, utilizing **Milestone Planning** and **Time Blocking** to enforce finite, manageable action. This disciplined approach systematically mitigated the **Estimation Deficit** and fragmentation of attention, conserving precious mental energy.

2. The Physiological Buffer (Book 4)

You introduced the non-negotiable science of hormonal synchronization, recognizing that the female EF system is dynamically influenced by neurochemical volatility.

- **Data and Advocacy:** By mastering **Cycle Tracking**, you transformed subjective experience into objective data, quantifying the decline in focus and organization during **low-estrogen phases** (e.g., the luteal phase).

- **Resilience:** You established a holistic physiological buffer—prioritizing sleep hygiene, nutrition, and stress reduction—to protect your vulnerable Executive Functions, ensuring that internal hormonal dips do not lead to external, functional collapse.

3. Emotional and Relational Mastery (Book 5)

The structural stability of the previous books provided the necessary bandwidth to tackle the deepest challenges: intense emotionality and external friction.

- **Emotional Circuit-Breakers:** You gained internal control by mastering **Distress Tolerance** (grounding, TIPP) and **Cognitive Reframing (CBT)**, consistently creating the crucial "Pause" between emotional stimulus and impulsive reaction. This work directly strengthens **Inhibitory Control (IC)**, providing the essential "brake" needed to manage intense feelings, including **RSD** (Rejection Sensitive Dysphoria).

- **Relational Resilience:** You utilized **Interpersonal Effectiveness** skills (**Mirroring, Validation, "I" Statements**) to reduce conflict and rebuild trust, actively dissolving the dysfunctional "parent-child" dynamic that plagues many neurodiverse relationships.

- **Financial Security:** You mitigated the long-term **Financial ADHD Tax** by implementing external systems to bypass compromised EF—automating high-stakes payments and simplifying decision points to combat impulsivity and time blindness.

Section 2: The Final Triumph:
Defeating Shame and Building Self-Efficacy

The true success of this journey is measured not just in productivity, but in the internal shift from shame to self-acceptance.

1. The Antidote to the Inner Critic

For a woman who has spent a lifetime internalizing her struggles and masking her symptoms, the greatest liberation is the knowledge that her difficulties were neurobiological, not moral. By consistently replacing self-blame with strategic, compassionate action, you have systematically dismantled the Inner Critic. The accumulation of small, visible successes—meeting Milestones, honoring a Pomodoro sprint, successfully navigating a conflict without yelling—provides **tangible evidence of competence** that builds profound **self-efficacy** and self-worth.

2. Reclaiming Your Narrative

You are no longer a passive participant in the cycle of overwhelm. You are now equipped with the vocabulary and the data to advocate for your needs in the world, commanding the necessary support from both partners and medical professionals. This knowledge allows you to embrace your unique neurodiversity not as a deficit, but as an operating system with specific needs that, when met with strategy and self-compassion, can achieve extraordinary results.

Section 3: The Empowered Commitment

The journey of the Empowered Woman with ADHD is a continuous practice, not a destination. There will be setbacks—missed resets, moments of overwhelm, and emotional flares. The true strength of your mastery lies in your ability to consistently return to your toolkit, treat the setback as valuable **data**, and choose strategic recovery over self-criticism.

You are now equipped with the ultimate toolkit:

- **A Clear Mind:** Focused, with distractions filtered, and time managed by external systems.
- **A Stable Body:** Hormonally buffered, well-rested, and regulated by physical self-care.
- **A Resilient Heart:** Capable of pausing during crisis, choosing love over impulse, and engaging the world from a place of genuine self-acceptance.

This integrated success, the harmony between your neurobiology, your environment, and your relationships, is the most powerful foundation for living the intentional, fulfilling life you deserve.

HERE'S ANOTHER BOOK BY VIVIAN WHITMORE THAT YOU MIGHT LIKE

WOMEN
with
ADHD
5-IN-1

APPROVED BY A LICENSED CLINICAL PSYCHOLOGIST

The Evidence–Based Guide to
Organize Your Life, Sharpen Focus,
Balance Hormones, and Master
Emotions, Money and Relationships

VIVIAN WHITMORE

Claim Your Free Bonus

As a thank you for reading, I've put together a powerful digital bonus pack to help you apply what you've learned — even if you only have a few minutes a day.

 Inside you'll find:

✔ Quick-access emotional reset tools
✔ A printable clarity map for focus and purpose
✔ 30 powerful journaling prompts
✔ Daily progress & reflection trackers
✔ A mini affirmation deck for calm and confidence

Access below to download your full bonus pack:

https: / / livetolearn.lpages.co / vivian-withmore-adhd-workbook-for-women-5-in-1-paperback /

Or, scan the QR code

RESOURCES

Introduction

1. https://advancedpsychiatryassociates.com/resources/blog/strategies-for-adults-living-with-adhd
2. https://lifeskillsadvocate.com/blog/pomodoro-technique-for-adhd/
3. https://add.org/adhd-paralysis/
4. https://www.sarahwest-adhd.com/blog/adhd-perimenopause-progesterone
5. https://www.zrtlab.com/blog/archive/supporting-teens-with-adhd-navigating-hormonal-changes-during-puberty/
6. https://add.org/emotional-dysregulation-adhd/
7. https://scholars.uky.edu/en/projects/estrogen-effects-on-adhd-and-cognition
8. https://pmc.ncbi.nlm.nih.gov/articles/PMC12145478/
9. https://www.additudemag.com/making-peace-with-your-clutter/
10. https://adhdandautismclinic.co.uk/unleashing-productivity-the-pomodoro-technique-for-adhd-management/
11. https://pubmed.ncbi.nlm.nih.gov/38039899/
12. https://lifeskillsadvocate.com/blog/time-blocking-for-adhd/
13. https://pmc.ncbi.nlm.nih.gov/articles/PMC10751335/
14. https://www.berkshirehealthcare.nhs.uk/media/109514308/4-adhd-guide-menopause.pdf
15. https://womensmentalhealth.org/posts/should-we-adjust-stimulant-dosage-premenstrually/
16. https://www.additudemag.com/adhd-and-periods-menstrual-cycle-hormones/
17. https://www.additudemag.com/how-to-improve-executive-function-adhd/
18. https://shahincarrigan.com/improving-communication-between-adhd-and-non-adhd-partners/
19. https://www.additudemag.com/dbt-skills-for-adhd-emotions-rsd/
20. https://www.simplypsychology.org/dialectical-behavior-therapy-for-adhd.html
21. https://chadd.org/attention-article/how-can-couples-with-adhd-keep-a-strong-relationship/

22. https://www.newportinstitute.com/resources/empowering-young-adults/body-doubling/

23. https://www.medicalnewstoday.com/articles/body-doubling-adhd

Book 1

1. https://www.helpguide.org/mental-health/adhd/managing-adult-adhd

2. https://add.org/executive-function-disorder/

3. https://add.org/adhd-paralysis/

4. https://advancedpsychiatryassociates.com/resources/blog/strategies-for-adults-living-with-adhd

5. https://www.additudemag.com/making-peace-with-your-clutter/

6. https://www.medicalnewstoday.com/articles/body-doubling-adhd

7. https://www.newportinstitute.com/resources/empowering-young-adults/body-doubling/

8. https://lifeskillsadvocate.com/blog/pomodoro-technique-for-adhd/

9. https://lifeskillsadvocate.com/blog/time-blocking-for-adhd/

10. https://www.iterateadhd.com/blog/the-adhd-tax

11. https://www.additudemag.com/how-to-improve-executive-function-adhd/

12. https://www.additudemag.com/how-to-calm-down-destress-techniques-adhd/

13. https://www.addrc.org/managing-rejection-sensitive-dysphoria-7-evidence-based-strategies-for-emotional-resilience/

14. https://psychiatry-psychopharmacology.com/en/marital-impact-of-adult-attention-deficit-hyperactivity-disorder-131265

15. https://shahincarrigan.com/improving-communication-between-adhd-and-non-adhd-partners/

16. https://chadd.org/attention-article/how-can-couples-with-adhd-keep-a-strong-relationship/

17. https://adhdandautismclinic.co.uk/unleashing-productivity-the-pomodoro-technique-for-adhd-management/

Book 2

1. https://lifeskillsadvocate.com/blog/pomodoro-technique-for-adhd/

2. https://lifeskillsadvocate.com/blog/time-blocking-for-adhd/

3. https://www.additudemag.com/how-to-improve-executive-function-adhd/

4. https://womensmentalhealth.org/posts/should-we-adjust-stimulant-dosage-premenstrually/
5. https://pmc.ncbi.nlm.nih.gov/articles/PMC6940517/
6. https://www.jmcp.org/doi/10.18553/jmcp.2021.21290
7. https://www.iterateadhd.com/blog/the-adhd-tax
8. https://pmc.ncbi.nlm.nih.gov/articles/PMC12145478/
9. https://scholars.uky.edu/en/projects/estrogen-effects-on-adhd-and-cognition
10. https://pubmed.ncbi.nlm.nih.gov/38039899/
11. https://www.additudemag.com/low-estrogen-adhd-hormones-theory/
12. https://pubmed.ncbi.nlm.nih.gov/39837362/
13. https://www.sarahwest-adhd.com/blog/adhd-perimenopause-progesterone
14. https://pmc.ncbi.nlm.nih.gov/articles/PMC10751335/
15. https://www.simplypsychology.org/dialectical-behavior-therapy-for-adhd.html
16. https://add.org/adhd-paralysis/
17. https://www.addrc.org/managing-rejection-sensitive-dysphoria-7-evidence-based-strategies-for-emotional-resilience/
18. https://shahincarrigan.com/improving-communication-between-adhd-and-non-adhd-partners/
19. https://www.medicalnewstoday.com/articles/body-doubling-adhd
20. https://adhdandautismclinic.co.uk/unleashing-productivity-the-pomodoro-technique-for-adhd-management/
21. https://www.berkshirehealthcare.nhs.uk/media/109514308/4-adhd-guide-menopause.pdf
22. https://add.org/executive-function-disorder/
23. https://www.newportinstitute.com/resources/empowering-young-adults/body-doubling/
24. https://add.org/executive-function-disorder/
25. https://www.additudemag.com/adhd-and-periods-menstrual-cycle-hormones/

Book 3

1. https://add.org/executive-function-disorder/
2. https://adhdandautismclinic.co.uk/unleashing-productivity-the-pomodoro-technique-for-adhd-management/

3. https://add.org/adhd-paralysis/
4. https://www.additudemag.com/how-to-improve-executive-function-adhd/
5. https://www.verywellmind.com/the-financial-toll-of-living-with-adhd-6744610
6. https://lifeskillsadvocate.com/blog/pomodoro-technique-for-adhd/
7. https://advancedpsychiatryassociates.com/resources/blog/strategies-for-adults-living-with-adhd
8. https://pmc.ncbi.nlm.nih.gov/articles/PMC6406620/
9. https://add.org/emotional-dysregulation-adhd/
10. https://www.additudemag.com/adhd-and-periods-menstrual-cycle-hormones/
11. https://chadd.org/attention-article/how-can-couples-with-adhd-keep-a-strong-relationship/
12. https://www.iterateadhd.com/blog/the-adhd-tax
13. https://lifeskillsadvocate.com/blog/time-blocking-for-adhd/

Book 4
1. https://pmc.ncbi.nlm.nih.gov/articles/PMC12145478/
2. https://pubmed.ncbi.nlm.nih.gov/38039899/
3. https://lifeskillsadvocate.com/blog/pomodoro-technique-for-adhd/
4. https://www.additudemag.com/low-estrogen-adhd-hormones-theory/
5. https://pmc.ncbi.nlm.nih.gov/articles/PMC10751335/
6. https://womensmentalhealth.org/posts/should-we-adjust-stimulant-dosage-premenstrually/
7. https://www.additudemag.com/adhd-and-periods-menstrual-cycle-hormones/
8. https://www.additudemag.com/how-to-calm-down-destress-techniques-adhd/
9. https://www.additudemag.com/dbt-skills-for-adhd-emotions-rsd/
10. https://www.additudemag.com/how-to-improve-executive-function-adhd/
11. https://www.ovid.com/journals/pnpbp/fulltext/10.1016/j.pnpbp.2025.111261~the-effects-of-psychostimulants-in-menstruating-women-with
12. https://www.sarahwest-adhd.com/blog/adhd-perimenopause-progesterone

13. https://add.org/executive-function-disorder/
14. https://add.org/emotional-dysregulation-adhd/
15. https://adhdandautismclinic.co.uk/unleashing-productivity-the-pomodoro-technique-for-adhd-management/
16. https://www.berkshirehealthcare.nhs.uk/media/109514308/4-adhd-guide-menopause.pdf

Book 5

1. https://add.org/executive-function-disorder/
2. https://add.org/adhd-paralysis/
3. https://www.additudemag.com/dbt-skills-for-adhd-emotions-rsd/
4. https://www.simplypsychology.org/dialectical-behavior-therapy-for-adhd.html
5. https://chadd.org/attention-article/how-can-couples-with-adhd-keep-a-strong-relationship/
6. https://www.additudemag.com/how-to-calm-down-destress-techniques-adhd/
7. https://www.additudemag.com/how-to-improve-executive-function-adhd/
8. https://add.org/emotional-dysregulation-adhd/
9. https://pmc.ncbi.nlm.nih.gov/articles/PMC10751335/
10. https://www.addrc.org/managing-rejection-sensitive-dysphoria-7-evidence-based-strategies-for-emotional-resilience/
11. https://www.additudemag.com/marriage-communication-adhd-spouses/
12. https://psychiatry-psychopharmacology.com/en/marital-impact-of-adult-attention-deficit-hyperactivity-disorder-131265
13. https://neurodivergentinsights.com/how-to-deal-with-rejection-sensitive-dysphoria/
14. https://www.sarahwest-adhd.com/blog/adhd-perimenopause-progesterone
15. https://pubmed.ncbi.nlm.nih.gov/39837362/
16. https://womensmentalhealth.org/posts/should-we-adjust-stimulant-dosage-premenstrually/
17. https://pmc.ncbi.nlm.nih.gov/articles/PMC12145478/
18. https://pubmed.ncbi.nlm.nih.gov/38039899/
19. https://www.additudemag.com/women-hormones-and-adhd/

20. https://www.verywellmind.com/the-financial-toll-of-living-with-adhd-6744610

Overall Conclusion

1. https://psychiatry-psychopharmacology.com/en/marital-impact-of-adult-attention-deficit-hyperactivity-disorder-131265
2. https://pmc.ncbi.nlm.nih.gov/articles/PMC6940517/
3. https://pmc.ncbi.nlm.nih.gov/articles/PMC12145478/
4. https://www.jmcp.org/doi/10.18553/jmcp.2021.21290
5. https://www.helpguide.org/mental-health/adhd/managing-adult-adhd
6. https://pmc.ncbi.nlm.nih.gov/articles/PMC10751335/
7. https://pubmed.ncbi.nlm.nih.gov/39837362/
8. https://www.additudemag.com/how-to-improve-executive-function-adhd/
9. https://www.simplypsychology.org/dialectical-behavior-therapy-for-adhd.html
10. https://www.verywellmind.com/the-financial-toll-of-living-with-adhd-6744610
11. https://chadd.org/attention-article/how-can-couples-with-adhd-keep-a-strong-relationship/
12. https://add.org/emotional-dysregulation-adhd/
13. https://www.iterateadhd.com/blog/the-adhd-tax
14. https://lifeskillsadvocate.com/blog/time-blocking-for-adhd/
15. https://www.addrc.org/managing-rejection-sensitive-dysphoria-7-evidence-based-strategies-for-emotional-resilience/
16. https://www.sarahwest-adhd.com/blog/adhd-perimenopause-progesterone
17. https://www.psychologytools.com/resource/mastering-your-adult-adhd-a-cognitive-behavioral-treatment-program-workbook

www.ingramcontent.com/pod-product-compliance
Lightning Source LLC
Chambersburg PA
CBHW060525150626
46550CB00020B/1437